A War Tour
of Viet Nam

A War Tour of Viet Nam

A Cultural History

ERIN R. MCCOY

McFarland & Company, Inc., Publishers
Jefferson, North Carolina

All photographs are by the author unless otherwise noted.

Library of Congress Cataloguing-in-Publication Data

Names: McCoy, Erin R., 1981– author.
Title: A war tour of Viet Nam : a cultural history / Erin R. McCoy.
Description: Jefferson, North Carolina : McFarland & Company, Inc., Publishers, 2022 |
Includes bibliographical references and index.
Identifiers: LCCN 2021049899 | ISBN 9781476682419 (paperback : acid free paper) ∞
ISBN 9781476644516 (ebook)
Subjects: LCSH: Vietnam War, 1961–1975. | Vietnam War, 1961–1975—United States. |
Vietnam War, 1961–1975—Music and the war. | McCoy, Erin R., 1981– —
Travel—Vietnam. | Vietnam—Description and travel. | BISAC: HISTORY /
Military / Vietnam War
Classification: LCC DS557.7 .M4127 2021 | DDC 959.704/3—dc23/eng/20211022
LC record available at https://lccn.loc.gov/2021049899

British Library cataloguing data are available

ISBN (print) 978-1-4766-8241-9
ISBN (ebook) 978-1-4766-4451-6

Front cover: DMZ area war memorial in Viet Nam
(Shutterstock/Claudine Van Massenhove)

Printed in the United States of America

*McFarland & Company, Inc., Publishers
Box 611, Jefferson, North Carolina 28640
www.mcfarlandpub.com*

For Joey

Acknowledgments

This book was a seven-year labor of love, and many, *many* people helped me along the way.

A big "thank you" is due to my folks in the English, Theater & Interdisciplinary Studies Department at the University of South Carolina Beaufort, who have been relentlessly supportive of this project. I'd also like to thank Dr. Amy Sears, without whom this book would not exist. Thank you as well to the University of South Carolina RISE Award Committees of 2015 and 2019; your funding made this book possible. Last but not least, thank you to my Sand Shark Veterans folks (USCB SSV); if I ever need a reason to keep going when I want to give up, thinking of y'all always works.

My friend Carrie Hodge, who came with me on my first trip to Viet Nam in 2012, deserves a warm round of applause for her support. I'd like to extend that gratitude to the rest of my Clemson people, my Wingate crew (especially Dr. Pam Thomas) and my Louisville folks (especially Dr. Mary Makris) who were with me for many steps of this journey.

In Viet Nam, I owe a huge thank you to Nguyen Thanh Phu, Ngo Xuan Hien, and Chuck Searcy at Project RENEW for their help (and helpful edits). Big thanks go out to Thang Troung Quach Thomas as well, not only for the continued friendship but also for introducing me to other new friends.

In Australia, I owe a "shout" to Rick and Gloria Butler, Dr. Nathalie Nguyen, Dr. Deane-Peter Baker, Dr. Bob Hall, and Mr. Derrill de Heer for their input, support, and overall generosity.

To my Viet Nam veteran friends (in alphabetical order): Ted Engelmann, Frank Gutierrez, Jim McGarrah, Mack Payne, and George Utter—your stories, support, advice, lunches, drinks, and talks kept me going, and I am forever grateful that each of you made time in your lives for me.

Of course, I am always grateful and thankful for my family—Mom, Dad, Allison, Peter, the McCoy family, the Wirz family, and all the Schumachers—for your support and love as well.

Thank you to McFarland for taking a chance on a kid from North Carolina with a dream—six-year-old me is who you really gave this book contract to.

And finally, with an overflowing heart, I thank my husband, Joey Schumacher, for his unwavering support, encouragement, and listening to me prattle on and on about this project for so many years—this one's for you.

Table of Contents

Acknowledgments vi

Preface 1

Introduction 3

1. 1940–1960 11

2. 1961 24

3. 1962 35

4. 1963 45

5. 1964 58

6. 1965 68

7. 1966 79

8. 1967 97

9. 1968 109

10. 1969 120

11. 1970 135

12. 1971 147

13. 1972 156

14. 1973 165

15. 1974 and 1975 176

Conclusion 186

Chapter Notes 191

Works Cited 193

Index 197

Preface

A War Tour of Viet Nam is a book about the Viet Nam* War—its history, players, and legacy. The Viet Nam War was complicated, misguided, and brutal. Fear of communism prompted the conflict, which dragged on from roughly 1961 to 1973. I say "roughly" because the United States sent aid and military advisors there much earlier and didn't fully leave until 1975. The Viet Nam War is still a difficult subject, and this book aims to combine lessons from the past with meditations on the present.

In this book, I attempt to be your tour guide through the chaotic and traumatic Viet Nam War. We can't go back in time, but I can show you what's still in Viet Nam, how they're telling the story, and what they think of the war now. The story is told somewhat chronologically: each chapter of this book focuses on an individual year of the war, musically and culturally in the United States, via the Billboard Top 100 popular music charts. Voices from the war—a West Point graduate whose class was the first to be allowed to select Viet Nam for their initial assignment, a Vietnamese college student, several Australian Viet Nam War veterans and scholars—are featured next to sites associated with the war, which includes places in Laos, Cambodia, Australia, and the United States. With regard to my Vietnamese sources, in chapters 3, 9, 11, and 15, I chose to use pseudonyms for college-aged Quin (a minor at the time of our meeting), as well as tour guides Nat, Mr. Anh and Mr. Thanh, whom I cannot reliably get in touch with outside of Asia.

There is so much more to Viet Nam—and the other places I just mentioned—than the Viet Nam War, so glimpses of those things, the real reason we travel, definitely have their place in this work. If you are on your way to Viet Nam, this book can tell you a little bit about what you might see beyond the more entertaining parts of the country. If you've already been, perhaps this book can illuminate something you saw or experienced.

My cultural and literary sources are limited, however; I can't speak Vietnamese (I've tried and am still trying to learn), and my time in Viet Nam, Laos, and Cambodia has barely scratched the surface of what can be found there. In addition, writing about any war (and definitely the Viet Nam War) becomes an endless pursuit. This book explores ideas like national identity, patriotism, and war tourism, and it relies heavily on "empirical data" I gained from traveling to Viet Nam War sites. *A War Tour of Viet Nam* does not descend into the particulars of military history or the deep catalogs of music, nor does it examine, in real detail, the anti–Viet Nam War movement, the civil rights movement, the women's rights movement, and so forth. These topics are broached, of course, but as an interdisciplinary scholar, I operate under the methodology of breadth versus

---

*See an explanation of this preferred two-word usage mid-page 7.

depth; I wanted to cover as much as I could without writing an encyclopedia. With regard to historical fact, I have cited everything but what is considered "common knowledge" (also known as information one can easily find in three or more sources); when you've spent the last decade of your life reading books about the Viet Nam War, what is "off the cuff" knowledge to me might not be so to you, and I've tried to add citations (in the form of endnotes) whenever possible without disrupting the flow of the narrative, which is a hybrid work straddling the line between prose and academic research reporting.

What is more important, in this book, is the position of the writer, a woman born after the war, and how she interprets the legacy of the conflict, often from a "front-seat" position with regard to sites of the war, as a scholar and solo traveler. This book aims to expand the scope of historiography of the Viet Nam War that departs from the dry historical texts that usually make up the bulk of Viet Nam War scholarship, instead providing an imaginative slant on what it's like to be a "tourist" of a conflict that ended 45 years ago and yet persists as a difficult topic in American and Vietnamese culture.

Introduction

I'm standing on the top of a windy hill next to Dutch, a Viet Nam War veteran (Navy), looking toward a thin stretch of road to the southwest. Our vantage point is a hill where the Vietnam Veterans Memorial in Angel Fire, New Mexico, is located, but our backs are to the memorial. Dutch alternates between looking through binoculars and talking to me about his time post-service, when he worked with troubled youth in the Massachusetts area. They'd all get on a big clipper and go out for 30 days, charging the kids with operating the boat. The kids would see stars spread out over the sea while on night watch; most had never seen a clear night sky before, which became a metaphor for the many possibilities their lives might have. Dutch is far from the first veteran I've met whose service didn't end when his time in the military did.

He stops and squints at the gap in the trees. I point to flickering lights in the drizzle: "Is that them?"

"They're on their way!" roars Dutch to the motley assortment of bikers behind us, and circles of light appear at the mouth of Carson National Forest. In the rush of activity and palpable excitement, I lose Dutch, as well as Blaze, who'd shown me John McCain's commemorative brick near the memorial's chapel. With un-ironic military precision, the minders and stagers and handlers move.

We've been waiting, in a bizarre combination of sun, wind, hail, and snow, for the "Run for the Wall" folks ("only at Angel Fire," someone laughs as the wintry mix comes down). I've come to the Angel Fire memorial to do research, and I've stayed past closing to witness this cavalcade of motorcycles, which stops at the memorial en route to the Vietnam Wall; it is a week before Memorial Day, and they do this every year. This year Dutch functions as a "stage" person alongside many other bikers who arrived a few hours before; their job is to meet, greet, and help the bikers, who started their journey from California. As they climb the slope, which is lined with bright American flags, many members of this leather-clad brigade appear wind battered and road weary (and there was a minor accident this year somewhere outside of Santa Fe—no one was seriously hurt), but they're smiling as we wave them in. Those who served salute them, standing stock still for at least 10 minutes. I stand on the side of the road and wave, and some wave back. Only one guy has his radio on. There are several women riders, but every bike—Indian, Harley, BMW, Kawasaki, "trike bikes"—have POW/MIA (prisoner of war/missing in action) stickers and U.S. flags waving. Also visible are the stickers of the Vietnam Service Medal, which is yellow with two green stripes at either end and three red stripes in the middle—I'm used to keeping my eye out for that sticker, but I've never seen so many in one place.

While I've spent most of my time inside the memorial today, this theater of the living makes me a little emotional, especially when I see the back of one biker's trailer stenciled with a KIA (killed in action) name and date above an "I ride for those who can't" sticker. This could mean the dead or those who simply can't ride a motorcycle, but the insistence of remembrance moves me; Viet Nam veterans got very little in terms of recognition upon their return from the war. These folks demand it. Loud pipes save lives. Squeaky wheels get grease.

One of the most persistent voices for Viet Nam veterans was "Doc Westphall," or Victor Westphall, the man who built this place. His son, David, died in an ambush in Viet Nam in 1968, and "Doc" used the insurance policy money from his son's death to construct a "Peace and Brotherhood Chapel," which is the stand-out feature of the memorial—it looks like a wing or a sail, white against the backdrop of the green Moreno Valley. It definitely provokes more calm energy than the black gash that is the DC memorial (though I like that one too). There's also a museum attached to the chapel, and it is pretty standard as far as military history goes: uniform ephemera, a library, a room to watch a film (*Letters from Home* played during my visit), a conference area, and, of course, a gift shop. The folks who work here are the nicest around, and they don't seem to mind me drifting in and out all day. One of the bikers asks me about a documentary—it takes me a moment to realize that he thinks I work at the museum, as I'm hunched over a notebook in the library. He makes a point of clarifying that he is not a Viet Nam veteran ("too young"); he's probably my parents' age (they graduated from high school in 1972), and he's come down from Denver to help. That's a long ride on a motorcycle.

When I met Dr. Stephen Trout, an English professor at the University of Southern Alabama, he was finishing up a book on the Angel Fire memorial. He chaired a panel on the memorial at the annual Texas Tech University Vietnam Center and Archive and Institute for Peace and Conflict conference, and that's where I found out about the New Mexico memorial. I'd never heard of it before. The people on the conference panel, as well as audience members, spoke so fondly of the Angel Fire site that I figured it had to be something special. A young Vietnamese woman, Carrie, whose father served in the ARVN (Army of the Republic of Viet Nam), anchored the panel; the inclusivity of the site also made me want to see it. In Australia, if you can prove you served in the war (before the recent conflicts in the Middle East, the United States and Australia shared the "American War" as their longest military engagement), you can march in the ANZAC parades. I can't imagine that occurring in the United States, where we seemed to quickly forget (if anti–Vietnamese immigration reports reveal anything) that the U.S. military worked with the South Vietnamese during the war. At Angel Fire, John McCain III's memorial brick is accompanied by those from Viet Nam, Australia, Thailand, and so on—anyone who had anything to do with the war is allowed space there.

As our veterans get older, we start paying them more attention. I used to get physically angry at the History Channel for running never-ending programs on World War II. Both of my grandfathers fought in it—one in the Pacific theater, the other went in on D-Day—but as a scholar of the Viet Nam War, it frustrated me that one war could be deemed "better" than the other. One was "right," the other was "wrong." I can only imagine how Korean War veterans feel.

We didn't learn about the Viet Nam War in school. Our high school history texts began with the Native Americans and ended at the Reagan era; World War II took up most of what came before the Gipper. Neither of my grandfathers spoke much about the

Vietnam Veterans Memorial, Angel Fire, New Mexico (2019).

war, even when asked: Grandpa (USMC, Japan) told funny stories now and then, but Granddaddy (Army, Europe) never said much other than how the Higgins boat he was in kept circling in the English Channel, probably saving his life. I very recently learned Granddaddy hopped in a P-38 plane—he practically had to sit in the pilot's lap—to get beer and cigarettes for his platoon somewhere in Europe. That's one of the problems with stories of war; they leak out into conversations rather than turning on like a tap, flowing with memories.

My first recollection of anything connected to Viet Nam is a hazy memory of a party—an adult party where the kids were allowed to run around in the yard—during which a guest got very upset and stormed out loudly and emotionally, and there were whispers of "Well, Viet Nam." This was in the early 1980s, not even a full decade after the war. On a school trip to DC, my mother did a rubbing of a name on the Wall for her friend whose father died in Viet Nam. She received the gift in tears.

Viet Nam wasn't something to be talked about, and characters on shows like *South Park* and movies like *Forrest Gump* (Lieutenant Dan) and *Rambo* portrayed Viet Nam veterans as unhinged, emotionally unstable, and damaged. The first Viet Nam War movie I saw was the haunting *Jacob's Ladder*, where the main character suffered hallucinations (one of them being the ceiling-fan-as-helicopter trope) that scared me. Everyone loved Tom Cruise, but his portrayal of Viet Nam veteran Ron Kovic in *Born on the Fourth of July*—my next memory of the war on film—jarred me; Tom Cruise was the ace pilot "Maverick" in *Top Gun*, not a weeping guy in a wheelchair. You didn't see any of that damage in the World War II movies. You didn't hear about PTSD (posttraumatic stress disorder), PTS (posttraumatic syndrome), or moral injury. We wouldn't want feelings and humanity to get in the way of "fun, travel and adventure."

To pierce the weird veil the United States grafted on top of the war, you have to dig deeper than Hollywood renditions and books and oral histories and stories. You have to go to Viet Nam ("a country, not a war!"[1]). And Laos. And Cambodia. And Australia. And Thailand. And perhaps you should go to Korea as well (they don't really like to remember their role in the war much, from what I'm told), along with New Zealand. Talk to one of the 30,000 Canadians who served in the war. Remember that Spain and Britain helped covertly. Read books about the women who served. Hell, read books about the Vietnamese who served as well as the civilians in Viet Nam who endured the war. But the easiest thing to do, maybe, is to start talking to veterans. Listen to what they have to say.

You can also eavesdrop (rude, I know). I watched one of the stage bikers flip through a giant book, *The Vietnam War in Photographs*, in the library that day at Angel Fire. He stopped at a page and pointed out a picture of a plane to his friend standing nearby: "That's the one I remember, that's mine." He flipped through a few more pages and then shut the book. "That's enough," he said, standing up to leave. As he was tall and clad in motorcycle leathers, I didn't expect to see him brush moisture from his eyes as he passed me; I caught myself expecting him, all geared up and big, to be tough and grizzled. I mistook his attire for a costume of a sort of masculinity that I know isn't real, but he fooled me. Maybe that was his intention.

Ten men from my home county—Union County, North Carolina—died in Viet Nam. The Angel Fire Memorial keeps giant binders labeled "Fatality Casualties Home State of Record" out. All their names sound like people I went to high school with. "How many of *my* classmates have died or been injured in Iraq or Afghanistan?" I wondered. On the back wall of the library, rows of portraits of the dead, often accompanied by notes ("From the Pen of Dr. Westphall"), are on display. I looked in the "Mc" section of the North Carolina binder, even though I know none of my direct kin served—but where do you start, really? William Wallace McGrew III gave me pause:

> "Mac was a pitcher for his Berne Union High School baseball team," his mother wrote to Doc Westphall. "When he wasn't playing sports, he liked to watch the cartoon 'The Roadrunner and Wile E. Coyote'.... When during a desperate situation [during a baseball game], the bench began to chant the Roadrunner's byword 'Beep Beep.' This signified that the bench wanted the pitcher to throw his renowned fastball. As often as not, this 'saved the day.'"

Cartoons? Baseball? "Mac" was just a kid. He was 22 when he died. Other veterans say "the real heroes" of the war are soldiers like him, but I beg to differ. I'm not saying Mac or anyone else who died, went missing, or came home injured is not a hero *at all*, of course. But Dutch, Blaze, and the other motorcyclists are also heroic; anyone who's been part of a war machine doesn't come out the same on the other side, and surviving that journey deserves respect.

Before I begin, a note on spelling: The spellings I use for Vietnamese locations are correct, but I leave out the diacritical marks. Diacritical marks indicate a variation on a letter's individual sound. I often use "acai" (uh-sigh) versus "açaí" (ahh-sigh-ee) as an example; the marks make two totally different-sounding words. But diacritical marks aren't very helpful to those of us who don't know what they mean. Vietnamese diacritical marks are so frequently used that they can be more of a hindrance than a help. Also, Vietnamese is a tonal (but not monosyllabic) language, and words are separated by syllables for issues of clarity, a confusion that stems from the switch from representing Vietnamese in Chinese for decades to using the Western (French) alphabet in the 1800s. "Hanoi" is "Ha Noi" and "Saigon" becomes "Sai Gon," and so on.

Similarly, because I am a bit of a lazy scholar, I often use the name "Sai Gon" for the place now known as "Ho Chi Minh City" or "HCMC." I've heard Vietnamese citizens and overseas Vietnamese still call the city "Sai Gon," and it's still technically a place, as the central district (District One) of Ho Chi Minh City is called "Sai Gon" (much like "London" is a broad term for a larger city in England, though the actual "city of London" is only a square mile). I trend to using the name HCMC only when writing about contemporary times; during the war I study and write about, the city was called "Sai Gon," so that's how I think of it. My favorite hotel is the "Sai Gon Liberty Central," and the airport code on one of my last flights to the city was "SGN," not "HCM" or similar. The name remains, even if it was officially changed to honor Ho Chi Minh in 1975.

While many academics debate the efficacy of writing "Viet Nam" versus "Vietnam"—neither is really a Vietnamese word—I like to write the country's Anglicized name as "Viet Nam" for two reasons. The primary reason is that (during the war, at least) the word was hyphenated or separated; we can easily see this treatment in government and political speeches in the United States, as well as in American 1960s news reports. "Viet Nam" was eventually condensed into "Vietnam" to optimize the speed of cabling information and reports around the world regarding the conflict; it took too much time to add the hyphen or space. My secondary reason for using the "Viet Nam" spelling is a gesture of respect for the Vietnamese. In my passport, my Vietnamese visas say, "Cộng hòa Xã hội chủ nghĩa Việt Nam." The English translation, below the Vietnamese, is "Socialist Republic of Viet Nam." In both Vietnamese and English, on a very official government-issued document, "Viet Nam" is rendered as a two-word entity. Plus, the United Nations uses the two-word iteration. I adore Viet Nam, and I hope this small gesture honors the innumerable treasures the people and country of Viet Nam have given me.

Writing about war requires a capacity for reflective thinking. War is too urgent, too violent, too mind-bending in terms of the spectrum of behaviors humanity is capable of; heroism and sacrifice by other names are brotherhood, while brutality in another context can be simply survival.

Many novels, memoirs, poems and films about the Viet Nam War, written from the point of view of those who lived through it and in it, exist. This book concerns itself with the concept of "breadth versus depth"; I may quote from the Nixon tapes, for example, but there are scores of books and articles written *entirely* about the Nixon administration. I always use music to help me tell the story of Viet Nam—it helps to "hear" what people enjoyed (or at least heard) in the background in American culture. While I have done significant work on Viet Nam War–era music, I have a colleague, Dr. Justin Brummer, who is tirelessly cataloging every obscure piece of music from the Viet Nam War era or about the Viet Nam War. His work is amazing and a far deeper dive into music than I can offer in this book. Dr. Brummer, however, most helpfully notes in his article "The Vietnam War: A History in Song":

> Vietnam has been called "the First Television War." But, as *Billboard* magazine reported on 4 June 1966, "few conflicts have evoked such a spate of musical production." As the magazine revealed, well over 100 Vietnam records had been released since that January alone. Fifty years

on, more than 5,000 songs have been recorded about the war, forming an international conversation about a conflict that tore apart the fabric of politics, society and culture.[2]

My focus in this book is mostly the top charting songs, which I assert tell us a great deal about American cultural psyche during the war. I also talk about peripheral bands, who were working and forming counter-culture movements but not necessarily on the Billboard Top 100. Country music got its own chart in the early 1960s, which means country artists usually get left out of the story of Viet Nam, except maybe Merle Haggard; I've tried to include a few outliers from the Top 100 in each chapter (or at least a song relevant to content).

How many voices tell a global cultural history of a contentious war? We know the Vietnamese and the Americans will be involved—the war took place in Viet Nam, and it is known as "the American War" *in* Viet Nam. Laos and Cambodia will come into play— we bombed them because they (willingly or unknowingly) allowed the Ho Chi Minh Trail to weave across their borders with Viet Nam. Australia and New Zealand also have some things to say, as they were major allies in the war and lost some folks to it.

We know the participants: leaders and followers of movements, politicians, soldiers/veterans, civilians, anti-war protesters. We might glimpse some "New Left" troubadours rubbing up against Dixiecrat traditionalists. We brush up against the children of the Vietnamese who left Viet Nam after the war, and sometimes those who left. We are acquainted with the spouses of the service people, the journalists, and the pundits. We have read the literature of those who studied the war from the critical distance of history, and we have read the novels and nonfiction of those who studied the war as it happened, as part of it.

What does it mean to be "part of" a war—culturally, and with reverberations into the present? Am I "part of" war by participating in it in a tertial way, by studying it, traveling around the globe to see it and talk about it? Do I perpetuate a version of the war through the choices I've made in my research? I know the answer to the last question—certainly.

I recently geeked out on a fellow educator's Twitter thread—she'd asked what sort of texts would serve as a good introduction to the Viet Nam War, for teaching, as well as texts that might expand her own ideas about it. Various people chimed in, with the top choice being Tim O'Brien's *The Things They Carried*. Admittedly, I teach a portion of that text every year in English 102, the literature side of two courses (English 101 being the partner) in freshman composition that my university offers. The O'Brien selection is an easy piece to teach; it synchs up perfectly with Viet Nam War scenes from *Forrest Gump*, which is a G-rated (and YouTube-available) bit of film to illustrate how the war looked. More important for my student audience, many scenes in *Forrest Gump* were filmed within an hour's drive of our campus. The Viet Nam War parts of the movie, for example, were staged on Huntington Island, a mere 25-minute drive from our school. But as much as I may like Tim O'Brien (for the record, I prefer his whirly-bird narrative *Going After Cacciato*), his story—a white male RTO in the army—isn't the definitive story of Viet Nam. As Viet Thanh Nguyen notes in 2017's *Nothing Ever Dies*:

> Because of the reach of American military and mnemonic power, of the entire American war machine lifestyle and its assumptions, I always run into American memories. No matter where I go outside Vietnam, if I want to discuss the war, even with intellectuals and academics, I often have to encounter their encounters with American memories. The Ivy League professor of contemporary literature who inquired about Tim O'Brien at my lecture on Vietnamese civilian war memories (because, she asked, what about actual war stories?[3])

American memories of the war are inevitable, but they're not the definitive story by any means. The Ivy League professor's question is dismissive and, in this new era of insistent and overdue inclusivity, racist.

Vietnamese civilian stories deserve equal value and weight as the American veteran stories—they tell us what it's like for an average person to be on the front of a war, what it's like to be afraid of bombs dropping on your home versus artillery fire on your foxhole. Both stories are important with regard to gaining a better understanding of the war, but skipping over the ones that we might not immediately identify with—due to national-ism or what-have-you—or cherry-picking only the literary "heavyweights" disregards an entire canon of literature. Second-generation *viet kieu** interpretations of the war, many emerging now in published form, give us a glimpse into what it's like to leave your home country and settle with your perceived allies, only to start all over again as an immigrant. I've spoken to a few Vietnamese youth in their late teens and early 20s, as well as people my age, and they always seem a bit mystified as to why I'm asking them about the "Amer-ican War." They acknowledge, wisely, that "no one wins in war," and then they cruise into a topic that they're more interested in, one that is on-brand with that age group. Why talk about the past when there's so much more to explore now?

One of the books I always recommend is *Novel Without a Name* by Duong Thu Huong. The main character, Quan, is 28 and a decade into his service in the North Viet-namese Army. His bright hopes that his military service would be filled with moments of revolution, brotherhood, and adventure have dimmed; he's foraging for food, and he hasn't been home in years. While the novel was published in 1991, the narrative's rubbery use of time echoes other literary devices on the war that many different authors over the years—and from different countries—have employed to describe war. It also is a remark-ably honest depiction of a Vietnamese soldier—not overly nationalistic, like they can be when written by the government. Quan could easily be Juan or John; the experience of the Viet Nam War soldier needs to include as many narratives as we can find.

To do that, we have to get over our built-in biases about one another. We can't fight wars unless we "other" each other. You have to make someone into a thing instead of a human; there's not even a Duke in our corner of the boxing ring, yelling in our faces, "He's not a machine! He's a man!" That's a reference to 1985's *Rocky IV*; if you haven't seen it in a while or ever, please take some time to check it out. It picks up with a brand of Reagan-esque 1980s anti-communism right where 1963's *Fail Safe* left off, complete with a hero clad in red, white and blue boxing trunks, battling a steroid-amped Russian super-fighter in Moscow. But the United States will at least get in the proverbial ring with Russians—we see them more as equals.

When we fight people who don't look like us, we give them "other" names. The Ger-mans called the Italians "macaronis" in World War I. The Americans called the Japanese "Japs" and "nips" in World War II; the Germans were "the Huns." The Vietnamese people called the American troops "chicken men" on occasion, while the Americans called the NVA and VC "gooks" in return. At the base of these names is racism, and it carries over into foreign policy.

In his "Remarks to the International Platform Association upon Receiving the

---

*Literally translated as "overseas Vietnamese"; sometimes these folks were born in Viet Nam and relocated when they were very young, or they can be second-generation Vietnamese born overseas.

Association's Annual Award" on August 3, 1965, President Johnson famously said of Viet Nam, "If this little nation goes down the drain and can't maintain her independence, ask yourself, what's going to happen to all the other little nations?"[4] While it's true that Viet Nam is not a large country, the diminutive "little nations" repetition reveals what Johnson—and many Americans—thought about Viet Nam: it was small and unimportant, part of a larger set of nations that made up a communist threat. The way Kennedy and Nixon talked about Viet Nam was no different. Kennedy took a patronizing, paternalistic view, forgetting that Vietnamese people and culture have existed for many centuries: "If we are not the parents of little Vietnam, then surely we are the godparents. We presided at its birth, we gave assistance to its life, we have helped to shape its future."[5] Fretting over the upcoming 1972 election, Nixon blustered:

> We should have flushed [Viet Nam] down the drain three years ago.… And it wouldn't have been too bad. Sure, the North Vietnamese would have probably slaughtered and castrated two million South Vietnamese Catholics, but nobody would have cared. These little brown people, so far away, we don't know them very well.[6]

Nixon's remark points to another longstanding problem in American foreign policy: because 99 percent of U.S. wars are fought outside of the United States, or even outside of North America, they always take place (to borrow a line from George M. Cohan's World War I pep song) "over there." People of a different color or political philosophy? We "don't know them" and thus can't understand them. Or so we think. But I think humans aren't that different across the world; we all really want the same things. We want to be happy, stable, and loved. We want our families safe and our food sources reliable. All of those elements of humanity are jeopardized in war, which can simultaneously bring out the best and worst aspects of the human character. The Viet Nam War exists as a perpetual puzzle for me—there are so many pieces!—but it also provides me, and anyone else who's interested, with a lens to view the larger human experience of a shared and complicated war.

1

1940–1960

The Vietnamese—and many American Viet Nam War veterans—refer to what we commonly call the "Viet Nam War" as "The American War." The Vietnamese name for the conflict speaks more to its place in a string of wars; Viet Nam had a lot of conflicts with a lot of different people. Post–World War II Viet Nam was marked by sustained turmoil and political unrest. The nation had been under French colonial occupation since 1887, and during World War II the Japanese took over from the French as part of a general Asian-expansion program. Since Japan was one of the Axis powers, the United States actually bombed Viet Nam during World War II—the Japanese were storing munitions and supplies around Ha Noi. Furthermore, in 1941, in the midst of World War II, the Viet Minh (meaning "League for the Independence of Viet Nam") formed under the guidance of Ho Chi Minh. At the end of World War II, Viet Nam was ravaged by famine, which was made worse by the influx of Chinese soldiers in the northern part of the country and British soldiers in southern Viet Nam. France, licking its World War II wounds, waited in the wings to see whether it might get its colony back.

Enter Ho Chi Minh. "Uncle Ho" had been traversing the globe, learning about communism and socialism, until the end of World War II. If we go by Ho Chi Minh's writings alone, it is easy to see his laser-sharp focus on the formation of an independent Viet Nam. While he knew Mao Tse-Tung and Josef Stalin, Ho also utilized the Viet Minh to help the United States find Japanese targets in Viet Nam during World War II, and he had the sympathetic ear of President Franklin Delano Roosevelt. Viet Nam's last emperor, Bao Dai, who'd been given the position at age 12 and was largely brought up in Europe, was essentially a Japanese prop. He abdicated his (limited, symbolic) power to the Viet Minh in August 1945, handing over his sword and seals and proclaiming that he was happier being an average citizen in a free country versus the king of an enslaved nation. The possibility of freedom in Viet Nam was reaching a fever pitch.

On September 2, 1945, Ho Chi Minh declared Viet Nam an independent republic in Ba Dinh Square (today heavily trafficked on all sides by motorbikes) in Ha Noi. Standing near him were, famously, American OSS (Office of Strategic Services) representatives—precursors to the CIA. The Viet Minh stepped into its power, implementing social programs and trying to redistribute food and supplies to its people. It worked on social reforms, such as literacy outreach programs, as well as moral policing (the Viet Minh banned opium smoking and prostitution). The British, frustrated with the Viet Minh, cut strategic cords (from "looking the other way" to outright letting French colonialists out of prison) in order to restore the French to power, which the French took—and tried to hang on to.

In the 1950s the French tried several different methods to keep hold of their colonies in Southeast Asia (they were also in Laos and Cambodia, collectively known as French Indochina) that included everything from torture to faux benevolence. The French broke years of Chinese tradition, especially in terms of government and education, to shape Viet Nam in the ways of the West. The 1936 novel *Dumb Luck* by Vu Trong Phung hilariously satirizes French attempts to "modernize" Viet Nam. Banned from 1960 until the mid–1980s,[1] but now almost required reading in Vietnamese schools, the book details how family dynamics, fashion, sport, and sexuality collided with French ideas of progress. The characters' names—Mr. and Mrs. Civilization, Mrs. Deputy Customs Officer, Mr. ILL—reflect how identity and keeping up appearances morphed with French social customs and a push for Western modernization. The book's claim to fame is that it told the stories of the common people ("Hooray for the common people! Long live the common people!"[2]), as opposed to elevated figures like emperors. The hapless protagonist, an orphaned street hustler named Red-Haired Xuan, floats through "modernized" Ha Noi, only to reveal how little Viet Nam really changed under French influence. Militarily, the French had a loose hold on Viet Nam until the spring of 1954, when they lost the historic battle of Dien Bien Phu. The mid–1950s was also when the United States started to send "advisors" over to Viet Nam. As my history professor, Dr. Benjamin Harrison (no relation to the president), at the University of Louisville used to say, "advisors do more than advise."

Prior to the Viet Nam War, Graham Greene's *The Quiet American* (published in 1955, on the eve of American involvement in Viet Nam) made pointed references to early American involvement in France's Indochina wars. The book's primary tension between Fowler and Pyle, a British journalist and American CIA operative, respectively, is over the affections of a girl named Phuong. But that tension acts as an extended metaphor of the incoming American experience in the country: frustration, cruelty, and suffering, with a dash of the exotic and a peppering of romance. Very "war," but with an edge; the American is clearly the "bad guy." The biggest irony is that he doesn't seem to know or think he is.

But Americans are not just quiet; they are also ugly during this period of history. In the historical semi-satire novel, William Lederer and Eugene Burdick's *The Ugly American*, Americans are innovative but smug, with intelligent outliers fighting bureaucratic messes. Western powers are fighting over control of the fictional country of Sarkhan, which the French have been occupying for quite some time. The authors, both navy veterans, published *The Ugly American* in 1958, and it is obvious commentary on the buildup to the Viet Nam War. In a trope-y "rogue American cowboy" type of scene, a bullish thinker, Ambassador MacWhite, ceases hobnobbing and bootlicking at an international political soirée to call out his hosts for missing an obvious part of their effort. The ambassador calls them out for not reading the works of one of the top communists of the 20th century, Mao Tse-Tung. The French—the West—are horrified at the implication:

> "Since December of 1946 the French have been fighting a war which has been maneuvered by the Communists precisely along the lines which Mao outlined in this pamphlet. You are a military man—you will please excuse my bluntness—but you make every mistake Mao wanted you to. You ignored his every lesson for fighting on this type of terrain. You neglected to get the political and economic cooperation of the Vietnamese, even though Mao proved long ago that Asians will not fight otherwise. Gentlemen, I have one simple—and possibly embarrassing—question. Has any of you ever read the writings of Mao Tse-tung?" [asked Ambassador MacWhite.]

"If you are suggesting, Ambassador MacWhite, that the nation which produced Napoleon now has to go to a primitive Chinese for military instruction, I can tell you that you are not only making a mistake, you're being insulting," the senior French general finally said.[3]

Self-assured superiority and smugness are ultimately the downfall of the French—and the Americans as well. The "primitive" Asian ideas are not worth a second thought. No one will even entertain the ambassador's idea, which is a metaphor for how the French and Americans viewed the Vietnamese as opponents. Fresh off a World War II victory (but with a little skirmish in Korea to keep in the rearview mirror), the United States was sure it would lick the communists in Viet Nam. The French, who admittedly took an "L" in World War II, were trying to cling to the vestiges of their empire. Their Indochine colonies made money, but they also represented French power across the globe; the United States would be more likely to help the people who, frankly, looked like them and thought like them. Gambling on the Vietnamese taking up democracy doesn't look like a safe bet when you already think of them, as a people, as inferior. It also doesn't endear you to people when you think of them as "less than" you. And really, how friendly and appealing can a colonizing country be to those colonized by it?

The arrival of the Americans, who are referred to as the "imperialists" in all public Vietnamese war history sites, museums, and literature, could easily be seen as filling a void left by the French. There were definitely Vietnamese who were anti-communist without the United States' help, but our presence in Viet Nam may have made some folks into communists. Forcibly moving people from their homes (strategic hamlets), bombing civilians (collateral damage), and poisoning civilians and their land (necessary defoliant use) do not create feelings of friendship. It's hard to reconcile the fear of communism to the things that the world did in the *name* of fearing communism.

While communism a governmental system that I certainly wouldn't want for myself, in my very limited experience of it, as a tourist, I really think communism is not as demonic as it's made out to be in literature and films from the early years of the Cold War. Communism doesn't so much take over the world as it does create entrepreneurs (which I'm pretty sure wasn't the goal envisioned by Marx and Engels); the squashing of political activity doesn't mean that people don't have the internet, and once you *see* other ways of being, you can't unsee them. And there's different flavors of communism—Ho Chi Minh's views were very different from those of Mao and Stalin. Plainly, I'm not advocating we give it a chance (which is moot because it's already existing), but rather I encourage everyone to worry about communism a little less.

◁▷ ◁▷ ◁▷

The current trend in Viet Nam War scholarship is to look back on the French Indochina wars, as France colonized Viet Nam from 1887 to 1954. This was the age of empires, when countries scrambled all over the world to plant flags in far-away lands and claim them—and their natural resources and people—as parts of a greater whole. Recent works, like Frederick Logevall's book *Embers of War* (2012) and the Ken Burns and Lynn Novick documentary film *The Vietnam War* (2017), take great pains to position the downfall of the French in Viet Nam as the start of the American war.

Per relics in the Dien Bien Phu Museum, this thesis holds. Materials, like bombs, are clearly U.S. products; you can see the manufacturer marks and English text on them (they could, arguably, be from the American war, or perhaps fake, sure). It's worth keeping a skeptical eye on museum placards in Viet Nam—there is a specific narrative the government wishes to project—but the truth is in the faded stenciled paint on the shell casings. Furthermore, we know that Presidents Truman, Eisenhower, and Kennedy supported the French effort in the fallout of World War II; in their view, communism had to be contained, or it might spread like a virus over the world, preventing the goodness of democracy and capitalism from attaining global dominance. This was called the "domino theory," and most U.S. politicians at the time believed that once a country fell to the perils of communism, its next-door neighbors and allies wouldn't be far behind. Viet Nam's proximity to China meant that it required a watchful Western presence, or else communism might creep all the way down the Pacific to another continent, never mind another country (hence part of the reason Australia and New Zealand joined the fight). The "red scare" was very real in the United States, and while many politicians were "Europe firsters" (meaning their worries about communism centered on the Soviet Union's activities in divided Berlin and the Balkans), there was also real fear surrounding the neighbors in South America. The Cuban Missile Crisis of 1962 cemented a deep fear of communism in the United States, so to war we went, to save the vulnerable Viet Nam from the clutches of the reds.

The Battle of Dien Bien Phu during France's fight to keep its colony in 1954 bears remarkable similarity to the battle for Khe Sanh in 1968; both battles involved heavy fighting, massive losses, and a big hill that the Westerners thought they could hold but ended up losing. The definitive battle at Dien Bien Phu took place on A1 Hill, which is now landscaped with one of my favorite trees, the royal poinciana—called "Christmas trees" in Australia, known as *flamboyan* in Puerto Rico—and walking paths. The big draw is the reconstructed trenches, complete with a few sad-looking French soldier mannequins in the bunkers. Sandbags, rendered in sturdy concrete, share space with singing stumps that line the walkways around the site; I don't know what songs were being played during my visit, but the plaintive female vocals and general ethos of the site led me to believe I was hearing melodies of loss and love of country. Near the edge of the hill is a massive and immaculately tended bomb crater, which illustrates both the destructive power of war and the illusions of war site recreation; I'd seen bomb craters all over the DMZ, softened by time and nature, so I could tell this crater was purposely designed (deep dark soil in contrast to the grassy hill, edges still sharp and defined) to emphasize the evils of the French versus the perseverance of the Vietnamese.

A1 Hill, where the Vietnamese prevailed, offers spectacular views of the small city of Dien Bien Phu, but while I marveled at the mountains, I realized that turning my gaze down and to the right allowed me to look into the Dien Bien Phu battle cemetery. I'd walked through it before huffing my way up the hill, and I was immediately struck by its uniformity. The black tombstones all looked the same; many didn't have individual names on them (some did, especially notable heroes of the battle), but rather "Liet Si" (martyr) written in yellow under a yellow star with a red background. Ceramic urns with blue designs sat before the tombstones to hold incense, and cream-colored vases holding fake yellow flowers (real flowers would wilt in the heat) rested to the left of the urns. Take away the incense and flowers and paint the tombstones white, and you'd be in Arlington Cemetery. As you enter the Dien Bien Phu cemetery, dark stone walls on either side of the entrance list the names of those who died defending Viet Nam in the battle, which echoes the Wall in DC. The similarities of the North Vietnamese cemeteries to the military cemeteries we have in the United States can be quite striking; we bury and remember our war dead in much the same way.

◄► ◄► ◄►

A1 Hill, Dien Bien Phu, Viet Nam (2019).

On my way home from work in Savannah, Georgia, I pass Battlefield Memorial Park, a memorial to the Revolutionary War "Battle of Savannah." It is little more than a hump of green grass with a sign reading "in memory of those who fought here." Admittedly, 1954 is a lot closer to the modern day than 1779, but the park is a pretty blip in a city scarred by multiple wars. The historical Colonial Park Cemetery off Abercorn Street in downtown Savannah is a Revolutionary War cemetery where Union soldiers set up camp during the Civil War, though many visitors to Savannah think it is a Civil War cemetery. It's not; upon hearing that the Union's infamous General Sherman, who was literally burning his way through Georgia, had advanced to the Savannah River, the city's mayor rode out to meet Sherman's troops to surrender. The deal spared Savannah from being torched to the ground. You'll hear this story if you take a guided tour, but if you're wandering around on your own, and unless you can decipher the weather-worn birth and death dates on the tombstones, you wouldn't know the difference. And if you live in the city, you know this locale mostly as "the cemetery that Lincoln Street runs through," not a historic landmark.

Similarly, in my hometown of Monroe, North Carolina, a World War II training camp, Camp Sutton, used to be indicated by a tall, old chimney on the side of Highway 74. The chimney eventually blocked a hotel sign, so it was whittled down to a stump you can't even see from the road, though you might glimpse it if you're waiting in the neighboring Bojangle's drive-thru. The Camp Sutton site used to have a nature trail, but it has since been taken over by the local hospital; Camp Sutton also served as a hospital, so that's okay, I guess. War sites morph and change and, ultimately, disappear unless we make a concerted effort to keep them visible and important. Dien Bien Phu makes every effort to ensure all visitors and residents remember the battle; the center of the city boasts the towering hilltop Dien Bien Phu Victory Monument, where a giant frieze of all the battle's events (elaborated on in the Dien Bien Phu Museum) flanks an imposing staircase.

The frieze shows Ho Chi Minh and the legendary General Vo Nguyen Giap making war plans amid scenes of medics tending to soldiers, cooks making food for the front, women fighters enmeshed in the war effort, warriors charging up hills, people constructing bunkers and fortifications, artillery being fired, and a group of surrendering French soldiers, morose and distinguishable from the other figures by their drooping moustaches. The Victory Monument itself, at the top of the staircase, features four figures, three facing the city. One is a soldier, happily hoisting a Vietnamese flag, and the other figure, also a soldier, holds aloft a jubilant child, whose hands are in the air, one holding what looks to be an exploding firework. Behind them, on the back side of the monument, is a soldier with his weapon pointed north, toward A1 Hill, forever guarding the city. His stern expression reminds me of the ubiquitous Civil War monuments in the South (many of them look the same because they were made by the same die-cast company). If you've not had the pleasure of seeing one, it's generally a tall, narrow pillar atop which a somber Confederate soldier stands, *always* facing the North and ready for the next battle, as the South will surely rise again! The Dien Bien Phu soldier, however, is less pitiful; his battle was actually won. But the fact that both monuments feel the need to be armed and ready for future conflict renders them less menacing and more fearful. Or prepared. Maybe both.

The Victory Monument sits on what was once "Hill D1." It's at least 10 flights of stairs up, with some vendors selling drinks and souvenirs at the bottom and the top. It's a pretty popular spot; I saw other tourists going up and down the stairs, and local kids used the base of the hill to ride their bikes. The top offers a nice view of the city, and the monument echoes an aesthetic I've seen in a lot of communist, propaganda-style art. It's blocky, and the features of the people are larger than necessary and impassive.

Dien Bien Phu Victory Monument, Viet Nam (2019).

The frieze at the bottom of the monument reveals more individual expression and emotion. I took a different way back down and found that winding walking paths traverse the sides of the monument and serve as *the* place for older Vietnamese people to walk together. As at the market, I received several random shouts of "hello!" My novelty as the lone white lady in town was also reflected at the Victory Museum, where Vietnamese tourists asked to take photos with me. Two of my new "photo friends" thought I might be French but appeared very pleased when I told them I was an American.

The Dien Bien Phu Museum's elaboration on the historic battle is equal parts informative and propaganda. For example, beneath a blurry black-and-white photo of about 4–5 French soldiers (easily identified, again, by their moustaches), the placard reads, "French soldier [*sic*] in miserable situation in Dien Bien Phu Battlefield (1954)." While I'm the first to agree that war is hell, the soldiers look dirty but not *miserable*; one is drinking from a cup (which could hold wine, as the museum boasts a sizeable collection of old French wine bottles) while, in the background, another is clearly *smiling*, which isn't my first thought when picturing the face of misery.

But after Dien Bien Phu, the 1954 Geneva Accords (which France, the Viet Minh, the Soviet Union, China, the United States, and the United Kingdom took part in crafting) stipulated that Viet Nam be divided at the 17th parallel—basically at the Ben Hai River— creating "North" and "South" Viet Nam overnight and oversimplifying the idea that Viet Nam was as crisply divided as, for example, the North and South during the American Civil War. Under the watchful eye of the world, the Geneva Accords stipulated that an election would be held in 1956. This was really to buy France and its newfound allies some time to gain support for a Western-friendly, democratic leader of South Viet Nam. About 80 percent of Vietnamese were prepared to vote for Ho Chi Minh,[4] and a democratically elected *communist* was not going to happen with America's blessing.

A lot of little dominoes—which would later fall differently than intended—were set up regarding the U.S. relationship to Viet Nam in the 1950s. In September 1954, the United States, along with Australia, France, Great Britain, New Zealand, the Philippines and Thailand, signed the Southeast Asia Treaty, pledging to defend the countries of Southeast Asia against communist "aggression." Shortly thereafter, in July 1955, China and the Soviet Union pledged military and economic aid to North Viet Nam. South Viet Nam, operating under President Ngo Dinh Diem, would receive provisions for military and economic aid when President Eisenhower put the Armed Forces Reserve Act in place; a clear battle between communism and democracy began to brew. U.S. forces also helped almost 500,000 anti-communist refugees relocate from the North to the South in 1955. But the moment of truth came in November 1959, when President Eisenhower increased the American "advisors" to the South Vietnamese army to almost 340 "assistants." Eisenhower's vice president, Richard Nixon, took note.

The United States emerged from the rubble of World War II financially intact, globally dominant, and assured of its status as a world power that carried aloft the torch of liberty for all to see. The destruction and global havoc of the war resulted in countries in upheaval, some being "redrawn" or annexed into different countries or absorbed as part of preexisting countries; several of these "new" countries, as well as East Berlin, came under the control of communist Russia. As a result, global anxiety over communism and its perceived evils came to permeate America. The new shadow of the Cold War amid the nuclear arms race was even more oppressive. Communism became the new enemy of American liberty, and anything or anyone "communist" was deemed unwelcome and unwanted in America. As the country launched a "quick war" against (communist) North Korea's invasion of South Korea, the shell-shocked veterans of World War II saw their younger brothers and cousins sent off into a war that, while initially supported by the American public, was quickly deemed unnecessary in the public's view. A general malaise brewed under the cloak of the communist threat: "Beat" poets emerged in the late 1950s, and the youth of the era began to act out (see 1955's *Rebel Without a Cause*) against the stifling social norms and fear-based political rhetoric. These trail-blazing kids eventually set the stage for the youth revolt of the 1960s and its accompanying anti-war music.

In the United States in the 1950s, things were heating up under the shadow of the Cold War. Late in that decade, a young Jimi Hendrix would buy his first guitar while Elvis retained his status as the top hitmaker on the radio. The music from the early 1950s is, to me, lovely or painful; there is no gray area. Sam Cooke's "You Send Me" (1957) is gorgeous, while "Hot Diggity Dog Diggity" from Perry Cuomo (1956) makes me groan. I love Johnny Cash (who was "[Walkin'] the Line" in 1956) and "Please Please Please" by James Brown (1956). The decade boasts definite creative highlights of American music history and culture. Three seminal jazz albums were released in the last years of the decade: Miles Davis' *The Birth of Cool*, John Coltrane's *Coltrane*, and *Jazz* by Sun Ra. But by and large the music leading into 1960 sounds rather stiff to my 21st-century ears.

In the mid–1950s, there was distinctive tension between two poles of political thought: communism and capitalist democracy. This conflict muddied the waters of the 1956 elections dictated by the Geneva Accords. In the decidedly anti-communist United States, a pervading fear of communist insurgency and espionage lingered around the edges of popular culture. The U.S.-backed president of South Viet Nam, Ngo Dinh Diem, had dutifully toed the line since 1955; there was no need to complicate things further with an election that would see a non-communist lose. Instead, the Western powers (France and the United States) arranged an election for Diem to win, deepening the divisions in Viet Nam and the country's general mistrust of Western pressure and influence.

Over the Pacific in the United States, folks were unaware of or uninterested in what was happening in Southeast Asia; they were enjoying the prosperity of postwar America. The early 1950s were marred by a brief entanglement with Korea, which seemingly confirmed the division of North Korea and South Korea, so perhaps the division of Viet Nam felt familiar and safe. The music charts were dominated by Elvis, whose "Heartbreak Hotel" and "Don't Be Cruel" took the two top spots of the 1956 Billboard chart. Doris Day scored her first number-one hit, "Que Sera, Sera," from the 1956 film *The Man Who Knew Too Much*. The detached, nearly Buddhist lyrical ethos of "Que Sera, Sera"—"Whatever will be, will be"—is topped only by the irreverent 1956 Henry Belafonte hit, "Day-O (The Banana Boat Song)," which goofily interprets a Jamaican folk song into a giggle-worthy Top 40 singalong. Or maybe that's the impression I have of it, seeing as I first heard the song in a comedic scene in the movie *Beetlejuice* (1988—I was seven) and still correlate the song with the film. Johnny Cash was on the scene in the mid–1950s, as "I Walk the Line" and "Cry! Cry! Cry!" entered the charts, and by 1957 Fats Domino's "I'm Walkin'" and the Crickets' "That'll Be the Day" entered the fray as the new genre of "rock 'n' roll" developed.

Elvis joined the army in 1958, so the late 1950s saw a marked decrease in his hits; by November 1959, U.S. military advisors (nearly 340) were aiding South Vietnamese troops. In February 1959, the Big Bopper, Ritchie Valens, and Buddy Holly died in a plane crash (an event dubbed "the day the music died"), and the pop charts mourned with Johnny Horton's hokey "Battle of New Orleans" at number one. The "Battle of New Orleans" sounds like a marching song and includes countrified words and images, like "a-comin'" and an alligator full of cannonballs as a weapon. The song stirs vaguely patriotic feelings, but it feels dated to listen to it now. I remember the Coasters' "Charlie Brown" and "Poison Ivy" from an oldies cassette tape that my childhood friend Crystal and I danced to as children; despite the lyrics about anti-itch lotions, the song "Poison Ivy" sounds edgy in comparison to other syrupy-sweet hits from 1959, like "Dream Lover" by Bobby Darin or "Waterloo" by Stonewall Jackson. Newport, Rhode Island, hosted the first Newport Folk Festival in 1959, which included performances by Odetta, the Kingston Trio, and an 18-year-old Joan Baez; folk music filled a space that would soon be seen as "counter-culture" music, even though groups like the Kingston Trio scored a Billboard chart hit with "Tom Dooley" in 1958.

By 1960, however, Elvis finished his military service and served up two hits—"Are You Lonesome Tonight?" and "It's Now or Never"—to cement his role in the new decade. He also starred in the film *G.I. Blues* and supplied the soundtrack for the film. The number-one song of 1960 was the soothing instrumental "Theme from *A Summer Place*" by Percy Faith. To me, it vaguely resembles elevator music, but it's not unpleasant. But 1960 boasted some memorable songs, and the year was memorable on a global scale—seventeen African nations gained independence in 1960, finally able to shed colonial rulers or loyalty to a crown. It's interesting to think, now, how young, for example, Somalia (England), Cameroon (France) and the Republic of the Congo (Belgium) are as nations *today*—in 2020, Madagascar was only 60 years old. That's young, especially for a country.

America turned 184 years old in 1960 (which is still pretty young, compared to, for example, European countries). January of that year kicked off with Senator John F. Kennedy of Massachusetts announcing his candidacy for president. He ran on the Democratic ticket and in November narrowly defeated Republican Richard Nixon, then vice president under Eisenhower. As a cultural historian, the short span of time between the Kennedy presidency—the mythologized Camelot, with youthful Jack and beautiful Jackie—and the eventual Nixon presidency (eight years) gives one pause; the 1960s revved the United States through so many changes. One of those rumblings occurred less than a month after young John Kennedy cast his hat into the presidential election: in February, in my home state of North Carolina, four Black students from North Carolina Agricultural and Technical State University staged a sit-in at a Greensboro Woolworth's lunch counter.

Around that same time, "Teen Angel" by Mark Dinning topped the charts. As the Southern United States entered a period of public protests against racial discrimination and antiquated Jim Crow laws, a young man penned a song about a girl who, ah, gets hit by a train. These are the foibles of history that transfix me; while some young Black men took a stand against injustice, at the same moment, people clapped along to the doleful strumming of "Teen Angel." The lyrics are marked by an easy (and perhaps ominous) romanticization of death—which, to be fair, is a thing in pop music, dating back at least to Scottish and Irish ballads of "poor" So-and-So who lost "a maiden fair" or what-have-you. By March, at the same time that the United States decided to send 3,500 soldiers to "advise" the South Vietnamese military, the "Theme of *A Summer Place*" began its nine-week domination of the Billboard charts. By May 1960, when President

Eisenhower signed the Civil Rights Act into law and the U.S. Food and Drug Administration (FDA) approved the first oral contraceptive, Elvis reentered the charts with bluesy "Stuck on You."

For Independence Day in 1960, the first flag with 50 stars flew to mark the celebrations, as Hawai'i became the 50th state in 1959. The Pulitzer Prize–winning classic *To Kill a Mockingbird* by Harper Lee was published that same July, which also marked the Democratic Party's official nomination of Kennedy to run for the presidency. That summer, songs of heartbreak—"Cathy's Clown" by the Everly Brothers, "Everybody's Somebody's Fool" by Connie Francis, and "I'm Sorry" by Brenda Lee—dominated the pop charts. By the end of the summer, the Olympics in Rome and the first televised presidential debate (Kennedy and Nixon) occurred, and *The Flintstones* debuted at the end of September. The most enjoyable Billboard chart top hit going into autumn was mid–September's "The Twist" by Chubby Checker. While innocent enough (it's essentially a dance song), the lyrics' obvious glee in the fact that Mom and Dad aren't around so two kids will be left alone to twist is something that struck me as a sexual metaphor at an older age. (I don't know how sexualized this song was intended to be, but I prefer the innocent, soda-shop version.) Sex appeal was an undeniable part of the Kennedy and Nixon presidential debate; Nixon, who famously refused makeup, looked dour and old compared to fresh-faced (and freshly powdered) Kennedy. Having just lived through the debacle that was the first Biden and Trump debate, the Nixon versus Kennedy discussion now looks positively prim.

Kennedy's close win hinged on his reassurance to the American people that he would not be soft on the evils of communism, which were at the forefront of the audience's mind; in mid–August, an American U-2 pilot was jailed in Moscow for espionage, and Cuban refugees were beginning to trickle in from the south in conjunction with the end of the Cuban Revolution, which inevitably placed known communist Fidel Castro at the helm of one of the United States' closest neighbor nations. The Kennedy clan also looked progressive on the issue of race, as Robert Kennedy, John's younger brother (henceforth known as "Bobby"), assisted Coretta Scott King in bailing Dr. Martin Luther King, Jr., out of jail in October. In that same month, the Louisville Lip—and future advocate for racial equality—Muhammad Ali (then known as Cassius Clay) won his first professional fight. By election day, the Drifters' perennially romantic "Save the Last Dance for Me" topped the charts. The song lyrics are slightly prescient; the singer's beloved can dance with whomever she wants, as long as she doesn't "forget who's taking [her] home and in whose arms [she's] gonna be."[5] But it's still a pop love song, a hallmark of the 1960s. Ray Charles made a quick chart appearance in mid–November with his soulful "Georgia on My Mind," a song that holds a special spot for me as a seven years' (and counting) resident of the Peach State.

The end of 1960 belonged to Elvis. "Are You Lonesome Tonight?" stayed at number one from November 28 until January 1961. It's a classic Elvis ballad, with his velveteen voice swooning up and around the lyrics. Elvis also takes on a speaking role, delivering a monologue loosely based on Shakespeare's *As You Like It* to detail how much Elvis loves his lost love; he finishes his speech with forlorn lines of life ending if the subject of the song's love ends. The smooth and familiar baritone of Elvis guided the beginning of the 1960s—a truly tumultuous decade—with a steady, practiced hand. At this time, President Eisenhower dedicated $1 million in aid to Cuban refugees, as 1,000 refugees a week entered Florida by the end of 1960.[6] On December 12, the U.S. Supreme Court ruled Louisiana's racial segregation laws unconstitutional and overturned them, while in the background Mississippi's own Elvis Presley crooned. The Viet Nam War, for the United States, was not in the public eye or on the top of Americans' concerns. The image of a lovesick Elvis (more respected now due to his new identity as an army veteran) singing a love song kept 1960 in lockstep with the end of the 1950s general American mood. Still patriotic, still dancing, still buoyed by sugary love songs, 1960 represented no audible threat to a growing and changing America. But the social and cultural events of 1960, along with the election of a shiny new Democratic president, laid the groundwork for change ahead.

◁▷ ◁▷ ◁▷

Up until very recently—I was editing this manuscript in 2020—one could not fly direct from the United States to Viet Nam. Something about "regulatory developments." So you'd likely get there, by plane, via a hub. My favorite route—if Tokyo-Narita isn't available at a low price—is through Hong Kong (though the protests and subsequent crackdown from the mainland Chinese government, which were just making headlines as I left the "fragrant harbor" last year, might eventually reroute me). You can also go via Seoul or Singapore, but I find Hong Kong's mishmash of Europe (remnants of the British Empire) and Asia delightful. Less than ten minutes from my beloved hotel, I can buy an acai bowl, visit a Buddhist temple, walk through a seafood market, or pop into a Circle K. And Hong Kong's airport is plush and expansive—and, oddly, I first thought, full of men my dad's age. Who dress a lot like Dad. And happen to be in textiles, again like Dad.

It's comforting to talk to someone in English when you're traveling alone beyond your country's official sphere. It's nice to talk to another American, even one you might normally never speak to on U.S. soil, after you've been away for a month or so—it is just enough familiarity to tether you back to your national identity, I guess. On several of my HKG-HAN or SGN-HKG flights, I've sat near a Dad-like guy; sometimes we're the only obvious non–Asians on the plane. A quick joke about the in-flight "snack" options, and you've made an instant friend. And it's nice, it seems, for these Dad-like guys, as I can use words like "creel" and "warper" (somewhat) confidently; I know these guys' trade more than the average traveler. I've noticed many of these men—often from the southern United States, like me—now have wives who live in Viet Nam. Sometimes their wives travel with them, making the trip to and from Hong Kong a shopping experience—or at least that's what one such guy was talking about on the plane to me a few years ago. Another Dad-like guy was much more Dad-like: he was traveling alone and hating every minute of it, but his company moved him between China and Viet Nam at least once a month. Ever check the label on your shirt—made of fabric that was "warped" at a textile plant—to see where it was made? Sixty percent chance it'll say Viet Nam.

The industrial part of Viet Nam—the textile plants, the Chinese and American buy-ins—didn't look to be a part of Dien Bien Phu. I wandered the streets after visiting the battle site and museum. Dien Bien Phu is beautiful, but it is decidedly un-Westernized in many ways. I walked through the open-air Muong Thanh food market. By "food," I mean vegetables, fruit, ducks, chickens, and people haggling and socializing. The market ends at a bridge—the Muong Thanh Bridge, which connects DBP's east and west sides over the Nam Rom River—that was marked with a blue historical dot on my map of the city. I've heard it referred to in some texts about the battle as "Bailey Bridge," but there was little to denote its importance besides the indecipherable blue plaque. Unlike every other city in Viet Nam, Dien Bien Phu didn't have much to offer in terms of restaurants—as I wound my way from the market to the monument, I passed many clothing shops and a few picnic-table-style mom-and-pop places, which I didn't have the stomach strength to chance on my visit. I decided a snack was in order, so I went to a baguette man on the main street. I only had larger bills—a twenty-dong note was my smallest bill—and through a series of pantomime and staggered English, the bread man conveyed that he couldn't break my bill, but he would give me baguettes in exchange. I walked away with a bag of five baguettes, assuring the seller that he could keep the rest in change. I dropped my bag of bread off at my hotel and, in the fading sunlight, went to find a more balanced form of sustenance.

After being turned away from two restaurants that looked appealing on Trip Advisor, I wandered the streets again. I passed a group of women dancing what looked a lot like the "fan dancing" that I'd enjoyed in China. I saw families eating together and teenagers racing through the streets on their motorbikes. There were several buffet-style open-air family spots, which is *the* way to make friends in Viet Nam, but my stomach doesn't survive these journeys, and Dien Bien Phu was leaving me tired; I cannot understate how exhausting it is to be a solo, obvious minority in a foreign country. It is not like being "Black in America" (which someone once asked me), but you are being watched, and you—the American lady—represent all of America everywhere you go. Politeness, humility, and overtipping are my go-to tactics. You also need to be willing to be ripped off on occasion without pitching a fit about it. I stood out in DBP in a way that just attracts more attention—positive, not creepy—but it's tiresome. I think everyone should go somewhere that renders them a racial minority. Go somewhere alone where you don't look like anyone there. Don't speak the language and enjoy the humility. Ideally it will be a positive experience, and it is definitely one worth having; it will open your mind to thoughts about race, class, and privilege *very* quickly.

I finally found a restaurant that looked like it would work. It was family owned, and while I sipped my fruit juice, a shrieking naked toddler shot through the restaurant, chased by his giggling young mother. Her mother was the owner, and she sat me next to a table where someone was obviously going over the restaurant's accounts. Some of the bills were smaller than what I'd withdrawn from the ATM before my trip. My phone nearly dead and carrying no book, I simply stared around the restaurant as I waited for my food, which I'd selected by pointing and reading off the menu (I felt confident enough in my Vietnamese to do so), and smugly watched as a gaggle of Chinese tourists, accompanied by one German couple in hiking sandals, were taken into a banquet room and served a prix-fixed meal.

Then my meal came. I had ordered a plate of plain potatoes. No butter, no salt. Plain cooked and sliced potatoes. I looked at the mound of starch on my plate and felt suddenly very tired and stupid. The restaurant owner's kids, including the young mother, were summoned and given what looked and sounded like whatever the opposite of a pep talk is before they all went into the banquet room. While the outside of the restaurant was a big open entryway, the inside of the restaurant looked like an old house, replete with a rich reddish staircase and bleached white crown molding. People walking by glanced at me, sitting alone with my pile of potatoes. After dutifully picking at them enough to make the cook not think I was wasteful, I paid for my meal and left.

When I got to my hotel, a man whom I'd seen earlier with his family in the hotel lobby held the elevator for me. We exchanged some small talk as the lift slowly climbed to the top floor, which I knew he wasn't staying on. So when he followed me off the elevator, I walked straight to the end of the hall, which had an open balcony. He followed me there, making a big show of stretching and acting tired. I stared hard and mute at the river until he walked down the hall. I went toward my room, trying to get in before he could tell which door was mine. "You have a friend in there?" he asked, and I shoved the door shut behind me, wedging a chair in front of it. My bag of baguettes, tossed next to the television, mocked me.

Dien Bien Phu didn't reveal any secrets to me. The story was that the French were terrible and lost, and the victors—especially those who died—would be forever honored for their contribution toward Vietnamese freedom. I could see why this was a popular place for Vietnamese families and tourists to visit; it was cheap to get there (my round-trip flight from Ha Noi was $82) and stay (my hotel was $20/night). The culture has yet to be polluted by too much outside Western influence, and the historical significance of the town acts as a layer of traditionalism that buries the whole space. The monument, museum, and replicated A1 Hill site were interesting, but as I moved through the city, I could tell that the young people living there were more interested in looking at their iPhones than history. But unlike some other historic areas of Viet Nam, Dien Bien Phu is very well kept, preserved, and enshrined. The city's sisters could be Philadelphia, Baltimore, or Boston, cities in the United States so thick with our origin story that we bubble wrap them—or at least their historical spots—with nostalgia and narrative.

It's true that the Battle of Dien Bien Phu was a turning point for the country, and it's obviously a source of pride for the Vietnamese. Gnawing on a baguette under the air conditioner, I thought again of the singing stumps and their piped propaganda. Perhaps what I was having trouble with was the bravado of Dien Bien Phu. It's hard for me to reconcile the amount of loss in the cemetery—which includes the memorial wall in the back and the rows of graves—with the amount of overall loss of Vietnamese to French colonial rule. The Vietnamese have every right to puff their chests up and erect a giant statue on top of a tall hill; their time under the French was often brutal. What is most potent about DBP, from my visit, is its role as *the place* where an independent Viet Nam looked possible. It is a victorious city, because the oppressed natives finally overthrew the white, European colonialists' power. There aren't many places in the world that can claim that victory, let alone claim it loudly and proudly.

2

1961

On January 2, 1963, around 4:00 a.m., one of the more notable battles of the Viet Nam War occurred. The Battle of Ap Bac—a strategic run on a Viet Cong radio transmitter a little over an hour outside Sai Gon—is often thought to be one of the first major battles of the Viet Nam War under American supervision. The immortal Lieutenant Colonel John Paul Vann (subject of journalist Neil Sheehan's infamous book *Bright Shining Lie: John Paul Vann and America in Vietnam*) was the U.S. advisor to Colonel Huynh Van Cao's notoriously brave 7th ARVN Infantry division. Lieutenant Colonel Vann's meticulous plans for the battle were undermined by none other than the ARVN commander-in-chief, President Diem, who preferred that his soldiers not die, or at least gain victory while simultaneously sustaining the lowest number of casualties. Vann watched the battle from overhead, in a helicopter, baffled and frustrated. Similarly, Vann's colleague Captain James Scanlon, another U.S. advisor, pleaded with ARVN Captain Ly Tong Ba to push his division into the scrum, only to see Captain Ly balk, unmoved, for a couple of hours—Ly having also been advised to lose as little life as possible by President Diem.

While we don't know, unequivocally, whether the ARVN troops could've been successful had Diem not intervened, we do know that the ARVN plans were leaked to the VC at the end of December 1962. Privy to the coming attraction, the VC set up a brutal ambush—complete with trenches containing surprise soldiers and anti-aircraft weapons—that ultimately won the battle. Aside from taking down three American advisors and 83 ARVN soldiers—in addition to five planes, several helicopters, and much loss of materiel—the battle marked one of the first divisions with regard to "truth" and the war.

Though Lieutenant Colonel Vann lamented the inadequacies of the ARVN, General Harkins at MACV (U.S. Military Assistance Command, Vietnam) saw the battle as a win for the South Vietnamese and U.S. advisors. How could the outcome of the battle be viewed so differently? Vann was on the ground, at the scene, and saw capable fighters retreat (inexplicably to him at the time) from the fight. By contrast, General Harkins was keeping score the World War II way—as the VC retreated into the night, the ARVN took over the territory that had been so ferociously defended for a terrifying 18 hours. The ARVN "won" in that they gained the territory in dispute. Unfortunately, that's not how the VC kept score.

The Ap Bac battle site leaves a little to be desired. There are the token dioramas of Vietnamese figures and placards depicting the "1.81 of the underground line" and trenches (none of which survive), as well as a section of tunnel that you can descend into. My guide, Thomas, did a wonderful job of reconstructing the scenario of the mighty

Diorama at Ap Bac Battle Site, Viet Nam (2017).

PAVN (People's Army of Viet Nam—that is, the North Vietnamese military) taking down the overconfident ARVN (Army of the Republic of Viet Nam—the South Vietnamese troops) and U.S. forces. But what struck me most at the site was its keeper. To get inside the complex, Thomas had to find the man who had the keys, who lived on site. While he was expecting us, Mr. Warden elected to wait inside, next to a fan (pro move). Thomas explained to me that the man, who had a kind face and swollen tan belly (which he quickly covered with a requisite green NFL-style uniform shirt), was a highly decorated war veteran. The man smiled and nodded at me politely when introduced, his grin mostly gums, and then padded back to his air conditioning. He obviously knew Thomas, and he also didn't seem to get too many visitors. I wondered whether his duty as site-keeper was truly an honor and a privilege or if it was a way for the government to reinforce the hero-ism of the party loyalists. It could be both. He didn't seem unhappy with the situation, so far as I could tell. I'd have loved to have spoken to him.

In Lieutenant Colonel David M. Toczek's 2007 monograph, *The Battle of Ap Bac, Vietnam: They Did Everything but Learn from It*, the author argues that the Battle of Ap Bac is a micro example of the major issues that eventually became the undoing of America's presence in Viet Nam. Toczek's argument that ARVN leadership was corrupt by virtue of its ties to the Diem regime holds water, but whenever I hear suppositions that the men in ARVN were subpar soldiers, I often wonder how much of that had to do with their lack of confidence in the American advisors as well as the obvious corruption in Diem's leadership. Diem, a Catholic, stocked his presidential cabinet with trusted cronies who followed his mandates, even if they were illogical. President Diem, per Toczek, was more interested in keeping the military as his personal bodyguards and protectors than having them in actual combat. Contemporary Viet Nam War scholarship, especially in Viet Nam, often refers to Diem as a "puppet" president and the ARVN as "puppet" soldiers. While I disagree with the latter assessment, I most certainly agree with the former. Personally, I don't doubt that the ARVN soldiers were fighting to keep communism at bay; there are too many accounts of Vietnamese citizens running from the VC, being terrorized by the VC, or just being plain uninterested in politics altogether.

The Vietnamese people definitely loved and favored Uncle Ho (and still do), but many weren't so keen on uniting Viet Nam under communist rule. Vietnamese fictional and autobiographical accounts of the war—*The Mountains Sing* (Nguyen Phan Que Mai, 2020), *The Sacred Willow* (Duong Van Mai Elliott, 1999), *When Heaven and Earth Changed Places* (Le Ly Hayslip, 1989), *Novel Without a Name* (Duong Thu Huong, 1991), and so on—each tell at least one story of a main character/narrator's family members being unjustly and harshly punished for "crimes" they weren't aware of committing. The public shaming, as well as the revoking of family farms under the guise of "land redistribution," was not popular with many Vietnamese people. In juries of their peers, many Vietnamese were exiled from their multigenerational homes, and the scorn and displacement left them with bad feelings toward the communists. While many escaped to the South, it is hard to tell how many ARVN soldiers were spurred into action due to direct communist intervention. What is clear, however, is that the soldiers of the Army of the Republic of Viet Nam felt they had a reason to fight against the PAVN and VC forces: an independent and democratic Viet Nam.

Some ARVN veterans, like Michael P. Do (author of *The Depths of Hell*, a memoir about his service and reeducation camp experience), still insist to this day that the South will rise again. Viet Thanh Nguyen's 2016 Pulitzer Prize–winning novel *The Sympathizer*, as well as his nonfiction book *Nothing Ever Dies*, detail enclaves of South Vietnamese soldiers who still believe that Viet Nam might be taken back. From the point of view of a white woman raised in the American South, such displays—"the South will rise again!" type of sentiments—make me sad. As I put this book together, I had arguments with friends and family about the removal of Confederate monuments across the Southern United States. My most repeated retort—"When you lose a war, you don't get to keep your flag!"—stings when I look at the South Vietnamese. I teach my students to recognize the flag of South Viet Nam (a yellow rectangle with three red lines in the middle), as well as the Viet Nam Service Medal (which adds green on the ends of the yellow ribbon), on local businesses and vehicles. It's one of those things you can't unsee, and my students will inevitably report back, "There are a lot of Viet Nam veterans around here," once they start noticing the flag. That same flag is illegal in Viet Nam, just as the East German flag is now in Germany—they used to call it the "secessionist flag" (*Spalterflagge*), and affixing it to one's car, for example, was a criminal act. My students always look skeptical of this knowledge; it is hard for them to comprehend in our Land of Free Speech. Also, we live in the South. At our small university in South Carolina, where a number of students still sport—loudly and proudly—Confederate flags on their cars and shirts, this isn't viewed as secessionist behavior, but rather a "celebration of heritage." From the South Vietnamese point of view, I can see that argument, but, unfortunately, I can't extend that compassion to the sons and daughters of the Confederacy. I think it's the inherent, unavoidable racism that comes with the ol' "stars and bars" that ultimately turns me off—but maybe it's because I'm half Yankee (my mom's originally from New Jersey) and I don't "get it."

The Cu Chi tunnels outside of Sai Gon continue to be a heavily advertised tourist attraction. Dug (at first by hand) by nationalists in the 1940s, the tunnels eventually traversed more than 150 miles from the edges of Sai Gon to the Cambodian border. Their selling point is that you can get in the tunnels, something I'd already done years prior in Vinh Moc, near the DMZ (pro tip: you see a lot more tunnel at Vinh Moc than at Cu Chi). The great expansive network of cunning tunnel warfare is only a brief part of the tour. The Cu Chi tunnels did not protect a village forced to live underground, but rather served as a supply route and guerrilla war–style ambush route. These tunnels told a far more combative war story than those near the DMZ. Both represent the obvious draw of war tourism.

My Cu Chi tour group included a couple from New Zealand, two American backpacker gals (one of whom rescued a flip-flop from doom with clever use of duct tape), a German couple, and an American family of four. The New Zealand couple were most kind to me; they wondered why I was traveling alone, and when I told them about my research, they immediately noted New Zealand's involvement in the war: "Our hands aren't entirely clean either." As we went farther into the Cu Chi area and learned about American atrocities during the war, I noticed the New Zealand couple sneaking glances at me to gauge my reaction to statements about American cruelty or how easy it was to find American soldiers by their trash and cigarette smoke. I remained impassive. It's hard to travel in a space where you're continually being told how terrible your country once was to another country, but this was my third trip to Viet Nam, and I was sort of used to it.

Before we made it to Cu Chi, we stopped in a village to visit a small family farm that dabbled in rubber manufacturing. Having only seen this process in passing, it was interesting to stop and look at the tree sap, slowly inching its way down the tree bark into little cup-looking containers. The Vietnamese rubber plantations were a big reason that France wanted to keep the country under its power: strategic rubber purposes. It's obviously a slow process, and it speaks volumes about the patience and dedication rubber farmers need to have to keep this type of industry going. I think we also tried to make rice paper, but I don't remember that endeavor counting as a personal success. My husband was arriving that evening in time for us to celebrate our first wedding anniversary, so my mind was elsewhere.

Until we actually started touring the Cu Chi site. After watching a short video in an open-air enclosure (as most tours in Viet Nam begin), we began walking through the site. The first thing we got to "try" was walking through a short bit of tunnel, which, our guide pointed out, had been enlarged to accommodate "tourists." The guide was the same height as me—around 5'5"—and probably weighed 100 pounds soaking wet; I wondered whether tourists just meant "non–Vietnamese people," but then I thought about other statistically "smaller" nationalities, like Peruvians or Italians. (I say this because in those countries my T-shirt size suddenly changes from a small to XXL.) I also figured the tunnels might be enlarged and fortified with concrete, like the tunnels in Vinh Moc, where you could pretty much stand up (I could) and find your way around via lanterns on the walls.

No such luck in the tiny portion of the Cu Chi tunnels. I'm a little claustrophobic, and as soon as I descended into the Cu Chi tunnel, I wanted out. (The corpse of an abnormally large insect next to the entrance had a lot to do with the sudden rush of fear.) Following the rump of one of the Germans, I sped through. At the end, our guide gave us a hand out of the tunnel, and the group tittered about the enclosed space. While I find the Vietnamese use of tunnels ingenious, I don't need to keep going in them; what the tunnels show you is how clever and self-sacrificing the North Vietnamese people were, especially with regard to utilizing the land they knew so well. The United States knew tunnels existed and bombed the crap out of the Vinh Moc area; the Cu Chi tunnels, due to their proximity to Sai Gon, didn't get as much shelling.

We were guided into an area where we could all look at a bomb crater, which was about 5 × 5 feet in diameter and rendered a fuzzy, grass-covered dent thanks to nature and time. I was distracted, however, by the repeated sounds of gunfire close by. Turns out you can shoot almost any Viet Nam War–era weapon at a firing range that's included in the Cu Chi experience. Looking into the jungle surroundings against the backdrop of barking AK-47s (four shots for a dollar!), I blocked out the group and focused on the sounds and scenery. Is this what it sounded like, being in the thick of the war? In films we often see soldiers walking carefully on jungle trails or amid rice paddies, but we also get to see depictions of people hacking their way through a jungle, like the one I was standing in, while gunfire cracks around them. I know that you can't transport yourself through time (yet), but I took note of what I was feeling: I was hot (a given), annoyed (the gun range noises drilled into my nerves), and a bit grumpy. We'd passed a diorama (another common piece of Vietnamese tourist sites) of waxen Vietnamese soldiers making booby traps and laboring to make uniforms—the famed black pajamas—for North Vietnamese soldiers who'd made it south. As our tour guide praised the soldiers who made the difficult trek to South Viet Nam to help the people there "rise up" against the "puppet government," I stared at one of the laboring diorama figures, who was categorizing ammunition liberated from the American troops. Juxtaposed next to punji sticks—bits of wood whittled to a point (which is usually urinated on or laced with some sort of substance that increases infection) and deployed into someone once they step on a booby trap—I felt a familiar surge of American patriotism swell in my stomach.

Again (and I think this point bears repeating at least once), it is not easy to visit a country that beat *your* country in a war that was, from everything I've seen, a pretty avoidable mess—at least from an American point of view. My New Zealand companions, as I previously noted, hailed from another country that might've done better at staying out of the affairs of Southeast Asia, but I have to remember that the fear of communism was a very real and very big thing. While the United States is still afraid of communism—a word Americans use, often incorrectly and interchangeably, with "socialism" and "fascism" on social media and on opinion-based news sites—we also have terrorism to contend with in the 21st century. But China and Russia, the biggest communists on the bloc (get it?) in the 21st century, continue to be bugaboos for many U.S. citizens and the U.S. government. Perpetual mistrust of both countries persists in the United States, but I don't always think it's warranted. Sometimes I think that, for example, Russia's meddling in U.S. elections wouldn't be such a problem if U.S. leaders were willing to admit that they needed to be a bit smarter, or even that they cared more, even if that meant admitting that their chosen candidate, Democrat or Republican, benefited from it. Having been to China for an extended stay, I know the people there aren't blindly following a doctrine they 100 percent believe in; people are pretty much the same everywhere. They just want to be able to do the things that make them happy, and they work within whatever government parameters they're stuck with in order to attain that happiness.

Half of our Cu Chi tour group trotted happily over to check out the gun range, while the rest of us meandered through the souvenir and food area nearby. The American family made a beeline to the shooting range. I was a little perturbed with them for doing that (We're *Americans*! How does it look for us to go to Viet Nam and immediately go play with firearms? Doesn't that send a message that is a little, I dunno, *typical* in the worst way?), but they had a young son who was begging to fire "an old gun," and, really, who am I to tell someone how to amuse their child on a hot jungle tour in a former warzone? He got to shoot an M16, the standard issue weapon for most of the American infantry troops, and he didn't like it. The AK was a much more satisfying toy, and he spent more time admiring it. I found that funny; many Viet Nam War veterans I know don't have really good things to say about the M16 either, though my pal George, for example, maintains that the performance of the rifle hinged on simply keeping it clean. Jazzed by his time at the range, the American son babbled on about the AK for at least the first half hour of our way back to Sai Gon.

It would be a fool's errand to expect an 11- to 13-year-old boy, traveling in Viet Nam with his parents, to be more interested in the 30-year-old history of a war site than the site's offering of guns to be fired. I wondered why his parents were even taking him, and his younger, more subdued brother, to Viet Nam in the first place. What was the allure for them? The parents pumped our guide for information about good places to eat in Sai Gon, and the places discussed were mostly expensive, tourist-trappy spots. The mother effusively commended Viet Nam's famous slow-drip coffee, and the tour guide kindly pointed out that she could find that almost anywhere in the city. "Well, there's a Starbucks down the street from our hotel," the mother mused. "Do you think we can get that coffee there?" Restraining myself from yelling "Why go all the way to Viet Nam to get fucking Starbucks?" I settled back into my seat and engaged in one of my favorite travel pastimes: staring out the window.

Watching the outskirts of Sai Gon whip by our van, I tried to keep track of how many wedding shops we passed or how many shop signs were in English and Vietnamese. Motorcycle helmets were required in Sai Gon, but not so much, it appeared, in the surrounding villages. While I judged the American family in my head, I made myself judge my own thoughts too. Didn't I, another American in Viet Nam, seek out comfort food like toast for breakfast, instead of trying the local delicacies? Didn't I also lose interest in the Cu Chi tunnels when I thought about my own countrymen getting hurt or killed by the booby traps? At one point on the tour, we were shown five different types of detonating and triggering devices used in conjunction with the various snares and sticks. We were also shown small mines, the fatal results of which the guide took great pleasure in describing. "Does anyone know what a 'bouncing Betty' is?" He smiled at us, and while I knew the answer—it's a mine that pops up out of the ground to almost waist height so that it can destroy your legs *and* torso—I kept quiet. One of the Germans suggested it was a mine that bounced, which made the group laugh.

Unfortunately, again, I felt a surge of anger. I thought of Americans, sure, but also of the many Vietnamese, Cambodian, and Laotian people I'd seen missing limbs because of mines. I'd been to Laos and Cambodia to study the legacy of unexploded ordnance (UXO) a few years before I went to Cu Chi, and I'm just not one for admiring weapons of war. They're too malicious, too indicative of the most depraved corners of the human mind for me. But I know they attract a lot of other people. I've taught a couple of war-based courses, and one way to get many college students' attention is to show them all of the "toys" in the American war arsenal. I invited veterans to guest lecture in one course, and when an Iraq veteran came to class with pictures of mortars and helicopters, students who'd looked bored for every other lecture perked up. My mind always reverts back to an old Donald Duck cartoon, "The Spirit of '43," that I had on video as a child. You can easily find it on YouTube now. The cartoon's mission was to gain support for World War II (or World War II propaganda, depending on your point of view), with emphasis on paying taxes "to defeat the Axis!" At one point the narrator intones, "Our taxes that run the factories…. *American* factories, working day and night. Factories making gun. Machine guns. Anti-tank guns. Long range guns…."[1] The narrator's voice gets louder, nearly orgasmic, exclaiming, "Guns, guns, all kinds of guns!" Then all the animated barrels shoot, and the familiar tones of Beethoven's 5th Symphony play as a ship bearing the Japanese "rising sun" logo sinks into the water.

That euphoric "guns, guns, all kinds of guns!" line sticks with me any time I see people getting excited about war. In the cartoon, as at Cu Chi, the guns get abstracted from the things they are actually intended to do. Sure, it's fun to shoot them, but the guns on display at Cu Chi are intended to represent relics from a war. Those guns—their make and model, not likely the actual guns themselves—were used to kill. It's estimated that well over 1 million people[2] died during the Viet Nam War. That number includes American casualties (over 58,000), the South (Army of the Republic of Viet Nam [ARVN]), and the North (the People's Army of Viet Nam [PAVN] and Viet Cong [VC]), as well as Vietnamese civilian deaths. Celebrating the various ways those people died—weapons, guns, booby traps, mines—never feels like the right thing to do. But I research a war, and weapons are a key historical artifact when you study a war. Outside Viet Nam War memorials in the United States and in Viet Nam, planes, tanks, and artillery supplies are always *proudly* displayed, giant metal reminders of the distances we put between the killer and the victim. I recall the old National Rifle Association line: "Guns don't kill people, people kill people." But doesn't the gun help? Isn't it easier to sight someone from yards away and pull the trigger than, say, put your hands around someone's throat or thrust a bayonet into someone's guts? I know there was some hand-to-hand combat in Viet Nam; the most well-known face-to-face fights in Viet Nam are those of the "tunnel rats" (soldiers who went into tunnels like those at Cu Chi), who were the most likely people to encounter someone up close and personal. In films like *Forrest Gump* or books like Tim O'Brien's *The Things They Carried*, the tunnel rat goes into a tunnel only after a grenade has been thrown into it and detonated, but sometimes that wasn't the case. Armed with only a pistol or knife, the role of tunnel rat wasn't necessarily a coveted position in a platoon.

But killing someone more intimately doesn't soften the impact of the horrors of war. In Ken Burns and Lynn Novick's 2017 documentary *The Vietnam War*, Dr. James Gillam, a former USMC "tunnel rat," shares one of his more harrowing moments in one of the tunnels:

> There are rules in tunnel warfare: don't turn on the light, and don't fire your gun. I chased somebody into a tunnel, met them at a bend in the corner in the dark. I thought I was alone, and then I smelled their breath, and we had a wrestling match in the dark and I got the upper hand and I crushed this person's trachea. Held him down while he died. And then got up. I beat and strangled someone to death in a tunnel, in the dark. But that wasn't the only casualty. The other casualty was the civilized version of me.[3]

Would it have been a more civilized death if Gillam had shot the man in the tunnel? Does it really matter, though? I mean, are *any* deaths during a war a "mark of civilization"? Gillam's civilized self was simply a person who'd never had to fight for his survival, one can argue. But because the United States put him in that tunnel, and U.S. foreign policy steered his fate to that point, the United States must take some responsibility for Gillam's "casualty." He only did what one must in a war zone, but it was of great cost to him.

While most people have heard of "PTSD" in the world of veterans' studies and mental health (short for posttraumatic stress disorder, which was once known, following World War I, as "shell shock" or "soldier's heart," though the condition can affect anyone who's suffered a trauma), a newer idea—"moral injury"—is now applied to many war veterans. The term simply means that people in the war did things that went against their personal moral code. Crushing someone's trachea in a tunnel, for example, might lead to moral injury. From what I've been told and read, moral injury quakes under the skin in the form of a debilitating combination of anger, fear, and guilt. It might never heal—it can only be coped with. Moral injury also carries with it a disconnection in one's sense of self; how can you be the same person as the one who did "that thing"? I think many morally injured U.S. Viet Nam War vets had their inner wounds exacerbated by their reception when they came home, which, at best, was social and cultural ambivalence. To paraphrase comedian Rodney Dangerfield, they didn't get no respect.

After returning from Cu Chi, we dropped off the American family second, right after the New Zealand couple, both of whom I cheerily parted with (I wasn't as moody and brooding in the background as it might seem, but as I read back this anecdote, it looks like I might have been). I'm often the only solo traveler on these group tours, and while I appreciate meeting new people, they're on vacation, while I'm taking notes and looking at everything with a critical eye—I'm not necessarily the most relaxing new friend to meet in Viet Nam. The American family was staying at a good hotel, and I got to watch them as our van driver tried to merge our van into Sai Gon's crazy rush of bikes, motorbikes, cars, and pedestrians. A doorman greeted the family and opened the door for them, the wife smiling and chatty with him. The older son jostled his brother's shoulder as they walked in behind their parents. When the younger boy looked up at his brother, the older son made an unmistakable pantomime of holding a gun and shooting it at a light fixture. The doorman noticed nothing. Was there anything to notice?

In graduate school, I was introduced to historian Walter Hixson's *The Myth of American Diplomacy*, which traces U.S. war history from its roots to the present and argues that the United States bought into the whole "beacon of liberty" message too aggressively. We don't really care, Hixson argues, about spreading democracy; we instead like to focus on creating democratic-ish nations that we can control (or at least get along with well). I started my PhD at Louisville the same year *Myth of American Diplomacy* came out—2008—and that was a year of great change. The United States elected its first Black president, Barack Obama, and fiercely critical books on America's busy-body reputation overseas were in vogue. We were still embroiled in a war that began well before September 11, 2001, but felt more urgent. The history department buzzed about Hixson's ideas, and I, new to graduate courses in subjects outside English, was eager to join in conversations. Now that I'm older and hopefully a hair wiser, I can find some holes in Hixson's work, but I still admire it, and I find that international audiences *really* enjoy his quotes in papers I've presented. Don't be mad at the international academic community; the United States is all over the world, and when we throw our weight around in international forums, it's a turnoff for other countries. Worry not—our food, sports, and culture have traveled far and wide—but it's a sad truth. As David Sedaris wrote in *Me Talk Pretty One Day*:

As an American abroad, you're bolstered by an innate sense of security. Something goes wrong, and you instinctively think, "We'll just call the embassy and see what they have to say." People know where America is on the map. They know that it's loud and powerful. With certain other countries there's no such guarantee. "Oh, right, Laos," I once heard someone say to a dinner guest. "Didn't we bomb you a couple of times?"[4]

Sedaris should know; though born in upstate New York, he grew up in the suburbs of Raleigh, North Carolina. While still a genteel area of the United States, Raleigh would've been a segregated, largely conservative space in Sedaris' youth. He, like many others, grew up in an era when the idea that "America is #1" was first called into question in a big, international way. In history's rearview mirror, the 1950s appear sedate compared to the 1960s. Looking back at chapter 1, we know that the 1960s didn't start out loud. The year of 1961 was similarly sedate, but a surge of soul and R&B hinted at the emergence of voices with more to talk about than love songs.

That's not to say that 1961 was the year that broke the love song. After all, the number-one hit of 1961 was "Tossin' and Turnin'" by Bobby Lewis, which held on to the top spot in the Billboard charts for seven weeks in the summer of 1961. The year began with the continued popularity of Elvis' "Are You Lonesome Tonight," but soon, by the end of January, "Will You Still Love Me Tomorrow?" by the Shirelles took the top spot. The Shirelles carry the honor of being the first all-Black girl group to gain a top single, and the dazzling song, punctuated by lead singer Shirley Owens' emotionally soaring voice over symphonic violins, remains a staple song of the 1960s. Written by Carole King, "Will You Still Love Me Tomorrow?" endures as a song of unsure love, and the lines comparing the night's activities to either a one-night stand or a budding love affair are pretty risqué for 1961, a year carrying residual social mores from the 1950s.

Things were starting to change. In his final State of the Union address to Congress, in mid–January, President Eisenhower—one of the last presidents to have served as both an army general and the POTUS—conveyed grave sobriety over the increasing Cold War tensions and his fears of the growing "military-industrial complex."[5] Eisenhower, who'd been one of the oldest presidents to date, would be succeeded by John F. Kennedy, one of the youngest. Though he had campaigned for Nixon—and Eisenhower's grandson David would later marry Nixon's daughter Julie in 1968—Eisenhower was dovish (more pacifist) than both of his possible successors, who were ready for a fight (hawkish). While the battle between doves and hawks would dominate the mid–1960s, Eisenhower, a West Point graduate, was a more complicated, wizened man. For example, he had been against the use of the nuclear bomb at the end of World War II, but he was all for its use when China started amplifying its forces in Korea. The Republican five-star general was a strong and vocal supporter of desegregation but was extraordinarily homophobic. He had little patience for Senator Joseph McCarthy's (R-WI) "red scare" communist witch hunt ideations, but he wholly believed in his own "domino theory" of the spread of communism. It's easy to see Eisenhower, ol' Ike, lighting a cigarette (he was also one of the most prolific smokers of his time) and kicking back to Lawrence Welk's "Calcutta," which peaked in the charts in the weeks after Eisenhower left office. It's not as easy to imagine him enjoying "Blue Moon" by the Marcels, which topped the April 1961 chart. The Marcels' doo-wop version of the 1940s Mel Tormé classic indicated that the old guard—exemplified by Eisenhower—was on its way out.

Before the end of April 1961, the disastrous Bay of Pigs invasion, a counter-revolutionary coup designed to oust Fidel Castro from power, made headlines. The event was sloppy and supported by the U.S. government, meaning after just a few months in office, President Kennedy had to take the failure on the chin (even though the plan was devised before he came into office). As April transitioned to May, one of the most classic 1960s songs entered the charts, though it never reached number one: "Stand by Me" by Ben E. King. The broad appeal of the lyrics—again a love song, but arguably conveying a more transcendent sentiment—and the assuredness of a friend in times of trouble to "stand by," served as a coda for the Eisenhower years and perhaps acted as a balm for Kennedy's ego. King, a soul and R&B producer, sang this song of brotherhood and companionship in a still-segregated America, where many people wouldn't "stand by" him by virtue of the color of his skin.

The year 1961 was one of transition and separation—apartheid continued, despite condemnation from the United Nations, and in June the Berlin Wall's construction would begin, separating the city of Berlin until 1989. But people—mostly young people—were actively pushing against separatist and racist agendas. In May 1961, the Freedom Riders started their infamous bus rides across the southeastern United States; they wanted to see whether the Supreme Court's decision to ban segregated public transportation stuck. The Freedom Riders met with resistance in the South throughout the month of May, ranging from baseless arrests for violating state-sanctioned Jim Crow laws to overt firebombs and outright violence from the Ku Klux Klan (KKK) *in concert with the police* in Anniston, Alabama, on Mother's Day 1961. The Kennedy administration, embarrassed by the images of brutally beaten young people, deemed the Freedom Riders unpatriotic upstarts and advised them to cease provocation. By the end of May, however, groups whose activism would grow to define the 1960s, like the Congress of Racial Equality (CORE), the Student Nonviolent Coordinating Committee (SNCC) and Southern Christian Leadership Conference (SCLC), gathered behind the Freedom Riders, pointedly *not* cooling down.

By fall, things were only getting warmer: Ray Charles scored a top hit in October with "Hit the Road, Jack," which still packs a punch today (those horns!). Then a Broadway musical and film about Puerto Rican immigrants—*West Side Story*—released its soundtrack, which would maintain the longest number-one run in history until Michael Jackson topped it 20 years later. The *West Side Story* songs were a childhood favorite of my mother's, so I feel warmly toward the record, play, and movie, even though Natalie Wood definitely wasn't Puerto Rican (casting was still very color-coded in the 1960s). The entertaining "Big Bad John" by Jimmy Dean dominated November 1961, a mythical tale of a big man from New Orleans who doesn't suffer fools and saves miners at the cost of his own life. Songs like "Big Bad John" weren't unusual in the pop charts, but Dean's song also made an appearance on the country music charts. In 1961, the Country Music Association formed, making its first point of business to induct Hank Williams, Jr. The "easy listening" chart also started in 1961; music now could be categorized and separated, which created strange sound and song juxtapositions in the latter part of the decade.

Two delightful songs—the Marvelettes' "Please Mr. Postman" (one of my very favorite songs of the 1960s) and the Tokens' "The Lion Sleeps Tonight"—carried the U.S. pop charts into 1962. But December 1961 also saw two army helicopter companies and 400 men, constituting the first U.S. forces deployed for direct combat support of South Viet Nam, arrive on December 11. Eleven days later, on December 22, the United States would see its first battlefield casualty: Specialist 4 James T. Davis. While the first casualty listed on the Vietnam Veterans Memorial in Washington, D.C., is Air Force Sergeant Richard B. Fitzgibbon, Jr., on June 8, 1957, Specialist Davis represents the first U.S. death in Viet

Nam under combat. The war between the United States and North Viet Nam had officially begun.

While Bobby Lewis' "Tossin' and Turnin'" lit up the charts in 1961, things were happening in my hometown of Monroe, North Carolina. Robert F. Williams,[6] a native of Monroe and USMC veteran, was also the president of Monroe's chapter of the National Association for the Advancement for Colored People (NAACP). Williams, whom I certainly never learned about in school or from family (my family did not arrive in North Carolina until 1962), pioneered desegregation of the city's pool and library, formed a "Black Armed Guard" chapter of the National Rifle Association, and represented two young Black men in the "Kissing Case," in which the two little boys kissed a white girl (their age) and ended up in jail. With regard to his time in the Freedom Riders, Williams' proclivity for violence (which went against the nonviolent ethos of the NAACP, SNCC, CORE, and SCLC) was met with force in Monroe, where a city-wide shootout occurred between Blacks and whites. Mobs filled the streets—streets whose names I know like the back of my hand—and Williams had the misfortune of happening upon a lost white couple from out of town who couldn't navigate the violent scene. Williams took them to his house for their safety, which turned into a kidnapping charge that got Williams on the FBI's "Most Wanted" list.

With his wife, Williams fled to Cuba, and he eventually ended up making a speech purportedly in favor of North Viet Nam gaining nuclear weapons in Ha Noi in 1965. This man—and these events—had never crossed my path until I was brushing up on the Freedom Riders for this book. As is the case for much of Viet Nam War–era America, I often am struck by how much I *don't* know (as opposed to being pleased with how much I do know). Of course, my rural, southern hometown would never glorify a Black man who instigated a city-wide firefight in the 1960s; that would be absurd, even in 2020. But you'd think Williams would at least have been mentioned somewhere for the good work he did. This is a lesson in what happens when one race and sex—white men—composes your local and national history. And that's worth remembering when I write about Vietnamese historical sites, whose authors and curators are bound by government rules, oversight, and agenda. The whole story about any event in Vietnamese and American war time in Viet Nam is never really told, even if it could be.

3

1962

I recently read an article about how the Vietnamese government has been cracking down on people speaking against the Communist Party. It started in 2016, when the successor to lead the party unexpectedly died, so the aging current leader tightened his grip. This development comes at a time when China is being touted as the emergent superpower due to its environmental and humanitarian outreach during the COVID-19 pandemic. But China is also cracking down on my beloved hub, Hong Kong.

All of my trips over the Pacific, save one, have required me to fly through Hong Kong. With regard to the Viet Nam War, Hong Kong was an R and R (rest and recuperation) location. It was also a place Vietnamese people fled to at the end of the war. On May 4, 1975, over 3,500 Vietnamese people arrived in Hong Kong as refugees via a Danish freighter. Later on in the 1970s and 1980s, the Vietnamese government started strong-arming trade and businesses to be state owned and state run, which resulted in more movement from Viet Nam to Hong Kong. Chinese and Vietnamese history intertwine in so many ways—the education system was taught in Chinese, historic pagodas all over Viet Nam have Chinese lettering, currently many Chinese businesses operate in Viet Nam and vice versa—but this particular instance of mass immigration is really only a hint as to the scope of the postwar Vietnamese diaspora.

It is useful to ask how a country's government and political philosophy impact you as a traveler. The first issue would be how you enter (or think about entering) a country. For my time in China, I had to send my passport to the Chinese embassy in New York for a visa (Zambia also required this step). For Viet Nam, you submit your "visa on arrival" (VOA) request online. (Pre-COVID, you could ask for a 30-day or 90-day visa, single or multiple entry, ahead of your journey.) About two weeks before your flight, you get an email with a document from the Vietnamese government to take with you. It's a little sketchy that this document also has the names and passport numbers of people entering on the same day as you. I've yet to have someone falsify a passport in my name, though, so I guess it's legit. You also get instructions to arrive bearing two passport-type photos and $45 in cash (that's the cost of a 30-day multi-entry visa; the 90-day option would cost more). You arrive in Viet Nam most likely via Ha Noi or Ho Chi Minh City, and the usual race to the baggage claim is interrupted by a marvelously slow bureaucratic process. You go to the arrivals area and submit your paperwork. You'll wait. And wait. And wait. In Ha Noi they used to yell out your name, but now there's a television that buzzes and flashes your name, plus your mug shot–esque passport-size photo.

The folks performing the task of gluing a visa into your passport are dressed in what

I think of as the uniform of the North Vietnamese Army, though they're now just "the army": deep forest green with red accents, epaulets and stars (the center of the Vietnamese flag is a star; so is the center of these folks' hats and the hat you'll end up buying at some point during your trip when you tire of the sun). There aren't people in uniform walking around with submachine guns (you can see that elsewhere in the world), but there are cameras and bored uniformed people with sidearms. After finishing a book, you get your visa and get in the customs line. You're unceremoniously stamped in (I've gotten more hassle in Canada), and you've hopefully already notified your ride (if you booked one through your hotel) that you're about an hour behind the schedule they set. Most hotels book your airport pick-up off your flight arrival time, not factoring in the visa process. Get WhatsApp or Skype so you can use your phone to call the hotel ahead of time; it's cheaper than getting super-ripped-off (ahem, Sai Gon) when you're just tired and need a ride.

The uniforms do throw me, a little, in a historical sense; I can't imagine what it does to veterans of the war or civilians returning to or visiting Viet Nam. Of course, I know that during the war, the men and women wearing the green-with-star uniforms were mostly likely in official or "pencil-pusher," behind-the-line-type roles. The folks in the thick of things were more likely in camouflage, dressed as civilians, or even wearing the infamous "black pajamas" of the Viet Cong.

Quick backstory: The Viet Minh was a nationalist revolutionary group that originated as opposition to the French (and Japanese, in World War II, from 1940 to 1945). The Viet Minh's residual members stoked the fires of what would become the Viet Cong, a communist revolutionary group that established the Communist Party in Viet Nam. The Viet Cong were the guerrilla "liberation front" of the North in the South, and their job was to slide around southern Viet Nam to get intelligence and support. The North Vietnamese Army, or People's Army of Viet Nam (NVA/PAVN), supported the VC, but they were the official army of the North during the war. In the 1950s, the communist forces went overboard with land reforms, scaring and shaming people from their homes and property. One could not be an apolitical farmer, and if you made any money—even if you were near destitute—it was expected that you'd give your earnings to the party. The memories of these traumas were still fresh by the early 1960s, so the Viet Cong tried different approaches, such as infiltrating villages to make political speeches or teach children nationalistic songs. Many Vietnamese citizens agreed that a unified, independent Viet Nam was worth fighting for, and the country was recovering from decades of colonialism and a brief spate of brutality by the Japanese—it was time to stand up for Viet Nam. Others, often left angry by the 1950s version of the party, placed their bets on democratic-leaning government initiatives and moved to the South (as did many VC troops, with the goal of eventually turning Southerners into true believers of Ho Chi Minh's cause).

Most of the time I enter Viet Nam through Ha Noi. It's the capital city of Viet Nam (it was the capital of the North when the country was divided; before that time Hue was the imperial seat of the country) and has an old town with ripples of urban sprawl. Ha Noi was the first Vietnamese city I learned to cross streets in—a sort of leapfrogging, slow mambo between traffic, as there are rarely crosswalks unless you're at a major intersection—as well as the first Vietnamese city in which I practiced (miserably) my developing

Vietnamese. For all of its eccentricities, Ha Noi remains one of my favorite cities in the world.

In 2012, when I first visited Ha Noi and still enjoyed going to Marlboro country, I would sit outside my hotel every morning and have a "Coke and a smoke" while people watching. I continued to do that until 2018, when I quit smoking and instead squatted outside of the hotel with just the Coke. In 2019, I observed that the Dinh Kim Ngan pagoda, diagonally across from my sitting spot, was now completely renovated compared to my 2012 visit. The "communal house" (that's how Google translates *pagoda*) was built in the 16th century and has many ties to the goldsmithing history of Hang Bac Street. I used to watch an older gentleman sit outside on a folding chair, reading the paper as people passed the pagoda indifferently; in 2019, I watched a few older folks go to the outside of the pagoda and pray.

The names of the streets in Ha Noi's Old Quarter correspond to the trades practiced—or that used to be practiced, in many cases—on each street. Trade remains a big part of the Old Quarter, but now there are more T-shirt and kitsch shops than perhaps merchants of old. A North Face outlet (another "Made in Vietnam" moment) sits across the street from one of my favorite restaurants. There's now a Burger King at the revamped Ha Noi No Bai Airport (the old airport had one little café), and a KFC directly faces Hoan Kiem Lake, the famous central lake in Old Ha Noi.

Even if I'm wishing Ha Noi would stay a bit unchanged for my own sentimental benefit, I have to admit that the growth is probably great for tourism, though the combination burger restaurant *and* tattoo shop I saw in town made me laugh. My nighttime stroll showed me more white folks sweating out the heat during happy hour than I have ever seen. And *Cu Rua*, the ancient giant soft-shell turtle that occupied the lake, died in 2016; the only constant in life is change.

My friend Frank, who is (among *many* things) a Viet Nam veteran and veterans' advocate from Lubbock, Texas, joked that I must listen to the old 1960s music while I'm in Viet Nam. I don't. I don't really listen to any music; I love the sounds and smells of the streets. Traveling alone also has its benefits; no one has any reason to talk to me (other than the street vendors), so the hum of commerce and life becomes a white noise that I enjoy.

The combination of French and Vietnamese architecture makes Ha Noi endlessly fascinating to the eye. Sweeping roundabouts and arched buildings, like St. Joseph's Cathedral, paint a sharp contrast of ancient and somewhat modern styles, and the French influence continues on everything from art on airplanes (one Jetstar plane at the airport sported a "30-year partnership" ad with a Vietnamese and French person holding hands under their respective flags) to the "do not disturb" sign on my hotel door. It seems ironic, as the Ha Noi Hilton, originally a prison for the Vietnamese during the French occupation years, is now a tourist hotspot that extolls the horrors of French colonialism in gruesome detail.

My three visits to Ha Noi (2012, 2015, 2019) reveal a city in perpetual growth. The ride into town from the airport used to have fewer hotels and such on the side of the highway, which was previously much smaller, but I'm glad to report that sidewalk barbershops and other vendors—butchers, flower sellers, fruit and vegetable stands—still exist. Today the majority of the motorbikers wear helmets; they don't have to in Ha Noi (they do in Ho Chi Minh City), but I guess it's safer now, as the city's surge in population led to more traffic.

During the Viet Nam War, Ha Noi earned its status as the capital of the country, and Ho Chi Minh (and, soon into the conflict, Le Duan) navigated the war from the old city. Photos at the Vietnamese History Museum, as well as many restaurants and even my hotel, illuminate the city's history. Street shots from late 19th- and early 20th-century Viet Nam show signs in English, French, and Vietnamese. Bicycles were the primary mode of transport (you'll definitely still see some cyclists). There were more conical hats, which are favored by folks who work outside—and silly tourists who don't know that they'll be toting that blasted hat as a carry-on for the rest of their trip—but the internal chatter and bustle of Ha Noi from the black-and-white photos still reverberates. The graceful and historical bones of the city can still be found in spots like the Dinh Kim Ngan pagoda. Once you're inside, the buzz of the city fades into a low vibration.

Once, as I was leaving the Hong Kong airport, I noticed posters of Chinese film stars promoting "traditional Chinese medicine"; you can still see that in Ha Noi as well. The city's residents insist (rightly, I would argue) on keeping some things about Viet Nam the same as they have been for centuries. I watched a woman slice up meat on a round butcher block on the sidewalk one morning, something that health codes in the United States would never allow. The undercurrent of "hustle" remains strong in Ha Noi, but the younger generations—able to watch foreign films and connect to global trends and events—have a bigger picture of what that hustle looks like. Instagram is popular, and Facebook is *de rigueur*. It's important to note (probably again and again in this book) that the majority of citizens in Viet Nam today were born after the war.

When I visited Ha Noi in 2015, I toured the Vietnamese Ethnography Museum with a young college student; in exchange for a one-on-one tour (and the student's time practicing English), you buy them lunch. The Ethnography Museum details the variety of ancestries in Viet Nam, including the Chinese, the Cham, and ethnic minorities like the Montagnards. It's a beautifully constructed space and, to my American eyes, underscores how much history Viet Nam has versus the United States—we don't have prehistoric tools and 13th-century housing structures to look at, nor do we have a clear marker of when our language became written (we do, of course, but in Europe, and much earlier than when settlers came to the United States). It's become a bit of a joke that Americans traveling abroad marvel at "how old things are," but it's good for us to acknowledge what came before us, as well as what's left out of our history education. Did you learn about Asia when you studied history? I certainly didn't. Or maybe I did, in art class—vases and paintings from ancient China and Japan made their way in, or I'd know nothing about the Ming Dynasty.

During our hot pot lunch, I asked my guide (whom I'll call Quin) about what she learned of about the war. After a small pause, she said, "Well, we were taught that America came to replace the French and that they were colonialist aggressors. But while Viet Nam won the war, no one really 'wins' in war, do they? Everyone loses something." She paused, her chopsticks hovering for a brief moment in the air, to see my reaction to her answer. Seeing none, she smiled, and we began to talk about her sister's wedding and how lucky her sister was to have a nice mother-in-law.

Of course, Quin is likely referring to loss of life when she talks about "losing" in war. I wonder, with regard to the prevalence of things like KFC, Starbucks, Instagram, and Nike in Viet Nam, whether I could argue that while Viet Nam finally got to be independent, U.S. influence ticked a box for commercial victory. Instead of French as the predominant second language in Viet Nam, English is now the most widely spoken second language. I'm not picking on my country 'tis of thee, as this situation isn't unique to the United States; everywhere that Britain went a-conquering, English influence persisted in some way. Pop quiz: Whose picture is on the money in Belize and Honduras? Queen Elizabeth. What is one of the official languages of those aforementioned countries, as well as places like Jordan and Jamaica? English. If you're an English-speaking traveler, this language perk works in your favor tremendously, and you won't hear me complain about it. It's good to recognize the privilege, though, and learn some phrases so you're not just another yelling foreigner. "Please," "thank you," and "sorry" go a long way.

◇ ◇ ◇

Globally, in 1962, Algeria, Uganda, and Tanganyika became independent nations, and the great Nelson Mandela was arrested for agitation (pushing for workers' rights) and given a five-year prison term that would quickly become a life sentence (though Mandela would eventually be released nearly 30 years later). Of course, there was the Cuban Missile Crisis in late 1962, a nuclear standoff between the United States, Cuba, and the Soviet Union, which still reverberates in modern society. In the United States, the Supreme Court ruled that mandating prayer in schools was unconstitutional and that naked male bodies are not inherently pornographic. The first Walmart welcomed customers in Rogers, Arkansas, in 1961; now you can find a Walmart in any midsize town in the United States. In the arts, Johnny Carson started his 30-year tenure as host of *The Tonight Show*, Andy Warhol debuted his iconic Campbell's soup can paintings, and one of New York City's landmarks—the Lincoln Center—opened.

James Meredith famously took the first step toward integrating the University of Mississippi (aka Ole Miss), escorted to class by federal marshals in September 1962. A few weeks later, Mississippi governor Ross Barnett spoke to a Confederate flag–waving crowd at a football game between Ole Miss and the University of Kentucky, proclaiming his love for Mississippi and vowing that "no school will be integrated in Mississippi while I am your governor!"[1] His hate-fueled words that evening—he also lauded Mississippi's white heritage and railed against segregation—would hours later incite "the Battle of Oxford," a race riot on the Ole Miss campus.

While the journey to stop bigots like Governor Barnett was only getting started, some American staples were ending, like the final CBS broadcast of some serial radio programs, which signaled the end of "the Golden Age of Radio" and ushered in the new "television age." On television that February, First Lady Jacqueline Kennedy hosted a tour of the White House. (Earlier that month, the United States had enforced a trade embargo on Cuba.) Jackie's tour of the White House, with its emphasis on historical artifacts, was the first opportunity many Americans had to see inside "our house." Chubby Checker's "The Twist" and Joey Dee and the Starliters' "Peppermint Twist" dominated the pop charts and dance floors that winter. Some metaphorical twists were also happening in Viet Nam in February: U.S. Military Assistance Command, Vietnam (MACV) was established in South Viet Nam against communist insurgents, in part a precautionary measure after the United States learned that the Viet Cong and North Vietnamese Army were getting training and equipment from China.

In the middle of March 1962, Bob Dylan released his first album: the eponymous *Bob Dylan*. His signature nasal voice sang folk tunes over the sounds of stripped-down acoustic guitar strumming. None of the songs made it to the charts, but this album would be only the first ripple in Dylan's decades-long career as a singer-songwriter. "In My

Time of Dying" is my favorite song from this record, but it wouldn't be until September, when Dylan played "A Hard Rain's a-Gonna Fall" at Carnegie Hall, that he began making music that truly spoke to me. In April 1962, Elvis was back in the charts with "Good Luck Charm," and Dylan was writing *Freewheelin'*; the emerging sounds of the 1960s proved to be quite a departure from the 1950s sounds of Elvis. But some vestiges of Americana still persisted via May 1962's top hit, "Soldier Boy" by the Shirelles.

"Soldier Boy" doesn't really mention a soldier in the lyrics; it seems like a pasted-in occupation for a song that's mostly about pledging one's love to a departed lover. It's another pop love song, but the title was a bit prescient. In March 1962, a plane chartered by the U.S. Military Air Transport service, carrying passengers who included army advisors en route to South Viet Nam, vanished. No wreckage was found. Then, in April, eight Marine Task Force helicopters transporting South Vietnamese combat troops were hit on the Ca Mau Peninsula. There were definitely "soldier boys" to sing about, but a massive surge in troops wouldn't occur for another few years. By the end of May, Acker Bilk's clarinet-laden instrumental "Stranger on the Shore"—the first British recording to reach number one on the Billboard Top 100—breezed through the airwaves, though stronger winds were building.

The summer of 1962 seemed innocent enough. The bawdy-trumpet and cymbal-crashing jazz song "The Stripper" by David Rose hit the top of the charts in mid–July. Sandwiching the instrumental were two love songs: June's top hit, "I Can't Stop Loving You" by Ray Charles, and July's sleeper hit, "Roses Are Red (My Love)" by Bobby Vinton. One of the most important 20th-century books about the environment, Rachel Carson's *Silent Spring*, began serialization in the *New Yorker* that June and would be published in September. The book's main argument—that humans are detrimental to the environment—is the cornerstone to pretty much every environmental initiative today (reducing the human footprint). The Students for a Democratic Society (SDS) released the "Port Huron Statement" from the University of Michigan in mid–June. Early in my academic career, I wrote a lot about the protest movements of the 1960s, and SDS remains one of my favorite groups. Formed from the pieces of another socialist "New Left" group, SDS's Port Huron Statement called for greater support of true participatory democracy in the United States and beyond (still a good idea). The document also recognized racial inequalities and imperialism in American culture and sought to reshape the world so that citizens would become the drivers of their informed lives. The Port Huron Statement is lofty in its ambition and pure poetry in its writing, but the group's membership wouldn't start to grow until the mid–1960s, when SDS became one of the most vocal anti–Viet Nam War organizations.

August saw Little Eva's "The Loco-Motion" peak at the top of the charts; it remains one of the most popular songs from the 1960s. Another favorite song, "Sherry" by the Four Seasons (about dating a reluctant girl), topped the charts in September, around the same time that Sonny Liston won the boxing world title after knocking his opponent out in two minutes and *The Jetsons*, a cartoon about a future world with flying cars, premiered on CBS. During the twelve-day Cuban Missile Crisis, a standoff between the United States and the Soviet Union, "Sherry" would lose its top spot on the Billboard chart to the hilarious Halloween staple "The Monster Mash" by Bobby "Boris" Pickett and the Crypt-Kickers.

My favorite telling of the Cuban Missile Crisis is by Robert McNamara in the film *Fog of War*; McNamara gets exhilarated while retelling the story of the nuclear weapons seen on Cuba and the breathless back-and-forth between President Kennedy and Soviet Premier Nikita Khrushchev.

> I want to say, and this is very important: at the end we lucked out. It was luck that prevented nuclear war. We came that close to nuclear war at the end. Rational individuals: Kennedy was rational; Khrushchev was rational; Castro was rational. Rational individuals came that close to total destruction of their societies. And that danger exists today. The major lesson of the Cuban missile crisis is this: the indefinite combination of human fallibility and nuclear weapons will destroy nations. Is it right and proper that today there are 7500 strategic offensive nuclear warheads, of which 2500 are on 15-minute alert, to be launched by the decision of one human being?[2]

Eventually, with U.S. nukes aimed at Russia via Turkey, the world leaders decided not to obliterate each other and delicately resolved the situation without either party losing face. It was the closest the United States ever came to nuclear war, and it's strange to think that "The Monster Mash" played in the background—for example, imagine that a hard-working Kennedy cabinet member, one of his historically hyped Harvard-educated "Wise Men" (let's say National Security Advisor McGeorge Bundy) gets in his car to go home, and during this harrowing moment in history, on his anxious commute in the face of looming nuclear annihilation, "The Monster Mash" comes on the radio. This daydream has no basis in fact, but it's always been interesting to me to think that crazy and/or serious things are *happening* when some fluffy nonsense song titters in the background.

November brought a little extra nonsense, though it wouldn't be revealed until later in the decade: Richard Nixon lost the California governor's race and proclaimed in his concession speech that the United States—people or media (perhaps both)—"won't have Nixon to kick around anymore," as the speech was his "last press conference."[3] Also, in November, President Kennedy sent Senate Majority Leader Mike Mansfield (D-MT) to Viet Nam, and he returned at the beginning of December with a less-than-enthusiastic appraisal of the situation. Mansfield was considered a U.S.-Asia relations pro; his long political career featured foreign policy work under Presidents Roosevelt, Truman, Eisenhower, Kennedy, Johnson, Nixon, Ford, Carter, and Reagan. Mansfield told Kennedy that "$2 billion in American aid funneled into South Viet Nam over the previous seven years was squandered.… The Diem–led government [didn't share power or] win support from the South Vietnamese people," and the influx of Americans in Viet Nam was seen, by many South Vietnamese, as taking "the place formerly occupied by the French colonial rulers."[4] Mansfield's dissent against America's involvement in Viet Nam would be one of the first on record, and it particularly annoyed Kennedy, as Mansfield had been on board with U.S. plans in Viet Nam prior to this visit.

The last big hit of 1962—aside from a late entry from the Tornados' "Telstar"—was another score from the Four Seasons: "Big Girls Don't Cry." This year also marked the release of the first single from the Beatles—"Love Me Do" in the United Kingdom in October—and the first chart entry for the Beach Boys ("Surfin' Safari" hit #100). In country music, Gene Pitney's "The Man Who Shot Liberty Valance" and Dickie Lee's "Patches" topped the country charts. Two songs written by the perennially earnest and sincere folk singer Pete Seeger, "Where Have All the Flowers Gone?" (Kingston Trio) and "If I Had a Hammer" (Peter, Paul, and Mary), reached the Billboard Top 100. Just in time for the holidays, Cuba swapped over 1,000 hostages from the Bay of Pigs invasion for $53 million worth of food, which spoke volumes of the Castro regime's success. How effective, wondered the Western world, could communism be if people were starving? Digging in its heels, the United States remained unwavering in its commitment to fight the evils of "the reds" as the calendar flipped from 1962 to 1963.

From 1959 to 1975, the Viet Cong controlled a network of covert jungle trails stretching from around Vinh, beyond the DMZ in what was then North Viet Nam, to Can Tho and Sai Gon at the southern edge of the country. U.S. military called the network of (in some cases) glorified footpaths "the Ho Chi Minh Trail." The Vietnamese named it the "Truong Son Strategic Supply Route," while some American soldiers referred to it as "the Blood Road" due to its six-month on-foot passage time—and the likelihood of not finishing that long walk. The entire spread of the trail covered around 12,000 miles and stretched into Laos and Cambodia. It was heavily bombed over the course of the war, but the Vietnamese stalwartly maintained its strategic presence.

When I visited the DMZ in 2012, Mr. Anh pulled the car over so we could look over the rails of a bridge donated by Fidel Castro (there were plaques reminding us posted at both ends). The trickling stream beneath caught the sunlight in slivers amid the hilly countryside—we were looking at a piece of the Ho Chi Minh Trail. Everything I've read or heard about the trail was pretty perilous, especially according to memoirs from the North Vietnamese Army and the Viet Cong. In 2015, endurance mountain biker Rebecca Rusch took a 1,144-mile journey in tribute to her father, who was killed in action near the trail in 1972; her experience was turned into the documentary *Blood Road*. Merrill A. McPeak, a member of the semi-famous Misty F-1000 squadron, described bombing the trail as "putting socks on an octopus"[5]; the trail was too long, too covered under triple layers of canopy, to be "killed."

The Vietnamese memory of the trail is purposeful; yet when I went to the Ho Chi Minh Trail Museum, I had to find someone to buy a ticket from, and she was quick to turn on the lights and fans in the exhibit rooms. My Grab driver was unsure of how to get there and took a little tour of the grounds himself, expressing delight at having found something he didn't know existed in his city. The ride itself—too long for a Grab bike, unfortunately—was a reward as well, revealing the dense and intense sprawl of Ha Noi; the city is much larger than the Old Quarter (where most of the tourism happens).

As I walked behind the woman who turned the lights on in the different rooms, I was taken aback by the creativity behind this museum. Much like the Vietnamese Museum of Ethnography and the Women's Museum, the Ho Chi Minh Trail Museum incorporated interesting paintings on the walls and more narratives alongside the typical ephemera you'll see in these types of places. And even though the museum carries the name of Ho Chi Minh on a map, I didn't know until I went there that the Vietnamese referred to the trail as the Truong Son Trail (after a nearby mountain range). The "Ho Chi Minh Trail" name is French in origin, as the trail started operating during the Indochina wars.

The museum celebrates the people who created the trail, as well as those who worked and died in hamlets along the way—and it was a long way. It was a supply route on a large scale (fuel, trucks) and a small one (think people on bicycles ferrying medical supplies or food in the dead of night). The United States bombed the *crap* out of it, which the museum is quick to tell visitors. The numerous operations—like Operation Barrel Roll (air bombing) or Operation Left Jab (ground missions)—the United States undertook to damage or control the trail could be their own book. What's more interesting are

Window detail, Ho Chi Minh Trail Museum, Ha Noi, Viet Nam (2019).

the photos of people on the trail; one of my favorites (captioned "A communication line across Ta Beng Stream, 1962") showed what looked like three Vietnamese hikers, with backpacks and walking sticks, making their way over a small waterfall. It looked pleasant, like an REI catalog. This picture revealed the amount of nature that the trail and its workers had to contend with.

The museum placed enlarged, sometimes non-captioned photos around the area, and I stood longest near one that had no description. It showed six Vietnamese girls—they looked to be in their late teens—smiling together, scarves tied around all their shoulders and wind moving their hair around their open faces. Maybe it's the overall theme of propaganda that pervades all Vietnamese war-related museums, but the vibe of the Truong Son Trail, per the museum, was that this was a group effort. Creating and maintaining this huge project brought people together! Everyone had a job! Everyone was working toward the independence of Viet Nam! What fun!

As I walked outside the museum to see the "main attraction," I thought back to a book I'd read, *Bare Feet, Iron Will* (by James Zumwalt), in which veterans of the trail described what it was like to be there. The fervor is present. But so is the malaria, lack of food, danger of bombs, and huge amounts of mud and rain. I wondered what duties the smiling girls were assigned and how many of them survived to reach adulthood. I wondered if, behind their smiles, there was the steely resolve of knowing they were doing something bigger than themselves, or was it just fun to be doing something, with other girls, while their country was embroiled in war? Those feelings, I decided, didn't have to be mutually exclusive.

The museum's biggest focus—out back behind the somewhat neglected pond area (and, bizarrely enough, rustic outdoor restrooms; the museum is in a very modern building, so I guess the toilets were an afterthought ... or perhaps a way for visitors to participate more in the sacrifices made by those on the trail)—is a monument to all those who died while keeping the trail alive. A plaque in front of the monument reads, in capital letters, "We Revere and Worship the Truong Son Heroic Soldiers." The plaque goes on to note, "During 16 years (from 1959 to 1975), Truong Son soldiers overcame innumerable difficulties and hardship to build and hold a strategic supply route.... The enemy's lethal weapons took the lives of near 20 thousands [*sic*] Truong Son soldiers and officers and over 32 thousands [*sic*] wounded soldiers.... We are eternally grateful [to them], who sacrificed their lives for our homeland." A frieze, not unlike the one at Dien Bien Phu

Monument at Ho Chi Minh Trail Museum, Ha Noi, Viet Nam (2019).

but smaller, depicts men and women in boats, riding on bicycles, pushing carts, and climbing trees. In the center is a group of smiling people, with a woman in the middle waving a small flag. The main monument—four pillars over an urn with what look to be flames on top—has a Vietnamese star prominently displayed. Around the main torch-like monument are walls with the names of those who died on the trail. Like the length of the trail, there are more names than I can count. I wonder whether any of the girls in the uncaptioned photo inside are on these walls, happy to be "revered and worshiped" as heroes to the homeland.

4

1963

Aside from the divisions within Viet Nam, the French and American (Western) presence seeped into Vietnamese culture by the 1950s and remains today. Even Ho Chi Minh, who had traveled the world by the time the Americans entered his country, preferred French cigarettes (outrage!). A country can't just wall itself off once its citizens have seen what else is out there. I saw the legacy of Western influence in 2012 on my first visit to Viet Nam. My friend Carrie joined me for the trip, which was a real champion friendship move. (I'd been in China for about five weeks, so I had adjusted to the 12-hour time difference—Carrie came over the Pacific and hit the ground running.) We spent a fair amount of our time in Hue, the former imperial capital of Viet Nam.

The main reason we were in Hue was to go on a full-day tour of the DMZ, which is nearly three hours away by car. We visited Hamburger Hill, Razorback Ridge, Khe Sanh, and the Vinh Moc tunnels, and we saw a section of the Ho Chi Minh Trail. Our guide, Mr. Anh, would add his own commentary to a British documentary about the Viet Nam War, which he handed us to watch on his iPad as we drove (it takes a while to drive around Viet Nam). The film began with the fall of the French and took great pains to emphasize the similarities between Khe Sanh and Dien Bien Phu, with the underlying message being "foreigners don't know the land of Viet Nam like the Vietnamese"—which seems obvious *now*. (I write more on the DMZ in chapter 15; for now, though, we stay in Hue.)

Our first big trip in Hue was walking across the city from our delightful hotel (always a fan of the cooling washcloth greeting) to the Citadel, because you kind of have to go there; it's the main thing on the tourist map, aside from commandeering and haggling with a boat or motorbike driver so you can race to see all the historic temples (a more streamlined process now). The Imperial Citadel was bombed during the war, and it's still being renovated, so there's that bit of time past being time present going on. I remember watching a man get outfitted in the emperor's robes for a souvenir photo in an opulent red-velvet-paneled room and laughing, and then walking 10 feet away and looking at a crumbling stone archway, in a perpetual state of disrepair since 1968. There was a stoic elephant on display by the outdoor café. (Asia, as a region, doesn't have its animal rights and welfare rules on lock the way other countries do—well, I've seen *Tiger King*, so I take that back. It's just more out in the open: Welcome to the Citadel, here is our visitor canteen, elephant by a banyan tree included. You can feed the elephant bananas for $2.)

We went to the Thieu Hieu pagoda, the one that is emblazoned on flags, iron streetlamps, and streetlight displays throughout Hue, just like the One Pillar Pagoda in Ha Noi is that city's symbol. We got there in time to hear the monks chanting, and I hovered near them, feeling a strange bliss mixed with the faux intoxicant of exoticism.

It was something I'd remember three years later when I heard the call to prayer in Istanbul. (There, however, after the first few days of enchanting echoes in a language I couldn't understand, my "wow!" quickly gave way to "oh, it must be around lunch time.") Thieu Hieu is also famous for having been a former residence of well-known Buddhist monk Thich Nhat Hanh. Hanh resides primarily in France; his views aren't favored by the Vietnamese government, though photos of his brief return in 2006 could be bought as postcards at Thieu Hieu. I bought a book of Hanh's writing from a monk at the pagoda, only to realize that night, at our hotel, that the book had been hastily put together; half of the pages were duplicated, and almost 40 pages were missing. I wondered whether this was a purposeful act, spurred by the government, or if I just got "suckered" as a tourist.

Inside the Vinh Moc tunnels, Viet Nam (2012).

At Thien Mu Pagoda, however, things felt more magical. We quietly wove our way through the immaculately kept bonsai gardens, enjoying some stillness by a reflecting pond with lotus flowers in it. We got there around sunset, so the heat was fading. Thien Mu continues to hold my personal honor of "most unique" relic at a Vietnamese site: the car that took Buddhist monk Thich Quang Duc to Sai Gon so he could immolate himself in protest of the South's brutal treatment of the Buddhist community. President Diem, a Catholic, didn't want Buddhists sympathetic to the people or the North to operate; many people converted from Buddhism to Catholicism to gain favor under Diem. Diem also did petty, stupid things, like forbidding the Buddhists to fly their flag on a Buddhist holiday or not allowing them to be private landowners. The latter was a French law that the Buddhists hoped would be repealed by their Vietnamese president; when it wasn't, and as anti–Buddhist laws and sentiments spread through Viet Nam, Buddhist protests—peaceful things, like hunger strikes—began.

The image of Duc, sitting upright while on fire on a Sai Gon street, a few blocks from the presidential residence, alarmed the world upon its publication (and the American journalist who photographed the event, Malcolm Browne, won a Pulitzer for the shot). People on the street cried, and even some policemen on the scene abandoned their duties and prostrated at the sight. A monk nearby repeated, in English and in Vietnamese, into a megaphone, "A Buddhist priest burns himself to death. A Buddhist priest becomes a martyr." It pains me to admit the first I heard of Duc was in 1992; his immolation is on the cover of Rage Against the Machine's self-titled debut album. The lyrics on *Rage Against the Machine* (particularly the refrain of the song "Killing in the Name Of") may or may not underscore the ethos of Thich Quang Duc, but from an early age, I understood that Duc's act was a powerful, last-resort act against oppression. Two years later, 82-year-old Alice Herz would set herself on fire in Detroit. She would be the first of at least four Americans to duplicate Duc's immolation as protest against the Viet Nam War.

War tourism and reflecting on the past gets heavy after a while, so Carrie and I tried to celebrate Viet Nam's present by going to different NGO (nongovernmental organization, usually nonprofit) and co-op shops. The provinces of Thua Thien Hue and its neighbor, Quang Tri, were heavily bombed and chemically sprayed during the war, which left many mentally and physically disabled people struggling to survive. As recently as 2019, unexploded ordnance was pulled off a beach near Hue. Carrie and I were unaware of that lasting legacy of the war in 2012; instead, we debated whether to get a massage by someone blinded by Agent Orange or shrapnel. This isn't meant to be flippant; blind massages were something advertised and geared toward tourists all over town. Eventually, a few years later in Hoi An, I would try the blind massage experience, but in 2012, we opted for getting custom-made silk items and items made from repurposed wire by victims of Agent Orange. My friend Jim, who got his Purple Heart not far from Hue during the Tet Offensive in 1968, encouraged us to grab a drink at the DMZ Bar, a place he'd gone on his only return visit to Viet Nam in 2005. We went during the day (we were told it got a bit rowdy at night) and dutifully wrote our names on the wall, as the custom goes. I've never been back to see whether they're still there, but my guess would be no, even though we artfully added a Clemson tiger paw next to our signatures. Those sorts of things don't last as long as ordnance or chemical weapons.

When Viet Nam War scholars talk about Hue, it's mostly in the context of the Battle of Hue. In March 1968, during the Tet Offensive, Hue was besieged from all sides by the North, and the U.S. Marines in the area (as well as a stalwart, understaffed ARVN platoon) held fast and ultimately secured the city. My friends in the Marine Corps tell me they were taught about this battle as recently as the early 2000s; the street fighting in the Battle of Hue would be something to revisit in the first decade of the new millennium, when block-by-block battles became a staple of fights in places like Fallujah. When looking back at historical battles, it is easy to romanticize war and its various players. The 1968 Tet Offensive marked a socio-cultural turning point in the Viet Nam War with regard to all involved; global anti-war movements showed marked growth after the horrors of Tet were revealed on international news outlets, and the rising tide of enlistments, bombings, and other military maneuvers led to angry responses from the U.S. anti-war movement in particular. The battle remains a clear historical pivot when regarding the Viet Nam War as a whole.

The Tet Offensive, while one of the most horrifying and bloody events of the Viet Nam War, has been repackaged with the trappings of war history romantics that have been seen in literature reflecting on the Battle of the Bulge, for example. Memories and memorials (personal and public) of the Tet Offensive cannot escape heroic deeds and moments of personal triumph, but the language used to describe the event borders on idealizing the gruesome horrors of war and can be careless and superfluous. Perhaps this is needed to combat the shame that is usually associated with the war, or perhaps this is an inevitable development when recounting stories of war.

Mark Bowden's *Hue 1968: A Turning Point in the American War in Vietnam* (2017) tells the story of the Battle of Hue, a rare instance of "street-fight" combat and regarded as an American victory during the Tet Offensive. In an excerpt from his book, published as a publicity piece in *Vanity Fair*, Bowden recalls *Stars and Stripes* photographer John Olson's Robert Capa Gold Medal–winning pictures—taken in February 1968, in the midst of the battle and later published in *Life*:

> With an artist's eye for composition, Olson captured seven Marines in a tableau worthy of Rembrandt. The palette is one of dark, muddy greens and blues and browns in a grayish light, with shocking splashes of red.... The most striking figure, at the center of the shot, in the foreground, is supine. He has been shot through the center of his chest. He is pale, limp, and half-naked. His shirt has been stripped away and his wound roughly bandaged. His head is the closest thing to the viewer in the frame. We see him upside-down, his eyes closed beneath dark eyebrows, his head resting on a wooden door that has been used as a makeshift stretcher. He has a full head of wet black hair, and a lean, handsome face with a long aquiline nose and a faint, youthful attempt at a mustache. He looks to be dead, or nearly so.[1]

Bowden sets the picture up most descriptively, noting Olson's "artist's eye for composition"—instead of merely documenting the terrors of the Battle of Hue, the photographer is now an artist in search of a muse. That he finds this inspiration in "seven Marines in a tableau worthy of Rembrandt" is simultaneously erudite and common; the attempt to conflate dying people and "a tableau" misses the mark. Rembrandt's forte was portraiture, so Bowden attempts to make this photo a portrait of youth and heroism. His emphasis on the "palette … of dark, muddy greens and blues and browns in a grayish light, with shocking splashes of red" continues to portray Viet Nam as exotic, rustic—other; this is a frequent literary trope used in Viet Nam War fiction. The "shocking splashes of red" Bowden refers to are open, bleeding wounds, not daubs of color on a canvas. The photo conveys the reality of war, and aggressive overinterpretation and embellishment only continue to falsely romanticize that reality. Blood on the battlefield is not shocking—one could argue it's rather par for the course. But perhaps the image shocked the American public; I am the historian looking backward, while Bowden's broader audience may remember the original publication of the photos, at the very least.

The "most striking figure" (not the most gruesome, the most somber, the most alarming, the most heart-wrenching) is a man shot through the chest in the center of the photo. The author doesn't mention the medic beside this young Marine, nearly cradling him, while another soldier holds a bottle of fluids and tubing that leads to the (most) wounded man's chest. These details—what is required for the "striking figure" to remain alive—are overridden by the soldier's "aquiline nose," "full head of wet black hair," and "faint, youthful attempt at a mustache." That he "looks to be dead, or nearly so" is the final sentence in the paragraph—poignant in its simplicity but also worded in a way that conveys a passive sadness at best. What we are looking at is a young Everyman, or "Anysoldier," who has a fatal wound and could be spending his last moments on top of a tank. His comrades will likely replay his death in their heads for the rest of their lives, the "tableau" a difficult memory.

The experience of war extends far beyond the moment a photograph was taken, and Bowden is aware of this fact. *Hue 1968*'s existence is a good thing, and it is a "pot-boiler" read; moreover, the book shows evidence of research, maintains some level of accuracy, and dissects a micro-example of the complexity of battle in the Viet Nam War. A rare "street fight," Hue did not represent a turning point in American or NVA military tactics—but it arguably did shift public perception of the war in the United States (hence the common narrative of Tet as a "turning point"). Historian Gregory Daddis commends

Bowden's excellence in "describing the horrific urban warfare.... He hammers away at the reader with a gritty mélange of decapitations, burns, amputations, and sucking chest wounds, enough to make even those with the strongest constitutions wince," and he applauds the book's "merit to unveiling the dreadfulness of combat."[2] Ultimately, however, Daddis also grows tired of Bowden's glossy takes on the war, pointing out, for example, Bowden's slipshod handling of General Westmoreland, chastising the author for adding "little to the debate, simply trotting out a caricature of the general associated with works from the mid–1970s and early 1980s." Furthermore, Daddis points out that frequent, flawed dramatic flourishes oversimplify the experience of war, such as Bowden's insistence on "dramatically maintain[ing]" that "the marines fighting and dying inside Hue really 'grew accustomed to the smell of death' ... did the marines truly cease to find death troubling or, rather, did they compartmentalize the horror?" A dehumanizing, grim romanticization of the realities of a combat zone overshadows the gruesome details of war; "*the* marines" do not share this memory with Bowden, never mind "*a* marine."

Memories *are* shared—accompanied by audio and visual stimulus—in Ken Burns and Lynn Novick's 2017 documentary *The Vietnam War*. Romanticization of war—particularly the Battle of Hue—is also present in this film. Burns admits that he knew while making the World War II documentary *The War* (2007) that "there was no way [he and Novick] could avoid telling [the story of Viet Nam]" and that the filmmakers were "really obligated" to make the documentary. With regard to timing, Burns notes that "historical presentation" requires "the kind of triangulation" of decades passing, while Novick asserts that the war is "unfinished business" of American history that can't be moved past without "understanding." The filmmakers make certain to frame the film as "not an answer, but a set of questions about what happened," but even this assertion—that the film is not taking a stance in any way, but rather just presenting facts—is made over the now legendary Ken Burns "zoom" video effect of a soldier standing, gun on hip, against a blue "anywhere" sky.[3]

But what happened was really just another war—at least in the Burns method of depiction. The primary image (used as the thumbnail on internet and TV downloads, the background to the website, and the DVD cover) from Burns' *Civil War* is a cannon. Neither "side" of the war is depicted (there are no people in the image), but one of the war's main weapons of destruction is shown against a sunset—poignant, beautiful, romantic and bygone. (The iconic sunset images of David O. Selznick's *Gone with the Wind* may have been an influence here.) For his film on World War II, Burns chose an "everyman" soldier to represent the film's DVD and accompanying book cover. The soldier is white, American, and haunted-yet-determined looking; again, a weapon is part of the larger picture, as the soldier has his gun slung visibly over his shoulder. *The Vietnam War*'s official cover photo features two people: a "reflected" Vietnamese farmer *under* an American soldier. The soldier's gun—like all the other weapons mentioned so far on all the other cover materials—is visible but not in use. In the distance, by the soldier's head, is a helicopter, a nod to the "first helicopter war" as much as a pointed reference to further firepower. These simple promotional images on the packaging for Burns' works tell us that war equals weapons. The weight of the individual who carries the weapon is the main story of war, per Burns.

The "Tet Offensive episode" of *The Vietnam War*, "Things Fall Apart," begins with a tribute to the helicopters, in which pilots reminisce on how flying in them "felt like being God"[4] and footage of helicopter silhouettes floating over rice paddies cements the distinct Viet Nam War image of the helicopter. The film then descends into a portrayal of (recalling Bowden) "horrific urban warfare." The film's inclusion of Vietnamese voices—in this excerpt, a North Vietnamese soldier—is one of its most critically lauded aspects. Truthfully, the Vietnamese perspective on the war has been greatly ignored or diminished by American narratives, and our allies, the South Vietnamese, are at best maligned players and at worst forgotten comrades. In Australia, if a Vietnamese person can prove they served in the ARVN, they are allowed and embraced in annual ANZAC celebrations and parades. By contrast, seeing a South Vietnamese soldier marching beside his American counterpart in a military parade in the United States is nearly unthinkable.

In Burns and Novick's film, however, the stories and experiences of the respective soldiers can at least be displayed side by side. In the film excerpt just referenced, the North Vietnamese are "trapped" inside Hue, well armed but thin, and many are wearing shorts (in February). They are portrayed in black-and-white film footage (likely government archive approved) as the narration from Peter Coyote and North Vietnamese veteran Nguyen Ngoc weaves through the film. The Americans, in contrast, are shown without a narrator and in color. The brief footage of a GI trying to light a cigarette—unsuccessful because of both his shaking hands and incoming enemy fire—is powerful. This is the reality of war: fear. Bowden's book and Burns' *Vietnam War* documentary take special care in handling the civilian massacre at the hands of the North Vietnamese Army, but only one NVA veteran, Ho Huu Lan, acknowledges it directly and, 30 years later, with fear: "We rarely speak of it; I'm willing to talk about it but many others are not. Be careful making your film because I could get into trouble."[5]

Due to its continued presence in the experience of humanity, it's a stretch to think that any one war retains any real uniqueness. Wars can be different from one another in terms of area, space, and time—cold wars lurk in submarines and subterfuge before morphing into "cyber" wars, and Viet Nam's jungles taught us different lessons than the deserts of Iraq or the shores of France. But ultimately the larger stories of war are the same. While both Bowden and the Burns/Novick team have made concerted and sincere contributions to the greater Viet Nam War narrative, they have all retained the urge to mythologize the war, as if not doing so would somehow make the trauma of it better. It does not.

I studied abroad for a semester in London for my undergraduate degree; it was one of the best times of my life. Upon returning home, my friends and I noticed that London was about a year ahead of the United States in terms of fashion and music. The jeans-tucked-into-boots look was all over England in 2003, as well as glitter-sprinkled skinny scarves, both of which would enter the local malls in 2004. We heard Kylie Minogue's "Slow" all over London; she'd only blipped on the American charts with 2001's "Can't Get You Out of My Head." The trans-Atlantic pop-culture lag year doesn't hold true as much today—hurray, internet—but in 1963 the United States was about a year behind England in terms of music.

The Beatles' single "Please Please Me" stayed at the top of the UK charts from February until November, when their new album *With the Beatles* knocked it off. The number-one song on the 1963 American Billboard charts was "Sugar Shack" by Jimmy Gilmer and the Fireballs (an insipid song about a crush on a poor girl, but with an infectious whistled hook); the number-one song in the United States in 1963 actually never made it to the top spot: "Surfin' USA" by the Beach Boys. In a distant graduate course that I ultimately withdrew from, I do remember the professor proclaiming that part of the Beatles' success was that they often wrote songs in the third-person narrative viewpoint, which "Please Please Me" is not. I think the "cuteness" of the Beatles was more part of their success than their narrative voice, but I could be wrong. What's undeniable (to me, at least) is that "Please Please Me" is better than "Sugar Shack"—but not "Surfin' USA." While not my favorite Beach Boys track, "Surfin' USA" always makes me move and smile. Also, *great* songs like "It's All Right" (the Impressions, with Curtis Mayfield), "You Really Got a Hold on Me" (the Miracles), "One Fine Day" (the Chiffons), and "Ring of Fire" (Johnny Cash) charted but never reached number one—competition was growing in the musical ranks, which tried to accommodate blues, R&B, country, rock, and pop in one chart.

The year 1963 was pretty rough, so perhaps moving and smiling was something the nation needed; there are several studies that say the worse things are in a country, the more likely people are to gravitate toward pop hits. Patsy Cline, a (country) music legend and treasure, along with Hawkshaw Hawkins, Cowboy Copas and one other person, died in a plane crash before winter was over. In January alone, the North Vietnamese won the battle of Ap Bac and Alabama swore in Governor George Wallace (the dictionary definition of a bigot), stirring up racial tensions that would start to boil in the summer. But the rough mood of 1963 couldn't be seen in the pop charts. The number-one song of January 1963 was the orchestral "Go Away Little Girl" by Steve Lawrence, a song in which the speaker wants a temptress to leave before he gets in trouble for seeing her—or she is trouble; it's not certain. The "forbidden love" theme that began 1963 gave way to a boost for the masculine morale with March's top tune, "Walk Like a Man" by the Four Seasons. Frankie Valli's trademark falsetto soared over scorned-love lyrics as the United States built a figurative wall between itself and Cuba in early February and tightened internal security with the creation of the CIA's (Central Intelligence Agency) Domestic Operations Division (DOD). The DOD's job was to spy on foreign targets within the United States, a directive specifically aimed at those perceived to be communist, hinting at the Cold War tensions occupying the U.S. government; the establishment of the "red phone" (the direct Russia-to-America hotline we see in movies) in June underscored Cold War divisions. President Kennedy's brother, U.S. Attorney General Bobby Kennedy, closed down the infamous Alcatraz prison in April; three people had escaped in 1962, so perhaps "the Rock" wasn't as secure as it looked.

By April 1963, the United States' racial relations issues got more visible and violent. On April 3, the SCLC began the Birmingham campaign, a peaceful sit-in protest against segregation. Sit-ins weren't unique to the 1960s, but I view them as the cornerstone of peaceful public protest: you simply go somewhere and sit—your only "crime" is taking up space. Alabama tolerated this act, but days later—April 12—SCLC luminaries, like Dr. Martin Luther King, Jr., were arrested for "parading without a permit"[6]—that is, *walking* (an Alabama judge had banned any sort of street demonstrations, but the SCLC rightly viewed the new rule as unjust). Four days after the arrest, Dr. King composed his "Letter from a Birmingham Jail," which wouldn't be published in full (or with King's permission) until June. The letter's trademark—the top "takeaway" I give it as an English professor— is that it is a response to another letter from eight white clergymen in Birmingham, who argued in their missive (titled "A Call for Unity") that the fight for equal rights belonged in the courtroom, not in the street. King insisted that the "sit ins, marches and so forth" were necessary due to the "broken promises" of civil negotiation with racist courts:

The purpose of our direct action program is to create a situation so crisis packed that it will inevitably open the door to negotiation. I therefore concur with you in your call for negotiation. Too long has our beloved Southland been bogged down in a tragic effort to live in monologue rather than dialogue.[7]

The image of a man scribbling these words—a call for dialogue with those whose narrow views ultimately imprisoned him—in the margin of a newspaper in a jail cell always strikes me as a visual metaphor for hope against all odds. Popular culture has "white-washed" Dr. King's legacy; he's become martyred for the cause of equal rights, which I think he deserves, but his insistence on nonviolence makes him more palatable to U.S. history than, say, Stokely Carmichael or Angela Davis. The calm, sober-faced minister walking with a crowd of people to Selma suits American sensibilities more than an angry Black person. But if you read "Letter from a Birmingham Jail" carefully—or out loud—you can hear the anger in it. And there would be more anger by the beginning of May, when Birmingham's public safety commissioner, Eugene "Bull" Connor (one of those textbook Southern good ol' boy racists), authorized the use of fire hoses and dogs against segregation protesters; the lucky ones—thousands—got arrested. The doo-wop hit "He's So Fine" by the Chiffons held the top spot in the charts during the events in Birmingham.

Hosted by Frank Sinatra, the fifth annual Grammy Awards in May 1963 crowned Tony Bennett's *I Left My Heart in San Francisco* as Record of the Year. I don't put much stock in the Grammys, mostly because I never saw my favorite bands (or genres of music) gain any recognition, and it's a historical failing of the organization. The early 1960s jazz scene, for example, is completely left out of the Grammy oeuvre; it's just not an accurate yardstick for popular music opinion (and yes, the Billboard Top 100 has its failings as well).

Across the Pacific, the inability of President Diem to maintain public support in South Viet Nam defined the summer of 1963. In early May, Diem embroiled himself (and his brother, Archbishop Ngo Dinh Thuc) in a stupid game of flag dominance with Buddhists. The situation rapidly got worse, but even U.S. protests and threats to withhold aid did not move Diem to change course. When Buddhist monk Thich Quang Duc set himself on fire to protest the Diem government's treatment of Buddhists, Diem's response was a muted plea for unity, while his sister-in-law, the villainous Madame Nhu, cruelly and publicly laughed it off as a "monk barbeque show."[8] The final nail in the coffin—almost literally—for Diem was the Xa Loi Pagoda raids in August. Essentially, Diem sent the ARVN to degrade, destroy and deface Buddhist pagodas all over South Viet Nam; slaughtering Buddhists who got in the way was also part of the mission. President Kennedy's team cabled its contacts in Viet Nam: get rid of Diem.

In the United States that summer, songs like Little Peggy Marsh's "I Will Follow Him" (brilliantly remade into an evangelical singalong in the 1992 film *Sister Act* starring Whoopi Goldberg) and Lesley Gore's "It's My Party" (the ultimate teen-birthday-party-gone-wrong song) charted high. Jan and Dean's "Surf City" capitalized on the "surf craze" of the early 1960s by the end of the summer, but these pop hits of love and surf life sound antithetical to the seriousness in American social and cultural politics at the time. On August 28, in front of the Lincoln Memorial, Dr. Martin Luther King, Jr., gave his "I Have a Dream" speech during the March on Washington for Jobs and Freedom, speaking to an audience of nearly 250,000. Musical guests included Joan Baez, Mahalia Jackson, Bob Dylan, and Peter, Paul, and Mary. It would be the largest protest to date until 1969, when it would be overtaken by the Moratorium to End the War on Viet Nam. That September would see the bombing of the 16th Street Baptist Church in Birmingham, Alabama, a brutal racist attack that killed four children and injured over 20 other people. The 16th Street bombing inspired John Coltrane's "Alabama" that year, confirming that the civil rights movement was now a part of popular music; racism in America could no longer be confined to the news. Sam Cooke began recording "A Change Is Gonna Come" in September, following in the tradition of Odetta's "Oh Freedom" (1961) and Billie Holiday's "Strange Fruit" (1939).

Malcolm X's mid–November "Message to the Grassroots" in Detroit called for revolution and racial separation, and Black unity: "[We must] put the white man out of our meetings ... and then sit down and talk shop with each other." In his speech, Malcolm X designated the white man as the "common oppressor, a common exploiter, and a common discriminator ... he's the enemy to all of us" and urged more violent protests, reasoning that "if it is right for America to draft us, and teach us how to be violent in defense of her, then it is right for you and me to do whatever is necessary to defend our own people right here in this country."[9] This sentiment would be echoed by Muhammad Ali and help build the Black Panther Party and, eventually (though with less emphasis on violence), be woven into Dr. King's "Beyond Vietnam" speech in 1967.

As Jimmy Gilmer and the Fireballs' "Sugar Shack" held the top spot in the charts in the autumn of 1963, things were falling apart in Viet Nam. On November 2, South Vietnamese president Ngo Dinh Diem was arrested and assassinated; the photo of him dead, bloody, and shoved in the trunk of a car horrified the members of the Kennedy cabinet, who nonetheless put their faith in General Guong Van Minh, the leader of the coup that ousted Diem. By the time "I'm Leaving It Up to You" by Dale and Grace ousted "Sugar Shack" from the number-one spot on the music charts, President Kennedy, like Diem, would be dead. On November 22, as Kennedy's motorcade glided through Dallas, a bullet tore over the waving crowds and into Kennedy's head; mere hours later, aboard Air Force One, with a blood-splattered Jackie Kennedy in shock to his left, Lyndon Johnson was sworn in as president.

On November 22, 1963, my dad was in a busy stairwell during the changing of classes at John D. Hodges Elementary School in Monroe, North Carolina—that's where he heard the news that the president had been shot; my mom, in sixth grade at Thomas A. Edison Elementary School in Fairlawn, New Jersey, heard the news from the school's principal over the intercom. The nation was shocked, and, in the hindsight only those of us who did not live through these decades might possess, the assassination of President Kennedy—in broad daylight, in front of an audience and next to his wife—looks like a prelude to the violence that the 1960s would ultimately experience. Anyone who lived through the Kennedy assassination knows where they were when it happened; it was such a sudden, jarring, terrible act. The impenetrability of the United States is often symbolized by the strong leader in power; to have him taken down (and then only days later see his killer shot, on television) shook the American public and rattled governments around the world. President Kennedy had occupied the Oval Office for less than three years; how would Johnson—and the rest of the nation—navigate the abrupt transition?

◇ ◇ ◇

Before the United States showed any interest in Viet Nam, it was (and still is) a country with a Buddhist religious majority. Communism is generally not a "friend" of religion, but in Viet Nam it doesn't appear to be a current pressing issue; one of my favorite things to do when I'm there is to take some moments, every day, of quiet in a nearby pagoda. In bustling, beeping Ho Chi Minh City, I love going to Chau Van Phat (aka the Temple of Ten Thousand Buddhas); I've been for "service" (I don't know what you call a gathering of Buddhists) a couple of times, sitting quietly in the back row. I don't know what's being said, and, similar to my memories of going to church when I was a kid, I don't know when to bow and when to respond. But I found myself swaying to the ringing bells under my pagoda-appropriate kimono (you'll either be given a robe or be unable to enter if you're in a tank top and shorts, but the same goes for a mosque). The Temple of Ten Thousand Buddhas boasts—you guessed it—10,000 Buddhas to look at; some of them are lit, most of them are golden, and the temple itself is on the third story of a building, so the big open doors behind the parishioners provide a welcome breeze. It's one of the coolest spots in the city. I know there are Buddhist holidays and special calendar events, and the Vietnamese often abide by Buddhist customs when burying their dead, but the marriages look pretty Western—big parties, big white dress.

Blending traditions and religions isn't unheard of in Viet Nam. Right off Pasteur Street in the HCMC center is the Sri Dandayudhapani Temple, another one of my favorite places to "sit a spell" when I'm in the city. I love the glowing Buddha, even though this locale identifies as a Hindu temple—but it's very normal to see Buddha make cameos in Hinduism. Buddha came from India, after all, and in at least one sect of Hinduism Buddha is an "avatar" (representation) of Vishnu, one of the gods in Hinduism's main triumvirate of deities (the other two are Brahma and Shiva). This temple is literally smack in the middle of everything, and yet, once you've passed through the door with your incense, it's quiet. I found similar solace in a pagoda in Hoi An, where I kept picking the same time of day to sit as another woman, who looked about 50 or 60 years old. She'd sit, barefoot on the floor, and just close her eyes for about half an hour. I've seen people prostrate themselves, using the predictable series of entry and exit bows—always three—and

Chau Van Pat (the Temple of Ten Thousand Buddhas), Ho Chi Minh City, Viet Nam (2017).

one time I saw a fellow white woman solo traveler whispering some script she'd brought with her, gesturing toward the pagoda's central Buddha statue with green glass beads. I'm not sure what she was doing, but no one cared. Pagodas are very open like that; should you see one, stop in if you can. And if you do it out of a pure desire to just sit down out of the sun, you won't be the first—I can't remember the name of one pagoda I went to in Ha Noi, but the respite it provided, from the heat and my own inner chatter, was much needed.

Cao Dai temple, Hue, Viet Nam (2012).

Aside from a few Catholic churches here and there, I also saw, in Hue, the Cao Dai temple of Vinh Loi. Cao Dai started in the 1920s in southern Viet Nam, and it blends Buddhism, Hinduism, Christianity, Taoism, Confucianism, and Islam. I don't know much about it beyond that, other than the Vinh Loi Cao Dai temple is like a pagoda on acid. The outside is brightly painted in yellows, reds, and whites; it wouldn't be out of place in a *Mario Bros.* video game. Buddhist swastikas always give me a moment's pause (thanks, History Channel, for all those Nazi shows), but the multicolored exterior didn't look like it contained an evil space. My pal Carrie and I happened upon it while walking around Hue, and when we asked whether we could go in (it was empty that afternoon, but I also have no idea when it's full), we were welcomed with great enthusiasm. The inside was painted in blues and golds, but the real experience started when our host switched on neon lights. The main altar (if that's what it's called) had plush blue curtains around it, and red lacquered wood surrounded us, along with dragons, mobiles with colorful flowers and pom poms, and intricate wood carvings. I have never before or since been to such a bright place of worship. But I wasn't sure how—or what—to worship there. I guessed whatever you wanted, as long as you were respectfully quiet. That remains the thread that connects all the pagodas and churches and temples in Viet Nam; all are perfectly acceptable places to sit still and soundless.

During the Viet Nam War, however, the "whatever you want, as long as you're quiet" sentiment wasn't really the scene. Seventy to ninety percent of Vietnamese people identified as Buddhist when the country was divided in 1954, so the American push to install a Catholic president of South Viet Nam, Ngo Dinh Diem, represented a pivotal point in the war. The French, who erected great cathedrals and brought the Catholic influence in Viet Nam, had no qualms with Diem. The Americans were more familiar with Catholicism (despite misgivings about President Kennedy's possible "church over country" allegiance as a Catholic); furthermore, at least it's a *Christian* sect, argued the conservative side of Congress and American public. While many Vietnamese are most certainly Buddhist, their main spiritual activities center around "ancestor worship." The main holiday in the Vietnamese calendar is the Lunar New Year (Tet), and one of the primary parts of the event is returning to the family home and taking a field trip to the cemetery to honor one's ancestors. That's part of the biggest party of the year—going to the family grave plot. Much less crazy than Christmas, I would argue, but I'm a bit of a Scrooge.

One of the reasons I'm not the biggest fan of Christmas is the commercialism; it's the same sadness that Charlie Brown lamented back in 1965 during the first airing of *A Charlie Brown Christmas.* Buddhism and ancestor worship represent worship that's the opposite of Western holiday capitalism. The biggest expenditures during Tet are on food, which everyone shares. The emphasis on family, togetherness, and honoring those who came before you renders the bulk of Vietnamese culture pretty inoffensive, in my opinion. But under President Diem, Catholicism overruled the virtues and values ingrained in Vietnamese culture. Diem put Catholics in key positions, flew the Vatican flag at some official events, and selectively armed Catholic Vietnamese villages against Viet Cong troops, which really helps win a war effort when most of your people *aren't* Catholic, right? (Note my sarcasm.)

Diem played his worst hand in 1963, when he decided to invoke an old French decree to deny Buddhists the right to fly their flag on the Buddha's birthday. On May 8, a crowd gathered in Hue to protest the flag ban, and the police and army fired into the crowd, killing nine people. Diem blamed the Viet Cong for the incident and attempted to brush the whole thing under the rug, but the Buddhists were incensed. By the end of May, over 500 Buddhist monks protested outside of the National Assembly in Sai Gon.[10] Protests spread around South Viet Nam, and police poured chemicals on the heads of praying, peacefully protesting monks. On June 11, Thich Quang Duc immolated himself in an act of resistance to Diem's anti–Buddhist policies. The image of Duc sitting upright on a busy Sai Gon street moved international powers to push Diem to work things out with the Buddhists. He hemmed and hawed over the issue, doing things like forming coalitions with the Buddhists and then not working with them or issuing orders for police to stand down against protests but not enforcing his own edicts.

Political propaganda labeled the Buddhists as communists, and by August Diem ordered the police to raid Buddhist pagodas in the dead of the night; over 1,000 were arrested, while others "disappeared" around the time of the raids. President Kennedy, through the U.S. ambassador to Viet Nam, Henry Cabot Lodge, pushed Diem to back down. Diem refused. By November of that year, an army coup had deposed Diem, who was found dead in the trunk of a car. The U.S. government was aware of this coup, but Kennedy reportedly blanched at the photographs of the outcome; eerily, he would soon be shot dead as well.

5

1964

Watching the 2018 film *Crazy Rich Asians*, which focuses on the Chinese-descended Singaporean mega-rich, one might wonder whether the Vietnamese are part of this pack of people on screen. They don't seem to be; often, Vietnamese people are maids (*Downsized*, 2017) or part of a Viet Nam War movie. The 2019 Best Picture Oscar winner, *Parasite*, strongly represented the Republic of Korea, but U.S. audiences don't see many Southeast Asian people in American popular culture. In fact, we really don't see that many *Asian* people—including from parts of Asia like India, Turkey and Russia—in American popular culture.

There are rich Vietnamese, of course. They most likely have been linked to the North and the Communist Party for a while, or they're involved in shipping and textiles. There are a lot of international business opportunities in Viet Nam; every time I go back to Viet Nam, they've moved forward in a way I didn't anticipate. Viet Nam Air, for example, is a pretty sweet airline, and the flight costs are largely in the budget category. Viet Nam is closer to Singapore than Hong Kong, but when I think "Asian Tiger" country, I think of Hong Kong—which actually might change as the government shifts more to full Chinese rule. But that's another book.

Tradition and lucky colors, familial responsibility and piety—these are all themes in *Crazy Rich Asians* that are shared with Vietnamese culture. Fast cars, cool haircuts—those are also part of Vietnamese culture. I'll never forget riding a tourist bus back from Ha Long Bay in the summer of 2019 and watching our jalopy of a ride get passed by Lamborghinis, Ferraris, and so forth. They were racing on the highway, which apparently is okay in Viet Nam. But those aren't cheap cars. Golf courses and resorts were also popping up along the coastal corridor, likely nudging natives out of areas they'd lived in for centuries.

The water in Ha Long Bay, aside from being full of jellyfish, is getting more polluted as more and more people travel to see the famous karsts. It took only five years for Cat Ba to go from a secluded, small enclave to a destination touted on the front of travel books. I've been twice. The first time in 2012 included trying to carry my heavy suitcase over a submerged bridge. On this trip, Carrie and I took our first motorbike rides, speeding through Cat Ba and into the hills of the Khe Sau valley. Our mission was to see Hospital Cave, a secret medical site that served as a hub for transport and convalescence since the end of World War II. The motorbike guys, however, first took us to the beach. They were confused as to why we wanted to see the cave, but through some pantomime and smiles, we all figured it out. Whisked up to the hillside entrance by our motorbike team, we climbed a steep staircase to the door—that's what our motorbike guys told us to do.

One of my favorite photos of Viet Nam is from the view at the top, in the mouth of the cave looking out into the jungle.

We were joined by a 30-something-year-old Frenchman and his father. The father couldn't speak much English, but his son made some small talk. He was also visiting the site for its historical significance; he admitted he hadn't learned much about the Indochina wars in school and wondered whether we had similar experiences with the Viet Nam War. I told him we did, and the serious look on his face—as if a suspected injustice was confirmed—dug into my mind. This look would, seven years later, lead me to investigate Dien Bien Phu. At this point in my studies, I was still writing a dissertation, so I didn't know much about the Indochina wars either. The French guy's look is something I've investigated but have yet to really delve into; part of learning about history, besides unlearning some things, is understanding that you have so much more to learn. As soon as you've peeled through one layer, another multilayered piece pops up.

This adventure to Hospital Cave came with a most memorable tour guide. I don't remember his name—just that what he couldn't speak in English, he made up for in theatrics. At one point he took photos of all of us with Vietnamese military helmets on our heads. He scared us with a fake spider. He brandished a stick at us. He also told us that Hospital Cave's importance came from its secrecy and claimed (and I can't always back this one up) that the cave began operating at the end of World War II, as a reaction to the Japanese occupation. I've mostly read that it was an "American War" space, but when people find caves and are at war for centuries, they're going to utilize them. I read up on Hospital Cave after going through my own notes and photos, and it appears (like most of

View from Hospital Cave near Cat Ba, Viet Nam (2012).

Cat Ba Island) to have been improved with dioramas and such. Our tour was very much poking around a cave; I think there were a few artifacts indicating where an operating room might have been or where patients recovered. My notes mostly concern the hilarity of our tour guide: "acted hurt, got an injection—'YEOW! Now cured!'" Mr. Guide (who I now know was likely a retired NVA veteran who'd been posted to Hospital Cave as an "honor") would not be deterred in having fun. I've since met other keepers of "American War" history who did not have the same level of interest or enthusiasm, but these guys—they're always men—aren't getting any younger. I wondered what sorts of stories they might tell, if given the opportunity. Do they like being, in a sense, living relics of the war, keeping it alive through their presence, as guardians of the sites? Seeing the cave showed me the undeniable resourcefulness of the Vietnamese people through the war, and I could see a remote cave being a bit more stable than a field medic tent. But what I really remember was the guide.

The larger area of Ha Long Bay grew as fast as Cat Ba. On my most recent visit in 2019, I saw hordes of tourists embarking on a variety of ships that took numerous tours through the United Nations Educational, Scientific and Cultural Organization (UNESCO) World Heritage Site. We still saw fishing villages, people sitting atop floating houses and waving. I always got most puzzled when I saw families with boat houses and dogs. Where did the dogs…? Never mind. The beautiful "junk boats," with their plumage sails, are now reserved for tourists who want the "real experience" of living on a boat in the bay. It's expensive, and I get seasick easily; I was fine with a day trip. On the boat my husband and I took for a day, the crew helped us make spring rolls, and our guide maneuvered us

Ha Long Bay, Viet Nam (2019).

through the valley to show us a beautiful limestone cave, complete with stalagmites and dark, dripping corners. As we boarded our van, a white dude on a motorbike, curly hair free from helmet, cruised by. I caught his eye to smile, but he gave me an undisguised smirk. *Bus people.* I rolled my eyes but smiled; I was him about seven years ago.

Arguably, 1964 was the year of the Beatles in American popular music culture. While the "Fab Four" had already enjoyed chart success in their native England, in the United States they had nine songs in the popular music charts. After setting television records with their performance on *The Ed Sullivan Show* in February 1964, by April the band had 14 songs in the charts and held the top five slots in the Hot 100 with "Can't Buy Me Love," "Twist and Shout," "She Loves You," "I Wanna Hold Your Hand," and "Please Please Me." That honor was previously the privilege of Elvis in 1956. The Beatles, alongside the Kinks, the Animals, and Motown acts like the Supremes, pushed the likes of Elvis out of the pop charts in favor of a new sounds and voices. This musical era was punctuated by other cultural milestones: the Ford Mustang was introduced, the infamous Whisky A Go Go music club opened in Hollywood, Muhammad Ali (still Cassius Clay) won the world heavyweight title, the TV game show *Jeopardy!* first aired, and Dr. Martin Luther King, Jr., received the Nobel Peace Prize. Ali would issue a best-selling album, *I Am the Greatest*, on Capitol Records on March 1, only days before announcing his conversion to Islam and name change; in retrospect, 1964 looks like the calm before a storm of change.

While it didn't top the charts in 1964, Bob Dylan's *The Times They Are a-Changin'* came out in mid–January. The record included a typical catalog of folk covers and ballads, but the anti-war song "With God on Our Side" and the prophetic "The Times They Are a-Changin'" set a new tone for the social and cultural role of music in the 1960s. The escalation of the Viet Nam War by the Johnson administration during 1964 and the continued battles of civil rights groups made 1964 a difficult year to separate current events from music lyrics. In South Viet Nam, the transition from the Diem presidency resulted in a mess of military coups and overthrows of power throughout the year, leaving the ARVN and South Vietnamese people under shaky leadership for the majority of the decade.

Sonically, 1964's first hit was a Bobby Vinton–revived 1945 love song, "There! I've Said It Again." (I didn't know of this version for a long time but was familiar with Sam Cooke's 1959 cover of the song, and I prefer that one, which is decidedly more R&B and less 1950s-era slow-dancey.) At the start of February, Indiana governor Matthew Welsh attempted to ban the Kingsmen's popular single "Louie Louie" as pornographic, prompting the recording's publisher to offer $1,000 to anyone who could find evidence to back that claim. At the same time, the Beatles hit the charts, sweeping the number-one spot from February until May with "I Want to Hold Your Hand" (February–March), "She Loves You" (the last two weeks of March), and "Can't Buy Me Love" (April–May). The Beatles have always been in the background for me; my parents owned their records and played them frequently, along with those of other artists you'll hear about as I move through this book. I truly loved the Beatles from a very young age; I remember examining the album covers for *A Hard Day's Night* and *Sgt. Pepper's Lonely Hearts Club Band* at about three or four years old, barely understanding that the people in the pictures were the ones playing the songs. You can't deny the guitar intro to "I Wanna Hold Your Hand"; it's infectious. To paraphrase a snippet from Emma Forrest's novel *Namedropper*, the Beatles always sound good because they always sound like *now*. I totally agree that their brilliance always feels current, and I have had plenty of arguments with people who claim the band is overrated.

Those naysayers would have been quite alone in the first half of 1964, when the Beatles dominated the charts. But there were plenty of less positive things happening: Black and Puerto Rican groups protested segregation in New York City in February, and Malcolm X, who'd long been at odds with the Nation of Islam's leader, Elijah Muhammad, broke from the Nation in early March. His plan to start a Black nationalist party scared some people, whose racist views made them fear any emerging civil rights protests. Malcolm X's "The Ballot or the Bullet" speech in Detroit emphasized the unification of the Black community and even briefly mentioned the Viet Nam War: "Let two or three American soldiers, who are minding somebody else's business way over in South Vietnam, get killed, and [the white man/Uncle Sam will] send battleships, sticking his nose in their business."[1] This sentiment was echoed earlier, in late March, when U.S. Defense Secretary Robert McNamara reiterated American commitments to South Viet Nam against the threat of communism. Indeed, the United States was getting more involved in Viet Nam's business as 1964 continued.

On May 2, the United States witnessed its first major anti–Viet Nam War demonstration: students in New York, Boston, Seattle, and Madison marched in protest of U.S. foreign policy. On the same day, the Viet Cong sunk the USNS (United States Naval Ship) *Card* in Sai Gon. More than a week later, on May 12, twelve men in New York City, identifying themselves as pacifists, burned their draft cards in protest of the Viet Nam War. The act of burning a draft card would be made a criminal offense in the next year, as the defiant act grew in popularity. The anti-war protest movement remained small in scale and acts in 1964, but these incidents were really a preview of coming anti-war events.

By May, the Beatles loosened their stronghold on the Billboard Top 100 charts, so "Hello Dolly" by Louis Armstrong, "My Guy" by Mary Wells, and "Chapel of Love" by the Dixie Cups enjoyed brief moments in the top spot. (It's entertaining to note that Ken Kesey and the Merry Pranksters set off on their LSD tour during the same month that "Chapel of Love" reached number one.) These sweet pop songs belied the decidedly unsweet direction the United States was going, however. In June, three members of CORE were brutally kidnapped and murdered in Mississippi by KKK members, prompting the federal government to go into overdrive. President Johnson signed the Civil Rights Act of 1964 into law in July, which officially ended racial segregation, but progress would prove slow; only weeks later, race riots would span six days of protest set off by (doesn't this sound too familiar today?) a white police officer (off duty) shooting an unarmed Black teenager.

The heat was on, literally and metaphorically, with regard to the Viet Nam War in the summer of 1964. On July 8, the U.S. military released the casualty numbers from the war: 1,387. In Sai Gon, the new interim leader of South Viet Nam, Prime Minister Nguyen Khanh, spoke on July 19 about expanding the war into the North; his sentiments were met the next day with a Viet Cong attack on Cai Be, the capital of Dinh Tuong Province, killing many, including 30 children.[2] Seven days later, the United States sent 5,000 more "advisors" to South Viet Nam. Twenty-one thousand members of the United States military were now in Viet Nam, lending an ironic slant to one of July's top hits, the Beach Boys' "I Get Around." On August 2, the *Maddox*, a U.S. destroyer (which was just hanging out in the Eastern Sea), was attacked. Or it wasn't; everything I've ever read about the Viet Nam War says this incident was less an attack and more of a human error. Nevertheless, the USS carriers *Ticonderoga* and *Constellation* bombed North Viet Nam in retaliation three days later. Within five days of the "attack" on the *Maddox*, the Gulf of Tonkin Resolution passed Congress with broad support. The U.S. government now had *carte blanche* to pursue aggressive action against the North Vietnamese. America's first order of business? Support the replacement (aka coup) of General Khanh with Duong Van Minh as South Viet Nam's new boss and have the U.S. Embassy help draft South Viet Nam's new constitution.

August kicked off with a new Beatles single in the number-one spot—"A Hard Day's Night," which accompanied a film by the same name. By mid–August, Dean Martin's orchestral "Everybody Loves Somebody" (which I knew as "the Allstate commercial song"), a 1940s relic redone with success by Mr. Martin, sneaked into the top spot. A week later, it was ousted by the Supremes' iconic "Where Did Our Love Go?" Bob Dylan released *Another Side of Bob Dylan*, best known (by me) for the beautiful song "It Ain't Me, Babe." The Kinks put out the single "You Really Got Me" at the end of August, previewing a louder, amplified guitar sound that would be a staple in future rock and pop songs.

Previews of a different sort occurred in Mississippi, where civil rights activist Fannie Lou Hamer famously berated the all-white Credentials Committee of the Democratic National Convention for trying to block the Mississippi Freedom Democratic Party, which she cofounded. The DNC attempted to stop Hamer's MFDP on racist grounds, but Hamer persisted, making an impassioned speech calling for mandatory integrated state delegations.[3] President Johnson, who'd only a month before signed the Civil Rights Act, strategically held a press conference so that Hamer's speech wouldn't be aired in real time.[4] By 1968, however, the integration requests of Hamer and the MFDP were realized, despite obvious gaslighting from those in power. The struggle for racial equality also spilled into the streets of Philadelphia at the end of August in a race riot; no matter the cause, people in the United States were showing signs of resistance to the slow pace of change.

In September, while John Lennon made waves for announcing that the Beatles would *not* play for segregated audiences, another British band, the Animals, scored its first number-one hit with a rendition of an American folk song called "Rising Sun Blues"; the Animals' version is better known as "House of the Rising Sun," and it featured the jangly guitar, trippy keyboard solo, and downright brutal vocals of Eric Burdon. The first time I saw a recording of "House of the Rising Sun," I laughed at Burdon. Dressed in a stiff suit and tie, with his shiny hair mussed in a Beatles mop, he looked no more than fourteen. But when he opened his mouth, that voice! Burdon's deep baritone remains one of my favorite voices in rock, and the band's "We Gotta Get Out of This Place" (1965) is one of the most-remembered songs of the Viet Nam War by U.S. veterans. The juxtaposition of Burdon's voice and appearance—the restrained ready-made suit and the wild, deep blues voice—remind me that appearances were deceptive in the 1960s; most of the members of the University of California, Berkeley Free Speech Movement, which germinated in a large protest in October 1964, looked like Burdon.

The clean-cut-looking kids resisting the police in California represented a micro-example of kids across the United States starting to rebel against social and cultural norms, and I can only imagine the shock the parents felt watching their children growing out their hair and speaking out against injustice. It had to be jarring, compared to the relative wholesomeness the 1950s famously broadcast. President Johnson, campaigning for election in the fall of 1964, may have had these youth in mind as he announced plans for his "Great Society" at the end of October. For all of Johnson's faults, his domestic plans for the United States were his best plans; the "Great Society" called for social reforms to combat poverty and racism as well as support for education and the arts. Broad and wide sweeping, many of the familiar social programs we know today—Medicare, Medicaid, the Public Broadcasting System, the National Endowment for the Humanities—stemmed from "Great Society" plans. In terms of inter-American work, the Johnson administration committed the United States to enact some truly groundbreaking actions.

But on the other side of the ocean, things weren't looking as "great" in Viet Nam. By the end of November, the U.S. National Security Council met with a view toward escalating bombing in North Viet Nam, which Johnson agreed to by the first of December. The United States felt secure in its air power and bombing capabilities, and Johnson, wary of getting China more involved in supporting the North, preferred the gradual, two-phase pace of Operation Rolling Thunder, which he described as a "seduction" instead of a full assault "rape."[5] Johnson's cabinet had been pushing for more bombing for a year; the more aggressive stance looked tough and satisfied pro-war hawks in Congress. Around the same time, the Shangri-Las' "Leader of the Pack" topped the Billboard charts, lauding the masculine image of a bad guy from the "other side of the tracks," in the parlance of rural North Carolina. The man runs his motorcycle off into the night, presumably to ruin, after the girl's parents force them to break up. The irony of a tough motorcycle guy picking up a girl at a candy shop can be forgiven, but the song's lyrics serve as a paean to the perennial pop music–approved appeal of "bad" guys to otherwise "good" girls who stood by their men. It would be a metaphor for U.S. citizens and their government by the end of the year, which included the arrest of nearly 800 students at UC Berkeley for holding a sit-in, the debut of the stop-motion Christmas special *Rudolph the Red-Nosed Reindeer* (personally one of my holiday highlights), the strange death of Sam Cooke, and a bazooka attack on the United Nations in New York City (Che Guevara was speaking). On Christmas Eve, the Viet Cong detonated a car bomb at the Brinks Hotel in Sai Gon, proving that American forces were not safe from the guerrilla strategies of their new enemy. The year closed with another Beatles hit, the sunny love tune "I Feel Fine," but the United States, in only a few months' time, would feel the opposite as the war in Viet Nam escalated.

One of my favorite films to illustrate the "thinking" of the Cold War is 1964's *Fail Safe*. Henry Fonda plays the president of the United States; his performance is that of a firm but measured man faced with a terrible situation. To wit (I highly recommend this movie, so I won't spoil the plot), a "fail safe" game of Cold War nuclear bomb chicken between the United States and the Soviet Union goes awry. The reactions of various characters—from pilots to a presidential cabinet to a professor—to this situation reflect the levels of fear in the United States (and Russia) regarding nuclear war between the two countries. One of the most chilling scenes involves the overconfident Professor Groeteschele (played by Walter Matthau) and USAF General Warren "Blackie" Black (played by Dan O'Herlihy). General Black opens the film; we learn that his wife would like to spend more time with him, and his closet is almost entirely dress uniforms—he's a dedicated officer and family man. Dr. Groeteschele is first seen opining self-importantly over drinks at a black-tie party in the wee hours of the morning; he's smart, but he's smug.

General Black and Professor Groeteschele face off in a meeting of the president's advisors. The professor advocates bombing the Soviet Union, even though they've done nothing to provoke an attack from America. General Black thinks the idea is absurd:

> PROFESSOR GROETESCHELE: Do you believe that communism is *not* our mortal enemy?
> GENERAL BLACK: You're justifying murder.
> GROETESCHELE: Yes, to keep from being murdered.
> BLACK: In the name of what? To preserve what? Even if we do survive, what are we? Better than what we say they are? What gives us the right to live then? What makes us worth surviving, Groeteschele? That we are ruthless enough to strike first?
> GROETESCHELE: Yes! Those who can survive are the only ones worth surviving!
> BLACK: Fighting for your life isn't the same as murder.
> GROETESCHELE: Where do you draw the line once you know what the enemy is?
> BLACK: You learned too well, Professor. You learned so well that now there is no difference between you and what you want to kill.[6]

General Black believes that a nation's communist status *alone* does not an enemy make, but Groeteschele wants to beat the Soviets to the punch if there is a war to be had. Black insists on a bigger meaning—"In the name of what? To preserve what?"—than simply being the one to throw the first punch. Reaction makes more sense to the general—"fighting for your life"—but he doesn't see differences between the United States and Soviet Union that the professor sees. Other characters in the film, like the high-strung military officer or the overdetermined pilot, underscore the pervasive message that everyone seemingly takes for fact: *Russia is the enemy and not to be trusted*. General Black and the president see each other on a more equal playing field. But what did average citizens think of the Soviet Union in 1964? The country was seen as a very real threat, which always baffles me due to our alliance in World War II; so soon we became enemies? But then I see *Rocky IV* (1985) and even the *Rocky* franchise's latest offering, *Creed II* (2018), in which Russia is, again and again, the cinematic enemy. Likewise, twenty-first-century James Bond movies have Russian villains.

Why has this trope lasted so long? Vladimir Putin is a pretty sketchy character, but I'm not afraid of a man who rides horses shirtless and poses with tigers; perhaps it's due to how my research dovetails with propaganda, but I'm not "afraid" of those obvious brays of power. It's narcissistic. The overt masculinity is tired. Russia's Putin, China's Mao, North Korea's Kim Jong-un—these rulers do nothing without putting their own self-interests first. Luckily, at least in the movies, the U.S. president and the Russian premier take calm approaches to the impending doom lurking across the Pacific, and the generals try to avoid war. But the fear that everyone else feels in *Fail Safe* is the same fear that the average U.S. citizen would have felt in 1964; it may look almost ridiculous now, but it was very real then. And it makes the idea of fearing a communist Viet Nam—which would help Russia and China dominate the Pacific—a little more plausible.

As David Halberstam illustrates in his comprehensive book *The Best and the Brightest* (first published in 1972), the Kennedy administration installed a cadre of Ivy League–educated smarties in the president's cabinet: Robert McNamara (secretary of defense), McGeorge Bundy (national security advisor), Dean Rusk (secretary of state), and so forth. These elites contrasted sharply with Texas-hewn Vice President Johnson, who was a traditional baby-kissing, glad-handing type of politician, as well as a graduate of a teacher's college instead of Harvard or Yale. But the spookily named "Wise Men" were who Johnson inherited as he assumed the office of president on November 22, 1963, in the wake of President Kennedy's assassination.

While I often pity Johnson (that's not really the way you want to get any job), his rush for the official swearing-in ceremony still seems off-key; couldn't he have waited a day? Legally, he was already president the moment JFK was pronounced dead, so it's not like the nation was entirely leaderless. The 37th president of the United States definitely wanted to be president—he'd run against Kennedy in the 1960 Democratic primary—but who wants to follow the slick guy in sunglasses, sitting against a waterfront backdrop at his stately Hyannis Port home while taking questions from Walter Cronkite? Kennedy was a young, glamorous president. Johnson was an older, wizened and seasoned politician. His jowls and drawl stood in sharp contrast to the pizzazz of Kennedy, but LBJ took the bull by the horns and decided to steer America the way he'd steered Congress—he's one of only four American politicians who've served (elected) as president, vice president, senator, and congressman.

Johnson's greatest legacy should be his "Great Society" plan. Whatever his foreign policy failings, Johnson put a demonstrable amount of effort into making America a better place. In 1956, while serving as a senator of Texas, he declined to sign the "Southern Manifesto" by the Dixiecrats, which rebuffed integration of schools; Johnson went on to sign 1965's Voting Rights Act (an effort to force states to make it easier for Black people to vote) and Immigration and Nationality Act (the cornerstone of current immigration policies in the United States). His big idea was "the Great Society," which called for all sorts of reforms to social programs like Medicare and public television. Johnson's heart was in the right place in terms of moving American lives forward. However, he didn't appear to care too much for moving the lives of the Vietnamese forward. Rather, he was simply uninterested from the start.

During the aforementioned Kennedy-Cronkite interview (September 1963), a confident President John F. Kennedy pronounced:

> In the final analysis, it is their war. They are the ones who have to win it or lose it. We can help them, we can give them equipment, we can send our men out there as advisors, but they have to win it, the people of Vietnam, against the communists.[7]

Kennedy, like Johnson, preferred to be hands-off in other people's wars. Kennedy was a "Europe firster" with regard to where he feared communism the most. He famously declared himself a "Berliner" in an anti-communist speech in West Berlin (June 1963) and preferred that foreign policy pivot to saving Europe from the perils of communism. But on the advice of the Kennedy advisors, Johnson ultimately accelerated the war in Viet Nam. The perils of communist dominoes falling caused the pro-war hawks to shift from "Europe first" to "Asia first," so that passing the Gulf of Tonkin Resolution in August 1964—which Johnson gleefully compared to "grandma's nightshirt" in that the resolution "covered everything"—was not difficult, though there was some opposition.

Senator Wayne Morse (D-OR) lamented the sad twist that "protecting democracy in Vietnam" had taken on the Senate floor in 1964. The senator beseeched his colleagues to find another way out of the war, pleading, "Surely when a nation goes as far down the road toward war as we have, it must know why it is there, what objective it is seeking, and whether the objective sought could possibly be achieved by any other means."[8] Morse's fellow senators, however, remained unmoved by his statements. They saw Ho Chi Minh as a prodigy of Josef Stalin and the small nation—a place most Americans couldn't find on a map—as a country in need of democratic firepower.

Viet Nam was not a rich country in the 1960s, and Ho Chi Minh was only a figure-head leader of the Communist Party by 1964; Le Duan (often portrayed as ruthless, or at least nefarious) assumed that role in 1960. The Japanese occupation during World War II, followed by the reinstatement of the French in the 1950s, meant that sorting out power and resources had just begun. The Viet Minh—later members of the NVA or VC—were committed to their cause of an independent Viet Nam, and American and French presence undermined their cause. They also happened to be communists (and funded by Russia and China). In essence, Viet Nam represented a proxy conflict within the larger Cold War for the United States: we were fighting communist influence on behalf of the people of Viet Nam.

Was everyone in Viet Nam a communist in 1964? Is everyone in Viet Nam a communist in 2020? In 1964, the answer would have been "not really," but in 2020, the answer is "that's the Party." A lot of things happening in Viet Nam these days look like what would be expected from capitalist countries (shifts of populations to urban areas, the rise of luxury goods, etc.), but it doesn't even call itself communist—it is the Socialist Republic of Viet Nam, thanks. However, there's freedom of the press in socialism, and Viet Nam will censor opinions unfavorable to the party. Both Nathalie Nguyen and Rick Butler (Australian folks you'll read about in chapter 7) had stories—firsthand and from others—about the government intervening on where guests of the country could and couldn't go, or sometimes what could be filmed at certain sites on certain occasions (an Australian commemoration of the Battle of Long Tan got shut down, for example). And the government doesn't really need to give you a reason; it can just say no. That's communism. Socialism has a softer touch.

Today, when I go to Viet Nam, I see entrepreneurs. I see people creating things and juggling multiple roles to maximize their earnings. In Sai Gon, there's a flashy upscale scene, though it's nothing like the haute couture *Crazy Rich Asians* lifestyle you might see in Beijing, Tokyo, or (in the case of the film) Singapore. Viet Nam, as we know it today, is also only 40 years old. There are still things to figure out. A theme emerged from a wide variety of sources (folks at Project RENEW in Quang Tri, a restaurant owner in Hoi An, a tour operator in Tam Coc, etc.)—namely, that *logistics* was still a problem. Getting clear and consistent lines of communication, for example, could be a hassle. But innovation, I think, is a skill the Vietnamese have in spades. The balancing act I've seen of towering objects on motorbikes attests to that. Seriously—that is a skill.

Viet Nam is still growing. I've seen so much change there in the past eight years, ranging from a huge update on the Ha Noi airport to the adoption of Grab (the Vietnamese version of Uber), which obliterated the haggling industry of motorbike hires. When I first went to Viet Nam in 2012, a friendly Vietnamese man told me that "Vietnamese success" was "one wife, two kids, three stories [of a house], and four wheels." That doesn't seem too different from the definition of success many Americans have; it's funny how humans across the world have so many more shared characteristics and behaviors than differences, but we most often focus on the differences.

6

1965

One of the things that strikes me about Da Nang—either driving through it or in my brief stay there—is the number of golf courses nearby. There are at least ten in a ten-mile radius, and the city is not that big. My friend Ted, a USAF veteran who has spent decades traveling back and forth to Viet Nam, informs me that the greens arrived around the same time that Chinese businesses—most often via Hong Kong—started investing more outsourcing to Viet Nam. There's not that much room for a sprawling 18 holes in many parts of Asia, but the verdant seaside hills of Da Nang provide for keeping one's multi-million-dollar company's assets in check while also hitting the links. It's a kind of funny side-hobby that many Asian tycoons picked up, golf; it's also interesting to me to think of the connection these courses might provide for southern textile guys suddenly doing business overseas. My dad, who's in textiles, did business on the golf course sometimes; I wonder how many other men like him find themselves teeing off in a place that was on the news (rarely favorably) in their youth.

My last visit to Da Nang in 2019 was accidental; I didn't know I was going there until I got hooked up with Project RENEW, which is based in Quang Tri. Hue is actually closer, but I hadn't spent too much time in Da Nang, and its ocean-front hotels were alluring. A week prior to my stay at the Ocean View (or some derivation of that name) hotel in Da Nang, I'd ventured into the waters of Ha Long Bay and gotten a nasty jellyfish sting. A few years prior, after a brief swim in Hoi An (about 30 minutes from Da Nang), I'd taken a swim and then a stroll along the beach, only to see jellyfish the size of my head lurking about ten feet off shore. I'd been warned that there are jellyfish "seasons" and that the ones in Viet Nam were pretty gnarly offenders in terms of their sting.

I stood on my balcony in Da Nang, rubbing ointment on the lingering jellyfish burn mark on my left forearm and staring out at the ocean over My Khe beach. Strains of happy music came from the pool and food area on the top of the hotel, and it felt oddly anachronistic to be staring at a beach where tourists frolicked when I knew I was looking at the same beach the U.S. Marines rolled up to in 1965. From my balcony in the fading daylight, I could also see the tallest Buddha statue in Viet Nam, the Lady Buddha. Cradled in the dusky Marble Mountains, she was a soothing beacon of calm as I tried to make sense of the lively seaside city. On the other side of the hotel, I could see the neon blink of a Ferris wheel, changing rainbow displays of light on the sides of buildings, and the famous fire-breathing dragon bridge (Cau Rong) up to my right. It only breathes fire on weekends, and I missed it because I got back to Da Nang too late.

Da Nang is where bases were. It's a place where soldiers regrouped and took in-country R and R. It's tropical and yet more lit up than the beaches near Hoi An. As

I walked along the streets, looking for a restaurant that didn't specialize in fish (ironic, right? Fresh seafood at the ready, and I just want Indian food), I found a really well-priced halal place. It wasn't unusual to find this type of food in the midst of a charlie-foxtrot of Chinese restaurants, as 90 percent of my fellow tourists were Chinese. There were swarms of them, tumbling out of buses that were illegally parked (and inducing a fanfare of horns from the locals), giggling in front of the hotels with their selfie sticks and sun hats, and lolling down the narrow, often under-construction streets, their all-new Nike athleisure wear–clad bodies sprawled in lobbies or under fans.

Because Chinese travel is often not done solo—think packaged group tours, where everyone has matching shirts or hats or, at the very least, follows a leader waving a tall, brightly colored flag—Chinese tourists mostly move in packs. Sometimes you'll see a family vacation, but it's still a sizable group, as Chinese family vacations appear to include more than just a nuclear family. Cousins, aunts, uncles—the more, the merrier! The dark side of seeing Chinese tourism is knowing that the groups' itineraries are planned and government approved; if you travel within China, you'll be subject to similar regulations. Every activity we had when I taught in Jiujiang, China, was preapproved; papers were pre-submitted at checkpoints. It wasn't as stilted in Beijing, but we weren't someone else's responsibility there.

My Da Nang hotel had a pool that overlooked the main drag, which was, of course, named after the venerated Vietnamese hero, General Vo Nguyen Giap (he led Vietnamese forces against the French and the Americans). Looking down at my fellow tourists, I noted that they were a jolly bunch, happily slurping boba tea. The near-silent purr of the ocean murmured in the background, reminding me that, to the ocean, our brief moments of "important" history exist only in our heads. The sea has a longer memory than humanity.

◁▷ ◁▷ ◁▷

In terms of music, 1965 was the first year during the Viet Nam War era in which the sounds perked my ears. The mix of Motown, pop, and rock is buoyant and creative, with a more original sound emerging like the Moog synthesizer (released the year prior, 1964) and the fuzz box guitar pedal (the impetus for the Rolling Stones' hit "[I Can't Get No] Satisfaction," written in 1965). The number-one song of the year was the saxophone silliness of Sam the Sham and the Pharaohs' "Wooly Bully"; like "Surfin' USA" in 1963, "Wooly Bully" never reached the number-one spot, but it was the biggest song of 1965. As musicians turned up the volume on their electric guitar amplifiers, in February 1965, 3,500 U.S. Marines arrived in droves on the beaches of Da Nang, turning up the intensity of the Viet Nam War. American troops were now on the ground, and support from Australia would arrive in August. After winning the 1964 election, President Johnson was sworn in for his first official, vote-won, full term in office in January. He would spend the greater part of 1965 dealing with big problems, both at home and abroad.

New and exciting things happened in 1965. The first spacewalks (Russian cosmonaut Alexei Leonov in March, followed by U.S. astronaut Ed White in April) occurred that year, and the Earth got its first photos of Mars. On Broadway, *The Sound of Music* opened, and Maria Callas performed *Tosca* in Covent Garden, London, as her last operatic concert. Petula Clark's catchy ode to urban life, "Downtown," temporarily unseated the Beatles in the pop charts, but it was quickly replaced by the Righteous Brothers' "You've Lost That Lovin' Feelin'" by Valentine's Day. About a week later, Malcolm X was murdered—shot 21 times at Harlem's Audubon Ballroom in front of 400 people—stirring up tensions within the civil rights movement and groups influenced by Malcolm, like the SNCC and SCLC. The activist's house had been fire-bombed a week prior to his assassination, and he had been under local and federal surveillance since 1953, due to his reputation as a subversive and radical figure.[1] His death would be the first of many among civil rights figures and anti-war protestors in 1965.

In March, as Operation Rolling Thunder commenced in North Viet Nam, the Temptations' classic hit "My Girl" gained the number-one spot, only lose it, like so many other songs in 1965, to the Beatles ("Eight Days a Week") and the Supremes ("Stop! In the Name of Love"). In the United States, another war was ramping up: On March 7, known as "Bloody Sunday," over 200 Alabama state troopers attacked over 500 civil rights protestors near the Edmund Pettus Bridge as they marched from Selma to Montgomery. Two days later, Martin Luther King joined the group, stopping at the bridge to pray and then returning to Selma under court order. By mid–March, police in Montgomery clashed with SNCC demonstrators, and civil rights supporters protested the violence in Alabama at the Montgomery courthouse. The late Georgia representative John Lewis, whose beaten head bore physical testament to the depravity in Alabama, remarked, "I don't see how President Johnson can send troops to Vietnam. I don't see how he can send troops to the Congo. I don't see how he can send troops to Africa and can't send troops to Selma."[2] By March 25, 25,000 civil rights marchers, including Dr. King, made the four-day journey from Selma to Montgomery accompanied by the Alabama National Guard and the FBI. Their fortitude inspired what would become the Voting Rights Act of 1965.

The civil rights activists weren't the only ones marching for a cause that spring; the Students for a Democratic Society (SDS) organized a "March on Washington to End the War in Vietnam" on April 17, drawing between 15,000 and 25,000[3] demonstrators to the Capitol. In response, President Johnson reinforced U.S. commitment to Viet Nam in his statement "Tragedy, Disappointment, and Progress in Viet-Nam [sic]," proclaiming that the United States "will remain [in Viet Nam] as long as is necessary, with the might that is required, whatever the risk and whatever the cost."[4] In over two short years, Johnson would withdraw from the presidency and his personal involvement with Viet Nam; perhaps he did not have "the might required" to stay mired in a mess he undoubtedly made worse. Freddie and the Dreamers' sassy-yet-sugary "I'm Telling You Now" was the number-one song that week, its saccharine sentiments ironic in the wake of recent events in the United States.

Johnson would need the fortitude he had spoken about in April; May began with a dramatic draft card burning and coffin march protest at UC Berkeley, stoking a fervor on the campus that produced a 30,000-strong teach-in by May 21. On May 22, the teach-in concluded with the burning of 19 draft cards and the hanging of an LBJ effigy.[5] The president's popularity was in jeopardy, but the Viet Nam War marched on. That summer, several immediately recognizable hits topped the Billboard charts—the Supremes' "Back in My Arms Again," the Four Tops' "I Can't Help Myself (Sugar Pie Honey Bunch)," and the Byrds' cover of Bob Dylan's "Mr. Tambourine Man"—before another wave of the British Invasion took over: the month of July belonged to the Rolling Stones' "(I Can't Get No) Satisfaction." The song's lyrics, which invoked dissatisfaction with commercialism and a general discontent over the limitations of modern life, echoed the malcontent of a whole generation of people. The song's entrance at the top of the Billboard charts underscored the emergent scene of young people—in America and beyond—looking for something beyond the pre-fab 1950s reality they were expected to continue. By August, however, cotton-candy love returned in the form of Sonny and Cher's international number-one single, "I Got You Babe."

During the summer of 1965, the Viet Nam War proceeded in a series of fits and starts. The Battle of Dong Xoai on June 10 resulted in a "successful" Viet Cong mortar attack that took over the Dong Xoai military base. An anti-war teach-in at the Pentagon in mid–June was largely peaceful, echoing the cheerful romanticism of "I Got You Babe," while the loss of a F-4C Phantom near Kang Chi (the beginning of several surprises on the United States Air Force during the war) reverberated the displeasure of "Satisfaction." At the end of July, Johnson simultaneously signed the Social Security Act (creating the public health initiatives we know as Medicare and Medicaid) and hosted a press conference announcing—per the advice of army general William Westmoreland, head of MACV—that troop presence in Viet Nam would increase from 75,000 to 125,000. Johnson also raised the draft numbers from 17,000 to 35,000, doubling the ability for the government to call men into selective service.[6] In 1966, Robert McNamara, in a desperate bid to keep increasing troop numbers in the escalating war, would implement Project 100,000 (aka "McNamara's Morons"), which accepted recruits with lower than average mental and physical aptitude test scores.[7] But the 1965 troop increases angered and worried many Americans. A lesser number of Americans were angered at Bob Dylan's set at the 1965 Newport Folk Festival, where the artist played electric guitar, eliciting boos from the folk music audience. Weeks away from their landmark performance at Shea Stadium, the Beatles' second movie (*Help!*) premiered at the end of July, proving that even the lovable mop-tops, weary from nonstop recording and touring, were feeling the weight of the mid–1960s.

By fall of 1965, American troops hadn't been in Viet Nam for a full year yet, but they were making their presence felt. In mid–August, the USMC overtook the Viet Cong in Operation Starlite, which would be followed by success between USMC forces and ARVN troops in Operation Piranha near the Chu Lai Marine base. Captain Philip Eldon Smith was shot down by a Chinese fighter in September and remained a prisoner of war (POW) until 1973. At the beginning of October, South Korean soldiers, acting as allied support for American troops, arrived in Viet Nam; in November, the Philippines sent soldiers to assist U.S. efforts. At the end of October, USMC forces would face a harsh battle with Viet Cong forces in Da Nang, but the most demanding battle—the first between U.S. forces and North Vietnamese forces—took place in the Central Highlands of Viet Nam, at the Ia Drang Valley. By the end of the year, President Johnson would decide to increase the number of U.S. troops in Viet Nam from 120,000 to 400,000, stoking the flames of the anti-war movement.

The last half of 1965 was filled with challenges to "establishment" America; there were many demands for change, including growing anti-war sentiments. The Watts Riots, motivated by unfair and brutal policing in a predominantly Black neighborhood in Los Angeles, resulted in over 30 deaths in the first weeks of August, and the end of the month saw President Johnson signing a law that made it a federal offense to destroy or burn a draft card. In September, the catastrophic Hurricane Betsy tore through New Orleans; the level of devastation would be matched only by Hurricane Katrina 40 years later. Anti-war activities included the self-immolations of Norman Morrison (a Quaker) and Roger Allen LaPorte (from the Catholic Worker Movement) as well as a sizable March on Washington in November. Carl Oglesby, president of the SDS, one of the major organizers of the November march, made a speech at the event that declared the North Vietnamese fight "an honest revolution" and lambasted U.S. involvement in Viet Nam as an action meant to "safeguard American interests around the world against revolution or revolutionary change."[8] While his words paralleled statements the North Vietnamese were making about the war and carried some truth, not everyone agreed; a pro-war march in October had garnered almost 25,000 participants, and many Americans felt that anti–Viet Nam War demonstrations were unpatriotic at worst and disruptive at best.

The period of burgeoning protest emboldened songwriters of the era to speak out against the war, and anti–Viet Nam War protestors used their songs as anthems in their crusade for peace. While the messages of the songs evoked what could be seen as "traditional" revolutionary rhetoric, the lyrics took bolder steps by naming politicians, specific cultural events, and so on, which earned anti–Viet Nam War protest music a reputation for aggressive and inflammatory behavior and unpatriotic sentiment. "The songs are sometimes satiric, sometimes sorrowful and sometimes indignant, but the tone is always negative," reported the *New York Times* in October 1967. "Nobody 'jabs' at the administration these days; it's more like a bomb for a bomb."[9] These "negative" and "satiric" songs' "jabs" at the administration continued throughout the Viet Nam War, encouraging the anti-war protestors to continue their crusade.

One of my favorite anti–Viet Nam War songs, if only for the theatrics of the music and lyrics, is "Eve of Destruction," performed by Barry McGuire. It uses a snarling narrator howling against those who do not believe the United States is on the "Eve of Destruction." The narrator foretells calamities the public is not aware of and urgently calls attention to them. He lists global catastrophes and pointedly attacks American naïveté concerning the impending doom through the desperately raging lyrics. The narrator clearly articulates his fear of witnessing human existence eradicated with the push of a button, or at least the start of nuclear war with some communist entity, which could be seen in films like 1964's *Fail Safe* (discussed in the previous chapter). Nuclear war lurks right outside the door in "Eve of Destruction," and the apocalyptic images of strife, hate, and death further underscore the massive crisis taking shape in a post–World War II United States. The U.S. cultural landscape experienced change in small pockets across the country. The civil rights movement, the women's rights movement, the increase in the number of anti-war and nuclear disarmament protestors, the rise of the New Left, and the various factions of counter-culture and "hippie" culture had coalesced by the middle of the 1960s, causing a rift in terms of American cultural identity.

The urgent lyrics of "Eve of Destruction" showcase the hypocrisy of a nation whose patriotism hinged on Christian morality and yet simultaneously was full of hate toward its own citizens, especially those of color, as seen in references to events in Selma, Alabama, in 1965. The lyrics also point out changing ideologies toward war—how come, the song argues, American peaceniks also carry guns? This does not echo sentiments of previous American war songs, which celebrated patriotism and voluntary military service, but rather bullies listeners into considering and acting upon their professed pacifist leanings. The bombast of "Eve of Destruction"—both musically and lyrically—likely caused the song's chart-topping success. The song "could project only a melodramatic foreboding without analysis of its political causes [and is] vague in its ideological orientation [by aligning] fear of nuclear disaster with both anticommunist and civil rights issues in suggesting an equivalence between all the 'hate in Red China' and that in Selma, Alabama."[10] While "Eve of Destruction" gains much of its effect through its loud presentation (complete with drums that sound like bombs), it also fosters fear of the changes and evils occurring all over the globe in 1965. "Eve of Destruction" is thus not a call to arms, but rather a call to action; the lyrics of this Cold War anthem illustrate the anger, hate, fear, and alienation that many citizens began to feel toward previously accepted ideologies concerning war. Yet the song, much like American culture during the 1960s, offers no definitive "answer" for its audience.

While less sonically aggressive than "Eve of Destruction," Buffalo Springfield's 1965 Cold War song "For What It's Worth" also encouraged Americans to act, though not necessarily in overseas combat. "For What It's Worth" instead urged U.S. citizens to pause and think about what was going on in their country. The lyrics contain images of foreboding and indistinctly perceived menaces; every corner presents possible danger. The police fill the streets, looking for easy targets in the form of confrontations with protestors or social undesirables. The streets are also filled with citizens marching, though a shadowy, gun-toting figure (the "Man" or the "Establishment"—the government) watches from a corner, whispering caution. The country, through the lens of the lyrics, is not safe, and authority figures are loosely drawn and vaguely threatening. In this incomprehensible American landscape, no one can agree on anything. America has no adequate or appropriate point of reference in its cultural memory to deal with such burgeoning turmoil. And while the lyrics of both "Eve of Destruction" and "For What It's Worth" speak to the inescapable fear that permeated American culture during the Cold War, the lyrics to "For What It's Worth" describe a cultural fate in which excessive fear affects one's life. The "sound" that the song's lyrics point out to the listener remains unidentified, just as the causes for fear are unspecified. This vague threat to America's cultural sensibilities allows listeners to color the "sound" with their own fears and experiences with the sounds of protest and war, no matter their views on a particular issue.

The combination of youth and music made the anti–Viet Nam War movement unique in the history of the United States. Many cultural historians cannot separate the music from the movement, and future protests in the United States would always have a soundtrack as a result of the legacy of the anti-war movement. Scholars such as Herbert Marcuse, an icon of the New Left movement that coincided with the anti–Viet Nam War movement, encouraged protest from a socially philosophical point of view. Politicians, musicians, and anti-war activists contributed to the overall ethos of the Viet Nam War era by following Marcuse's directive that "we *must* protest against [the war] even if we believe that is hopeless"[11]; this spirit of earnest social action remains an integral part of American society today. The anti–Viet Nam War movement embodied this earnestness, reaching its apex in the mid–1960s, when conflict in Viet Nam escalated to the point that American troops began entering the country in droves. Journalist Dorian Lynskey considers 1965 a watershed year for the movement, which gained momentum as combat intensified:

> Following Operation Rolling Thunder, a sustained bombing campaign over North Vietnam, the first U.S. ground troops set foot on Vietnamese soil on March 8, 1965.... The antiwar [*sic*] movement coalesced with impressive speed. Just six weeks later, Students for a Democratic Society (SDS) organized the first national demonstration in Washington DC.... The marchers numbered twenty-five thousand, roughly equal to the number of troops stationed in Vietnam.[12]

As mentioned in the previous chapter, when the United States formally escalated the conflict in Viet Nam through the Gulf of Tonkin Resolution in 1964, Senator Wayne

Morse (D-OR) took the Senate floor on August 5 to protest. Even though he was a decided minority among those on Capitol Hill (only Ernest Gruening [D-AK] stood with him) in his belief that war in Viet Nam was wrong, he spoke out strongly against it:

> Does anyone mean to tell me that with a population of 15 million, and military forces consisting of 400,000 to 450,000 South Vietnamese troops, of various types and various services, they are incapacitated, and that we must send American boys over there to die in what amounts basically to a civil war? Mr. President, criticism has not prevented, and will not prevent me from saying that, in my judgment, we cannot justify the shedding of American blood in that kind of war in southeast Asia.[13]

Senator Morse's brave challenge to the authority of the White House fell on deaf ears, and the United States committed to shipping troops to "defeat communism" in South Viet Nam over the next five years. Morse, however, would gain allies in Washington by the end of the war, and anti–Viet Nam War activists would continue to support his views through marches, teach-ins, sit-ins, be-ins, and concerts across the United States for the duration of the Viet Nam War.

I was returning triumphantly to my hotel from the sandy streets of Da Nang. I arrived, tossed my bags down and confirmed a car to Project RENEW, and then ran out to find a place—bank, pawn shop, whatever—that would transfer some Thai baht I had into Vietnamese dong. Now flush with cash, I had my eye on a fruit smoothie from the hotel, out of the heat. The beach-side area of Da Nang was a little rustic and beat up compared to the glossy city. I half expected to see one of those beach stores, like "Wings," a chain on the GA-SC-NC coast that sells hermit-crab starter kits and tacky towels. But only seafood restaurants appeared on the ocean-front stretch.

As I walked, I thought about what a young Vietnamese man had said to me a few days earlier, in line at the airport. He'd asked me why I was in Viet Nam, and so on, and I told him about my research and the war. As we parted ways following the security pat-down, he asked me whether I thought the Viet Nam War was a "civil war." This is a loaded question in Viet Nam. Your answer might hinge a lot on the age, hometown, and political acumen of the person you're talking to. If you don't know the person very well— say you've known them 20 minutes, in an airport—then you must be precise.

I slid my eyes upward and to the left, as if I was thinking. "Kind of …" I said, watching his face for any changes. A slight smile; I could keep going. "It depends. But in many ways yes," I finished. He shook my hand and wished me a pleasant journey, and he even waved to me again when I went to get on the bus to take my fellow passengers and me to our plane waiting on the tarmac. Had he frowned when I said "kind of," then I would have known that he was one of many Vietnamese people who fervently believe there was no division in Viet Nam—geographical, political, or otherwise—and blamed any divisive history on the Western interlopers who stirred that pot. *Most* people I speak to in Viet Nam think there was inter-Vietnamese strife before America got involved. *Most* people I've spoken to, but definitely not all, and it's good to be careful.

Here is why the answer is complicated: When Americans think of "civil war," we see the "war between the states," in which the Union, north of the Mason-Dixon line, fought against the Confederacy to the south. The South wanted to keep its free labor, while the North wanted to keep the country together (don't let the anti-slave rhetoric of the Union fool you, and look at President Lincoln's track record on slavery if you don't believe me). Anyway, the war was a clear divide between two opposing sides in the same country, locked in arms over "states' rights." The North had Lincoln in the White House, the South elected Jefferson Davis, and for four years the forces fought until General Robert E. Lee surrendered at Appomattox in April 1865.

Viet Nam, by contrast, was divided geographically, on the 17th parallel, per the 1954 Geneva Accords. The division was only supposed to last until 1956, when a fair democratic election was to take place, but that didn't happen. Furthermore, before 1956, the Vietnamese had already killed one another in the name of Vietnamese independence. In 1946, fresh off several victories against French and Japanese colonial forces, the revered General Giap and the Viet Minh killed and purged nationalists, anti-communists, and those who had worked with the French government. These events happened largely in the North, so a nice division of "north versus south" doesn't fit so well. Also, the people Giap purged were not armed, per se—this made the Viet Minh a bit scary to the average Vietnamese farmer, one might imagine. While the "VC" nickname is dismissive, it is interesting to note that there's a nice little coffeehouse in Ha Noi named the "Cong Café"—apparently the Vietnamese "own" that moniker now.

The Viet Cong would actively recruit members during the war. While the United States and President Diem of South Viet Nam boasted about the success of their "strategic hamlet" programs, the people who'd been taken from their land—and thus their ancestral graves and heritage—were not so thrilled. Capitalizing on that anger was what many good VC did, recruiting new soldiers in the march toward an independent and communist Viet Nam right under the noses of the Americans. Finally, the VC utilized the famed Ho Chi Minh Trail, as well as a host of other methods, to post people in the South. Per Ho Chi Minh's right-hand man, Le Duan, planting VC in the South would be crucial for the eventual uprising of the people. However, during the Tet Offensive (1968), VC forces in Hue were not met with a throng of communist-loving, gun-toting militants. And, once again, Giap's orders were to shoot those who did not join the party and rise up.

There was a civil war in the sense that people within a shared country were fighting each other—at the very least ideologically. Except this version of civil war often resulted in the brutal slaughter of innocent people, not an armed militia. So how "civil" is that, really?

Many Vietnamese relocated from the North to the South, and vice versa, between 1954 and 1955; they had 300 days to pick a side, and the small Catholic portion of the North most definitely fled south, as Catholicism wasn't welcome under the communist regime. Revolutionaries who were 100 percent all in with Ho Chi Minh often went north, and anyone with any affiliation with the French almost always ended up heading south. Northern landowners who were really just independent farmers—definitely read *The Mountains Sing* (2020) to gain more perspective on this group's point of view—were denounced as capitalists and nearly driven out of their hometowns, and they gradually moved south. To sum up, those who weren't overtly and fervently *with* the Viet Minh were *against* the Viet Minh, in their view. Lack of cooperation or stubborn attempts at neutrality were not rewarded.

Again, there was a civil war. Just not between two armed forces.

It's tricky, because if we look at this question carefully, then we have to ask "What, precisely, was the United States was doing in Viet Nam in the first place?" Backing a democratic government and protecting our interests against the evils of communism is generally the first answer given, but Diem's presidency was not one born from a democratic election: it was rigged. People did vote, but who pulls off a 98 percent victory? The United States was plainly backing whoever might keep communism from taking over, following the fears stoked in the "domino theory."

If we ask "What was the US doing in Viet Nam, again, exactly?" the question will lead to an inevitable discussion when talking about the Viet Nam War: you cannot talk about the war without including the voices against it. The anti–Viet Nam War movement remains a multifaceted, fractured, interesting topic, and most movies you see about the Viet Nam War include at least one long-haired anti-war person, who is usually wearing a (suede, maybe fringed) vest. If they are male, they have a beard. However, America's anti-war movements are far more interesting and complicated than cinematic renditions. Furthermore, there was a global anti–Viet Nam War faction. When I went to Ha Noi in 2012, there was a huge temporary exhibit dedicated to global outcry over the war at the Military History Museum. Similar tributes to international angst over the Viet Nam War have been displayed in mini-exhibits I've seen at the War Remnants Museum in Sai Gon, the Dien Bien Phu Museum, and even places like the Air Defense and Air Force Museum (Ha Noi) and the Long Phuoc Tunnels (near Nui Dat). The fact that a lot of people all over the world didn't like the Viet Nam War and spoke out against it is a very important part of history that the Vietnamese government would like you to know.

And they're correct in this reminder. Global anti–Viet Nam War demonstrations clearly occurred, and the anti–Viet Nam War movement surely happened. But what happened *before* this widespread protest movement? Before diving deep into any anti-war sentiment, I needed context—at the very least from the United States' point of view, because that's what's most familiar to me.

So, the short version: Every war in U.S. history had some opposition, if for no other reason than the Quakers, who take pacifism very seriously and conscientiously object to all war. It's not personal. Growing up in North Carolina, our elementary school chorus group learned an "old Quaker spiritual" as part of a Thanksgiving show for a local old folks' home. Here goes:

> 'Tis the gift to be simple, 'tis the gift to be free
> 'Tis the gift to come down where we ought to be,
> And when we find ourselves in the place just right,
> 'Twill be in the valley of love and delight.
> When true simplicity is gained,
> To bow and to bend we shan't be ashamed,
> To turn, turn will be our delight,
> 'Til by turning, turning we come 'round right.

In a similar vein, "Simple Gifts"[14] is an 1848 song from the Shakers (related to the Quakers, just a little livelier) that preceded the Civil War and the Spanish-American War. The song really emphasizes simplicity and how "bow[ing]" and "bend[ing]" aren't shameful, though these things run counter to a lot of American ideas (and, arguably, those of any country driven by economic power). But the Quakers saw freedom as a gift, albeit one gained by "com[ing] 'round right" and in "the valley of love and delight." It sounds pretty hippie, if you read it right. However, this was a pious song, or at least that's what the Wingate Elementary Choir soberly conveyed to the residents of Guardian Care in the late 1980s. Our performance occurred during the Reagan-Bush era, so we pledged allegiance in the morning and said grace at lunch. When I heard that the Quakers always protested war, I went back to this song and thought, "Of course you did."

Aside from the Quakers, each war in U.S. history had pushback in some form. World War I is an interesting example of anti-war American history. We know the Quakers were there, of course, but women's leagues and suffragettes also protested the war—the 19th Amendment didn't give (white) women the right to vote until 1920, so in 1917 women took to the streets instead, for a variety of causes. Then there were also some unions and socialists against the war—and those two words perk Americans' ears; socialism is considered dangerous in the United States. We kind of already have it (in the form of the VA, Social Security, vehicle taxes, etc.), but it's still scary. In 1917, as the United States entered World War I, ideas like socialism scared Congress into passing the Espionage Act, followed quickly by the Sedition Act in 1918. People you've probably heard of but don't know who they are (I don't either unless I look it up), like Eugene V. Debs and Kate Richards O'Hare, were jailed for doing things like obstructing the draft (like Viet Nam, World War I had a draft) or sending subversive, scary, socialist things in the mail. Or talking trash about the Constitution, which, as I mentioned before, didn't grant white women the right to vote until 1920 (it's important to remember that the Constitution was and still is a living document; Black women didn't get the right to vote until 1965, to extend the example). Anyway, socialism: The International Workers of the World (IWW) came into being during the World War I years, and they are described as "radical" in at least 20 history books I've read. People were jailed for aligning with the IWW under the Espionage and Sedition Acts; freedom of speech was attacked and assigned federal crime status.

While not an anti-war action, another curious push against the government took place over a decade after the war's end. In 1932, more than 15,000 World War I veterans (bringing enough friends to make a head count of over 40,000) organized in front of government buildings all over Washington, D.C., to demand back pay.[15] President Hoover called the military on the protest sites, and two veterans were shot and died.

Using the World War I experience as a micro-example of American anti-war tolerance, it would be fair to say that the United States doesn't take kindly to anti-war sentiments, nor does it shirk from using the military to disperse its own citizens in protests it dislikes. We see echoes of this attitude in anti–Viet Nam War movements, but one of the examples that piqued my interest was the veterans who spoke out against the war or the active-duty folks who went AWOL or refused to fire their weapons. When I first read about military members protesting the military, I was shocked. I was at least 10 years younger than I am now, and rebelling against authority was still a new and provocative concept; I watched the film *Sir! No Sir! The GI Movement to End the War in Vietnam* (2005) with some confusion. I'd seen photos of Viet Nam veterans throwing their medals over a wall in 1960s history montages, but I was floored when I heard about the Fort Hood Three, a group of army defectors locked in the Presidio Stockade for being unwilling to go to Viet Nam. A naval nurse, Susan Schnall, helped drop defection leaflets around the Bay Area military bases. A nurse! Ballsy!

One of the more persistent drivers of GI disobedience was race. In *Sir! No Sir!*, Viet Nam veteran Gary Payton reflects on his realization of enemy-othering during training: "[The military] used 'gook' like they used 'nigger'—they talk to them like they talk to us." Then there's the Vietnam Veterans Against the War, who have been outspoken against *all* wars, much like the Veterans for Peace (VFP) organization.

U.S. Veterans for Peace artifact, Viet Nam Museum of Revolution, Ha Noi (2015).

I think veterans who spoke and continue to speak up about U.S. foreign policy—especially if what they have to say goes against the common dialogue—are quite brave. It takes a lot of conviction to speak out against the U.S. military-industrial complex; it's an organization that prefers to keep things internal, and it doesn't reward dissent. But that's why a lot of people from the Viet Nam War era appear so revolutionary from a rearview mirror perspective in 2020; that refusal to back down against injustice is still alive around the world today.

7

1966

In 1966, Australian "diggers" faced one of their largest battles during the Viet Nam War: the Battle of Long Tan. Long story short, Australian soldiers were stationed near a rubber plantation at a base called Nui Dat, in the province of Phuoc Tuy in South Viet Nam. They received enemy fire. A patrol went out and found that the Australian forces were fairly outnumbered, and a fierce battle was waged. By the end of August 18, 1966, the men of D Company, 6th Battalion of the Royal Australian Regiment were victorious; 18 diggers and 240 North Vietnamese died.

The word *digger* is Australian slang for military personnel. The origins of the word stem from those who dug trenches at Gallipoli, one of the most important battles in Australian military history. As part of the British Commonwealth, the people of Australia and New Zealand often had to participate in wars that weren't of their own making, just as soldiers from India and South Africa were part of the UK forces in World War II. The diggers stationed on the famed Turkish peninsula during World War I had to endure nearly a year's worth of fighting, and the number of men lost in the war was so great that Australia and New Zealand fashioned a holiday to commemorate the event: ANZAC (Australian and New Zealand Army Corps) Day. While Australia and New Zealand already participated in Armistice Day observances (known Veterans Day in the United States), ANZAC Day is unique to the two countries in that it remembers Australian and New Zealand losses specifically and is a pretty pointed nod toward forming national identity.

The holiday is not without controversy; until I went to Australia, I figured everyone was in on the gig. However, I spoke to some people who thought the occasion had turned too nationalistic and watched a documentary that argued the particulars of the Battle of Gallipoli. Lastly, I read *The One Day of the Year*, a play written in 1958 by Australian playwright Alan Seymour. *The One Day of the Year* took the stars from my eyes with regard to ANZAC Day—I still email my Australian folks on the day, of course, but Alan Seymour's portrayal of the ANZACs revealed a generational fissure that I wasn't aware existed in Australia. As in the United States and much of Europe, the 1960s were a time of upheaval "down under."

The One Day of the Year became popular in the 1960s, as Australia entered the Viet Nam War. Prime Minister Robert Menzies, another follower of the "domino theory," increased military spending to shore the country up against the ever-present threat of communism in the early part of the decade. Australia and New Zealand were also involved in the "Indonesia-Malaysia Confrontation" in the early 1960s, which (a) ensured that the military would remain a growing entity and (b) arguably better prepared Aussie and Kiwi soldiers for the jungles of Viet Nam. If you want the full story, check out the mighty brick of a book that is *Australia and the Vietnam War* by Peter Edwards. I have read it, and it is a magnificently detailed account of Australia's eventual decision to get involved in Viet Nam.

Australians are still involved in Viet Nam; only an 8-hour plane ride away (that's about how long it takes me, on the U.S. East Coast, to get to Europe), the tropical climate and budget accommodations make for an alluring tourist destination. Interestingly enough, I also noticed that China, which is about a 10-hour flight away, had a lot of tourists in Australia. It's very telling when your tourist attraction signs are written in English and Chinese. But in Viet Nam, while there are definitely Chinese tourists, there are also many Australian ones, along with Australian NGOs and restaurants; even in Cambodia I got a decent hamburger from an Aussie-run restaurant. I saw the most Australian outreach in Hoi An, where I found a rugby-themed restaurant *and* a charity tea shop that taught Vietnamese youth various service-industry skills (like KOTO in Ha Noi; thanks for the recommendation, Dr. Cedeño!) as well as English. I found this

Australian memorial near the Long Tan battle site, Viet Nam (2017).

connection interesting and extremely helpful. Struck down by food issues in Hoi An, I found that the Australian café about a five-minute walk from my hotel provided some life-saving toast. Similarly, when I got lost and frustrated, more than once I chose to duck into the bar with "The Blacks Play Tonight!" scrawled on an outdoor chalkboard next to a neon Foster's sign. These symbols meant I'd find English spoken (if not native speakers) inside. The Vietnamese people are unfailingly helpful, but sometimes you just need some toast and jelly.

I am fortunate in that I received awards that funded the travel I did for this book; it is far easier to keep researching the Viet Nam War on a global scale when someone else deems paying for that plane ticket worthwhile. Of course, one of the glitches in getting research grants is that sometimes, by the time you get the award notification, plans have to be changed. People who could be involved are no longer available. Your eligibility to sign up for, say, volunteering with Agent Orange victims at the Friendship Village near Ha Noi becomes void (true story), so you have to be able to improvise. This was the case for my time in Australia.

In June 2017, I landed on "the last continent" (if we don't count Antarctica, the South Pacific was the final piece of my "continents I've visited" collection). The trip was a difficult one to pack for—I'd flown first to Viet Nam (via Hong Kong) and then on to Australia, where I'd start my journey from its northern (warmest) coast and move down into colder weather. I needed to be prepared for at least two climates. I was still a smoker at the time, so I remember pushing myself through the Sydney airport, in a Valium-eight-hour-flight daze, trying to get outside to a smoke-friendly zone ASAP. I was bummed that my passport didn't get a stamp, which I'd secretly hoped would have a kangaroo in it. Nevertheless, I grabbed a Coke on my way out and parked my luggage and self near an ashtray, surveying the "land down under"—the final frontier.

After checking in to my airport-adjacent hotel and taking a shower, I went foraging for food. It was cold. Once I discovered that cigarettes were *twenty dollars a pack(!)*, I began to quit smoking, which I would maintain for the majority of my time in Australia. I don't drink for the first few weeks when I'm trying to quit smoking. This might seem like an insignificant detail, but when people find out you didn't partake of the amazing hops and barley brews of Australia, they seem a little put out—you went all the way down to big beer land and drank not a drop? What fun are you? I took solace in a final Marlboro as I watched bizarre birds—parrots? cranes?—roost in the trees at a park. My hotel's address included the fascinating word "Woolloomooloo," which I repeated to myself as I walked in the fading light to a Thai restaurant I'd looked up. For a while, I was the only white person in the restaurant, and then a woman in her mid–60s came in. She was bundled up from the cold in what looked like layers of flannel, and she was friendly. We eventually struck up a conversation, whereupon she gave me the name of an Australian war "activist" who surely had some stories to share. I never followed through; knowing now, however, that Australians are some of the *nicest* people on the planet, I should have.

My Australian journey truly began in Cairns (pronounced "cans"—I didn't know until someone corrected me). I'd tentatively planned to meet with a colleague near there when I'd submitted my grant, but he got his own grant and was in Europe. My tour guide to the Long Tan battle site, Thomas Trang, had an Australian associate—and Viet Nam War veteran—who lived near Cairns. Rick Butler (and his wife, Gloria) ended up driving all the way to Cairns to pick me up on a full-day Australian adventure. I dedicate this chapter wholly to them, for I am so incredibly grateful for everything I learned from them, as well as their generosity and kindness. I should've driven up to see them, about an hour away from Cairns. But I didn't bring my glasses—I have one eye that's starting to lose steam, and it's most difficult to drive at night—and I was also too chicken shit to "drive on the left." I'm sure it wouldn't have been too hard to do, but there's a thing called a "hook turn" where you have to drive into traffic to turn—it scared me to death. Luckily, Rick and Gloria had friends in the area whom they visited before picking me up.

They took me all over some parts of Australia that I don't think are in the travel books but are worth a drive, like the Tablelands. Rick knew where all the war memorials were, and we saw as many as we could. There was a new memorial to the Iraq and Afghanistan wars, the Avenue of Honors in Yungaburra, that Rick had "wanted to see

Rick and Gloria Butler at the Afghanistan Avenue of Honor, Yungaburra, Australia (2017).

anyway." It was small but tasteful—more like a garden walk—and obviously cared for; the land around it was rolling and verdant, a quiet space that encouraged respect. I told Rick and Gloria about my friend and USCB student, Nick Becker. He'd died in March 2017, the same year I went to Australia. Nick was a year older than me and an army veteran; he had a ceaselessly witty sense of humor that drew from a wellspring of intellect, and we liked similar bands, so it was fun to talk to someone "my own age." In his suicide post on Facebook, he referred himself as the "22nd man," which is a reference to the U.S. average of 22 veterans suicides a day. In spite of his buoyant personality and sharp sense of humor, he suffered from PTSD (which has recently been shortened to "PTS," per my veteran friends). We lost a lot when we lost Nick, and it was comforting to talk to Rick and Gloria about it. Rick had brought along RSL (Returned and Services League, an Australian military veteran support system) magazines, and I learned about the RSL's "Mates for Mates" program, in which veterans are matched with other veterans for a variety of reasons. Sometimes it's just a connection so vets have someone to talk to, or it can be for helping veterans returning from war transition back into society. Australia, like the United States, shares a long commitment to the Middle East conflicts; there is even a heartbreaking memorial at the National War Museum in Canberra dedicated to all the IED-sniffer dogs lost in Iraq and Afghanistan.

Rick took me to the World War II Trail in Atherton, which since 1942 held more than 100,000 troops. Per the Atherton tourism website:

> With a cooler climate than Cairns, [Atherton] still provided excellent jungle warfare training for those heading off to places like (Papua) New Guinea and Bougainville. Servicemen were also treated for malaria at camp hospitals. The Atherton Tablelands was the largest Australian military base with camps at Tinaroo, Kairi, Wongabel, Herberton, Wondecia, Ravenshoe, and Mt Garnet as well as Atherton/Tolga area.[1]

Troops in Atherton also did some Viet Nam War training, because the Australians (unlike the Americans) made a concerted effort to train in conditions that mimicked the terrain they were going to fight in. While I know that many U.S. Marines trained in Viet Nam–like conditions at Parris Island (which, in July, is very close to the heat and humidity in Viet Nam), not everyone had the opportunity; many U.S. veteran accounts of the war immediately remark on Vietnamese weather—hot, wet, sticky.

We made a quick detour on our war memorial route to "Far North Queensland's Curtain Fig Tree," a massive ficus tree that seemed to me near the middle of nowhere. Rick told me that he'd trained in areas like this for his time in Viet Nam. Over lunch, I heard more about Rick and Gloria's life—including fun stories, like how Rick quit smoking due to a combination of roof repair and sweat melting off his nicotine patches—at an RSL restaurant (another rare treat), where Gloria taught me what a proper shandy is.

While contemporary Rick treats friends to an enviable Facebook feed of travel and family, Viet Nam–era Rick was just a 20-year-old guy starting out on one adventure but taken on another. In 1964, the Australian government started mandatory conscription (like the United States), but they picked a slightly older age (20) than the United States (18). While Rick and I were talking, we both agreed that the older age was probably a good thing; by 20, versus 18, the average person has gotten a little more living done, which leads to more familiarity with their own mind. Many Australian service people's letters I perused in the archives in Canberra were exchanged by married or engaged couples—many Aussies serving in Viet Nam wanted to come home to see their lovers, per the letters I read. You'll see similar threads in U.S. letters home, but you'll also see more letters to parents, because many U.S. soldiers were too young to really have an established sweetheart. Rick told me about massive birthday parties—everyone was drafted by their date of birth, so there'd be a lot of guys with the same birthday—that the diggers would have, as well as what types of service he and people he knew did while in Viet Nam.

One thing Rick and Gloria had gotten involved in—and this is where the link to Thomas comes in—was taking veterans back to Viet Nam. Their photos of these journeys revealed a lot of joy; many of these men were really boys while they were in country. Rick told me about one man who wanted to return to Australia as soon as he'd landed in Viet Nam; his wife awoke the day after they'd arrived to find him packed up and ready to return. Being in Viet Nam was freaking the guy out, but after a couple of days, he felt right at home; meeting with some Vietnamese veterans for a beer helped bring him out of his shell. "Nowadays, we're all just old soldiers," said Rick. I looked at a picture of smiling guys around a table—all once warriors, now simply beer buddies—and thought about the effect of age and time on emotional wounds. Perhaps those never heal, but it's easier to cope with them over some shared brews.

The goodwill in Rick's photos isn't limited, as I've said earlier, in the continent of Australia. A Long Tan veterans group runs a school near their old battle site (the kangaroos on the sides of the buildings give it away); you can buy a stubby holder (coozie) at a nearby food and beverage shop. I went to Long Tan—by way of Vung Tau—on a day trip with Thomas Trang. What I remember most about my time with Thomas isn't the history of the sites we went to (which I know he told me); it was stories that weren't necessarily part of the trip. Thomas loved travel; he was working on speaking Spanish when we met (he's now fluent), and he's taken travelers all over the world, from the Middle East to Latin America. He told me that he'd read *Dumb Luck* in school, but I found that the characters' names in Vietnamese were *slightly* different (which I put down to translation). Thomas taught me some of the differences between northern and southern Vietnamese dialects and informed me of the recent growth explosion in HCMC. Vung Tau, now a seaside

Site of the Battle of Long Tan, Viet Nam (2017).

My guide on my Long Tan excursion, Thomas Trang, with Kiet (driver) and me, near Vung Tau, Viet Nam (2019). (Photo by AK, courtesy of thomastravelvietnam.com)

resort area, was a popular R and R spot for Australian troops. The Long Tan area, however, reminded me of my trip to the DMZ: here in this spot a great battle was once fought; now it is a field. It was raining, so we didn't get to walk around the area much, but we did brave the rain to lay flowers at the white cross erected by the diggers at the battle site. The red clay mud stuck to my shoes, which I tried to tap together before getting into the car. As we drove past rubber tree farms and rural Viet Nam, I thought about how much of the scenery has changed since Rick and his fellow diggers came through the country.

At our lunch stop, we had a traditional meal of rice with "lots of bowls of other things"; some bowls were familiar and some were not, but all were delicious. In the bathroom of the restaurant, I noticed the wallpaper border was a cheerful Disney *101 Dalmatians* cartoon print. It was both an amusing and a jarring detail. *How did that get here?* I wondered as I washed my hands. What was the appeal of this four-inch strip of decoration versus, well, anything else? I sneaked a photo of it. As we left, Thomas and I started talking about the Vietnamese national anthem (I wanted to know the lyrics) and building websites. At the end of the tour, Thomas admitted that he'd thought I would be an old man, and it was funny that instead he got … me. Why would a 30-something American woman have any interest in Long Tan? He'd only taken a few Americans—veterans, couples—on this tour. When I told him about my research, Thomas and I had the serendipitous conversation that ultimately led me to my introduction to Rick. After we waved goodbye and became official Facebook friends (me off my hotel's Wi-Fi), I thought back to the rainy spot in the jungle where the white cross stood, accompanied by a few wilted plastic poppies. I wondered who the next visitor to Long Tan would be but felt comforted to know that the dead there were remembered and commemorated, even if their family was an ocean or a lifetime away.

◄► ◄► ◄►

Australia arguably has a better relationship with Viet Nam than the United States does. I think part of that is the proximity; one of the reasons the Australians entered the war was fear that the evils of communism would continue down the Pacific and into the Land Down Under. That was a common train of thought in that era, and Australia, coincidentally, had a sizable anti-war movement accompany its commitment of men and materiel to Viet Nam.

The Viet Nam memorial in Canberra is similar to the U.S. Vietnam Veterans Memorial in that it's black and jagged. The Australian memorial is smaller, and it doesn't do the individual name thing. But you can walk into it, and the effect is going into a dark cave with only a small chasm of light coming on top of you. It reminded me a little, in terms of design, of Lower Antelope Canyon, in Arizona—just without the spectacular "the earth made this itself" aspect (and colors). Like the United States, Australia's national war monuments are clustered together, lining the end of a mall (maw) that looks from the Parliament building to the War Museum. It's pretty. It's also a pretty bold move, to connect your government directly to war, spatially. But war is something worth studying in Australia; as a Commonwealth country, it has been involved in a number of colonial wars alongside Britain—like the Boer War, which I have to admit I don't think I'd really heard of until I went to Australia.

My first meeting in Canberra was with Dr. Deane-Peter Baker, who teaches philosophy. He took me on a tour of the academy, and then we had lunch in the canteen. Like many other faculty members at the University of New South Wales–Australian Defence

Viet Nam War Memorial, Canberra, Australia (2017).

Close-up of Australian War Memorial, Canberra (2017).

Force Academy (UNSW-ADFA), Dr. Baker spent time in the service; he had previously taught at the U.S. Naval Academy and retired as a major in the South African Army Reserve (I learned the last part because I couldn't decipher his accent at first.) We spoke a little about war ethics and philosophy, and he taught me about just war theory right there in the canteen, among the crows that flew in and out of open windows. Dr. Baker was extraordinarily accommodating and helpful, introducing me to colleagues and telling me about the programs that UNSW-ADFA offered, as well as his thoughts on the Naval Academy versus the Australian Defence Force Academy (one big hint: no one checked my ID at a checkpoint for me to get into the buildings). He later took me to speak to Dr. Bob Hall and Mr. Derrill de Heer, both veterans and scholars of the Australian Viet Nam War experience.

Dr. Hall and Mr. de Heer are the leaders of UNSW-ADFA's *Australia's Viet Nam War* project. It is massive. There is an interactive battle map that includes veteran photos and interviews, and they have artifacts and more content to add. When Dr. Hall and Mr. de Heer showed the map to me, I knew I was in deeper territory than I'd expected. These guys *knew* their stuff, and they clearly really cared about it. In 2019, at the annual Viet Nam War conference in Lubbock, Texas (sponsored by Texas Tech University, and future site of a Viet Nam War Museum), the UNSW-ADFA project was on display, warming my heart; I was so happy to see the project still in motion.

In a generous gesture, on the way to my drop-off at the main bus terminal, I broached the subject of Australia's Aboriginal people with Drs. Baker and Hall, who gave me rides back into town. I'd visited the Australian Capitol building and noticed a sizeable "protest" on the lawn proclaiming sovereignty over land stolen from the Aboriginal people. It sounded like a cross between the Black Lives Matter movement and the Native Lands Acknowledgment that Canada and the Pacific Northwest folks do. I didn't know about the fierce racism issues in Australia until I went there, and I didn't know whether it was something spoken about or still a quiet issue. Both Dr. Hall and Dr. Baker seemed to feel the Aboriginal people got a raw deal, elaborating that equality for this population was long overdue.

Like many Americans—maybe like many people who have no tie to Australia—I didn't know much about the Aboriginal situation, never mind just a loose history of Australia. Something vague about Captain Cook? Prisoners? I'd learned a bit before I visited, and I knew about poppies and ANZAC Day from watching Kate Middleton (aka the Duchess of Cambridge, UK) wear outfits on royal tours. Jim Jeffries, the Australian comedian, would throw in bits about his home country in the short-lived *Jim Jeffries Show*, but I didn't see that until after my 2017 visit. It turns out there's a history of racism in Australia as well, which points to why, as I write this book, Black people all over the world are speaking out against institutional racism in their countries. It wasn't until 1965 that Aboriginal people got the right to vote in Australia. Institutional racism, forced sterilization, and segregation are things Australia and the United States share.

Sometimes I'm a budget traveler; when I'm trying to stretch a grant as far as it can go (especially when I'm paying upfront and awaiting reimbursement), I will trade comfort for some extra cash. I'd heard that Australia's Greyhound bus system was miles ahead of the shabbiness that U.S. Greyhound is known for. I've been on nice bus trips in the United Kingdom, Ireland, and Panama, so I gave the Australian Greyhound a go—I took the overnight bus from Canberra to Melbourne. Our bus only had about 12 people on it, so everyone got their own double-seated spot on the bus to stretch out in. We stopped once, at about 3:00 a.m., and our bus driver kindly ushered us in and out of a rest stop, our faces puckered with sleep and wind chill. We rolled into the Melbourne bus terminal around 7:00 a.m. I'd twisted myself around and gotten some sleep on the bus, but I was definitely not rested. I got a Coke and croissant in the terminal, trying to shake off my grogginess and get my bearings. I had an 11:00 o'clock appointment with Dr. Nathalie Nguyen at Monash University, and I needed to be on top of my game.

First, I dashed to my Airbnb apartment to drop off my things. I quickly noticed it had a heated floor. Gauzy mouthed and dazed from lack of sleep, I tried to pull together a decent outfit and head over to Monash via the bus, which I took the wrong way at first. My outfit was not professional enough; the administrative assistant thought I was a student trying to get an advising appointment. But Dr. Nguyen was more than accommodating to my unprepared questions and vaguely announced visit. I'd read her books and just wanted to talk shop. Dr. Nguyen is of Vietnamese descent and arrived in Australia as a child refugee. Her scholarship covers topics like women, memory, and veterans' oral histories (check out her books *Memory Is Another Country* and *South Vietnamese Soldiers*)—it's beautiful work and carefully done.

Dr. Nguyen was delightful and insightful. We spoke for just over an hour about her work (telling the stories of Vietnamese Australians as part of a great story of Australian history) and her experiences taking students to Viet Nam as part of a Monash study abroad program. I learned that the Vietnamese government liked to approve (or at least view) the topics that would be taught during studies abroad at in Ho Chi Minh City. At the time, I didn't think much of the government oversight on curriculum, but as a more seasoned professor *now*, I would be upset to have anyone dictate what and how I taught. Dr. Nguyen cautioned me not to seek out certain topics brazenly and to be careful regarding whom I talked to. I thought I'd recorded the whole conversation, but I'd not learned how to use my recording device properly (or was sleep deprived); I'd just hit "record" and then "pause." I didn't take notes—I think it's rude to do that when someone's talking—but I remember Dr. Nguyen's dedication to telling Vietnamese stories and her insistence that the Vietnamese point of view, in Australia and beyond, should be told. For a newer scholar, it was a superb lesson in inclusivity. I left thinking I had so much more to learn.

Melbourne reminded me of London, where everyone dressed in monochromatic shades (or all black) and bustled everywhere. You could also get lost in thought there, which I did as I circled the vast Monash campus, angry at myself for screwing up the recording with Dr. Nguyen. My taxi drivers to and from the Melbourne airport told me that the city was becoming increasingly difficult to live in, and my companion and guide to the William Ricketts Sanctuary and Dandenong Rainforest, while a relentlessly cheerful individual, did admit it was getting harder to live in Melbourne—but he'd never want to live anywhere else. Per my trip to the Immigration Museum in Melbourne, I knew that Australia had a storied and interesting past regarding immigration; the diversity in the city could only be attributed to its acceptance of refugees and immigrants. There was even a "Little Viet Nam" section of town, lit with lanterns and full of typical Vietnamese wares and cuisine.

I opted for an Airbnb in Melbourne to have a bit more privacy. My cozy little flat—a studio with an attached bedroom, to be transparent—was located in the Hawthorn neighborhood, on the east side of the city. At the Little Mushroom Burger restaurant (now defunct, per Google Maps) down my new street, I was persuaded to try a magnificent gift: a Tim Tam milkshake! If you're familiar with Tim Tams, Australia's bewitching snack cookie, then you understand my awe and happiness. I typically avoid desserts/foods that get too much hype, often saying things like "I don't like chocolate peanut butter cheesecake" when what I really mean is "if I even taste this, I will rocket into an orbit of sugar that I cannot cope with." I had demurred on Tim Tams long enough, and the happy chef and owner of the Mushroom Burger had me in a good spot for manipulation: little sleep, little food, cold, confused, and in need of some comfort food. A burger and a milkshake it was. I remember blissfully sinking into the little mismatched chairs and leafing through an artsy magazine, my body thankful for nutrients and, really, carbs. From my cozy seat, I watched the people of Melbourne—or Hawthorn—go about their day as the tram crossed by them in the background. It looked like folk song should sound, rooted and choral; I sipped my Tim Tam milkshake with the unrestricted joy of simply being warm, safe, fed, and in a new place.

◁▷ ◁▷ ◁▷

When I taught English in China, I played "California Dreamin'" by the Mamas and the Papas for my fifth- and sixth-grade classes, and they surprised me by knowing all the words to the poetic tribute to California sunshine. Not many kids in Jiujiang knew much American popular music, but "California Dreamin'" was featured in a very popular Chinese film—thus my unintended singalong (we had a blast and did "hippie dances"). Like other songs from the 1960s, "California Dreamin'," the top song of 1966, never made it to the number-one position on the Billboard chart; however, the Mamas and the Papas' song "Monday, Monday" did hold the top spot in May. I prefer "California Dreamin'"—I like the verse about stopping in a church; it feels heavy and immediate, but also poetic. Those qualities are also in the first number-one song of 1966: "The Sound of Silence," by Simon and Garfunkel. Neither "California Dreamin'" nor "The Sound of Silence" are bubble-gum, poppy love songs; they both have substance and creative lyrics, and the guitars (and a very enthusiastic flute solo) strum prettily. This was a first for the pop charts—songs with lyrics not about heterosexual love but a more purposeful poetic nature. The Beatles' "We Can Work It Out" (rumored to be more about the band's relationship than a romantic one) vied with "The Sound of Silence" for the top spot through the entire month of January; this mix of folk and pop rock would be the hallmark of 1966 in music.

Around this same time, a young man named David Jones changed his name to David Bowie, and "acid tests" were starting up in San Francisco. The first took place at the Fillmore in San Francisco on January 3, igniting the popularity of combining a psychedelic experience with music (the Grateful Dead was the house band for several events), which would peak within a few years' time. In other parts of the United States, however, the expansion of the mind was met with gritted intolerance. In a move underwritten by racism and segregation, the Georgia House of Representatives denied Julian Bond his seat in the statehouse. Bond was the cofounder of the Student Nonviolent Coordinating Committee (SNCC), and he agreed with SNCC's anti–Viet Nam War statement, which angered the (white) establishment. The Supreme Court, however, ruled that Bond's right to free speech had been violated, and Bond thus began a long and distinguished career in politics. Progress was slow but present: the first Black presidential cabinet member, Robert C. Weaver, was appointed U.S. secretary of housing and urban development around the same time Bond was fighting for his seat with the SCOTUS. The Viet Nam War also kept moving; after reiterating America's commitment to Viet Nam in mid–January, President Johnson met with South Vietnamese prime minister Nguyen Cao Ky in Honolulu on February 7 to discuss ways forward in Viet Nam. The opportunity for talks was a welcome change from the constant bombing campaigns the year prior, but everything I've read about Ky paints him as a shady character. That reputation was bolstered when Ky (a Catholic) fired rival general Nguyen Chanh Thi (a Buddhist) in a power grab in early March, prompting the Buddhist Uprising of 1966 in South Viet Nam. From March until mid–June, Buddhists clashed with ARVN and U.S. forces in central Viet Nam, including skirmishes in Hue and Da Nang. More self-immolation protests occurred, this time not just in protest of the government but also opposing American imperialism in South Viet Nam. Using the massive firepower at his disposal, Ky ultimately quelled the uprising with deadly force.

In April, the South Vietnamese government pledged to hold elections by the end of the year, the vagueness of the date aggravating the Buddhist Uprising, which led to more protests. In the United States that May, the March Against the Viet Nam War drew 8–10,000 people to Washington, echoing the anti-war movement's calls to end the war that had occurred in March, during the International Days of Protest (Tokyo, Oslo, and London were involved). The civil rights movement also maintained a busy calendar, including the shooting (luckily not fatally) of James Meredith. Last seen as the first Black student to attend the University of Mississippi in 1962, Meredith was injured during the March Against Fear in Mississippi. By the end of the year, Bobby Seale and Huey P. Newton founded the Black Panther Party, whose ethos of Black Power would create a new dimension in the civil rights movement.

Throughout the spring, the top hits included "Good Lovin'" (the Rascals) and "When a Man Loves a Woman" (Percy Sledge), but early summer's number-one song, "Paint It Black" by the Rolling Stones, felt more in line with the reality of 1966 than sweeter pop hits. The haunting introductory guitar motif is accompanied by grim lines ("no colors anymore/I want them to turn black"); the song is sexy in sound but depressing in lyrics. The year 1966 marked a clear moment in experimentation with popular music. Seminal albums that explored darker themes of loss, anger, and the turbulence of the global environment, like *Blonde on Blonde* (Bob Dylan), *The Doors* (the Doors), *Pet Sounds* (Beach Boys), and *Freak Out!* (Frank Zappa and the Mothers of Invention), also came out in the summer of 1966. The Beatles would release their "acid" record *Revolver* in the fall, just as LSD became classified as an illegal substance in the United States.

"Paint It Black" sounds honest against the historical events that occurred while the song topped the Billboard charts. At the end of June, the Johnson administration began bombing North Viet Nam, escalating the war. Cleveland saw its first race riots in July. A former USMC sniper took out 14 people from a tower on the campus of the University of Texas in Austin. It was a "black" year. And, of course, there were events in Viet Nam that made the world feel "[painted] black": the Battle of Long Tan, the Binh Tai Massacre, and the Binh Hoa Massacre. The Binh Tai and Binh Hoa massacres were the work of South Korean forces—U.S. and ARVN allies—who killed at least 600 unarmed citizens in the two villages between October and December 1966. I've heard (mostly from Viet Nam veterans at the annual Viet Nam War Conference in Lubbock) that the Koreans had a reputation for being particularly mean. I've also heard that said about the Puerto Ricans; I'm not sure how much stock to put into hearsay.

The Viet Nam War isn't spoken about much, if at all, in Korea. My friend Ted spent several years teaching in international schools in the Republic of Korea (South Korea) and Viet Nam. At one point he was told, in no uncertain terms, *not* to talk about the Korean forces who fought in Viet Nam. The Korean veterans of the Viet Nam War, thus, have no support structure (never mind recognition) in Korean society—another instance of painting history black. And we, today, in the United States, get mad about Civil War monuments being moved to museums. At least museums preserve memories and statues, as opposed to blotting the history out entirely.

The year 1966 ended with the premier rollout of the Toyota Corolla and the first airing of the animated *Dr. Seuss's How the Grinch Stole Christmas!* and *It's the Great Pumpkin, Charlie Brown*. It wasn't entirely "Paint It Black" despair in 1966. Rousing songs like "Reach Out, I'll Be There" (Four Tops) and "Good Vibrations" (Beach Boys) played out the end of the year; New Year's Eve's top song was the undeniably fun pop smash "I'm a Believer" by a television-created band, the Monkees. The Johnson administration, however, believed in winning Viet Nam. In December 1966, NVA divisions, composed of tens of thousands of troops, moved to Quang Tri Province near Khe Sanh, one of President Johnson's most beloved outposts on his war map. Fierce fighting from the DMZ to Sai Gon began, and the administration increased the number of troops in Viet Nam to 385,000. Additional soldiers, of course, were difficult to muster when some of those who'd served and returned were protesting the war. Furthermore, by 1966, the American people were starting to tire of the war—we're nothing if not an impatient nation—and the war's drop in popularity meant a loss of interest from potential soldiers to fight in it. To the average recruit in 1966, the Viet Nam War didn't look like a good way to spend 1967, or beyond.

◁▷ ◁▷ ◁▷

Perhaps it is because I am a sarcastic, dry-humored sort of person, but I initially found Sergeant Barry Sadler's 1966 one-hit wonder "Ballad of the Green Berets" hilarious. I think it's because the video (which I saw at the same time I heard the song) is so stiff, and I am nothing if not a child of the music video generation: the golden-haired muscle man in uniform, singing of valor with the thrumming of the marching band behind him, looks like a World War II propaganda video—just with a different uniform. But it's an important song; unlike many songs of the Viet Nam War era, Sadler's song portrays war favorably and unconfrontationally. "Ballad of the Green Berets" is a tribute to American soldiers and American national identity. I think it's worth devoting a moment to the song, which held the top spot for the entire month of March and first week of April, because it reveals a lot about how (the majority of) the United States wanted to see itself during the Viet Nam era—and arguably beyond. The song highlights traits of honor, valor, and bravery, as well as other qualities prized in the ideal American soldier. A member of the Green Berets has bragging rights; it takes a great deal of grit to become a member of this elite Army Special Forces unit.

Sadler's "Ballad of the Green Berets" uses Christian savior elements found within American national identity (and cultural mythology, but that's another book), including the masculine sacrifice. The first three lines of the song reveal breathtaking pretense (even though they're just doing what paratroopers do, which is, admittedly, something I would not want to do); like angels, these Green Berets appear to be dropped from the heavens. But these men are not harbingers of God's peaceful message of brotherly love— on the contrary, their actions have purpose, and their words are plain and simple in meaning. They're not dropping in on you to say hello; these guys have a mission. The elite nature of the Green Berets surfaces through the repeated chorus of the song, in which Green Berets are further identified with the symbol of silver wings, the insignia given once training is sufficiently passed. Only a fraction of those who try for the Green Berets will be chosen to bear these wings or wear the distinctive green beret so coveted. The image of the American soldier offered in Sadler's "Ballad of the Green Berets" regards U.S. troops as heaven-sent entities wearing silver wings, and they are identified multiple times as the United States' "best"[2] caliber men. The mythology in this song points out that

America values a certain overinflated Christian motif for its martyrs; as part of Manifest Destiny, the soldier embodies the warrior, gifted to the world from the sky, bearing silver angelic wings that deliver liberty for the oppressed. The job of the American soldier, according to this mythology, is to do God's will.

Later in the song, the image of the American soldier morphs into a vision of a Grizzly Adams–type character, living off the land and meeting foes with only his fists. The idea of the soldier sent by God becomes inflated in these lyrics, for the ideal, mythological American soldier becomes resourceful after his elite Green Beret training. A product of American education and guidance (which definitely includes the possibility of combat), the Green Beret uses only what surrounds him; he needs nothing more than nature's gifts to survive. This warlike figure is relentless and driven, his privilege and masculinity pushing him toward deified heights. According to "Ballad of the Green Berets," American soldiers, in their pure, God-given form, live to fight.

What these soldiers fight (or fight for), exactly, does not warrant identification. The enemy remains undefined because, historically in American cultural mythology, an enemy disagrees with or attacks American value and belief structures. The duty of the American soldier is explicitly articulated in these lyrics. It is worth noting that the inevitable, yet glorious, death of the American soldier receives two distinct mentions, and the soldier's dying wish is that his son also receive the silver wings of the Green Berets. This rhetoric of sacrifice highlights the complexity found within the theater of war. The Green Beret decrees that his son will be eventually fulfill his greatest duty: fighting for his country.

This glimpse into the ideal American soldier identity reveals a theology that permeates American mythology, and it outlines the cultural values of America that seemed, frankly, out of place in the Viet Nam War. American soldiers who died in the Viet Nam War did not die for oppressed Americans, nor did they necessarily die in hopes of saving the South Vietnamese. This myth does not signify a cultural truth, nor does it attempt to offer a solution to the conflicting sides of the Viet Nam War. As Americans watched the carnage in Viet Nam, their opinions concerning their national identity and mythology changed. Many citizens' old beliefs regarding war, bolstered by a masculine national identity and supported by an equally hegemonic cultural mythology, created a tension with new opinions resulting from the televised reality of the Viet Nam War. Barry Sadler's "Ballad of the Green Berets" offers a comforting message of old: the soldiers always do the right thing, because God would not have America's best acting any other way.

The most decorated Australian unit from the Viet Nam War (four Victoria Cross recipients, a merit equivalent to the U.S. Medal of Honor) is the Australian Army Training Team Vietnam (AATTV). The AATTV fought with the South Vietnamese, assisted the CIA and U.S. Special Forces, and worked with farmers. I recently read in a 2020 news article that it is lobbying the "Federal government to approve an Australian bush site as the first official national war memorial outside Canberra." The AATTV selected a space called "The Grove," where "1,006 native trees" have been planted, "one for each member of the AATTV who served between 1962 and 1972." The trouble with the Grove is that it's also part of the Land Warfare Centre at Canungra (near Brisbane), which is currently used by Royal Military College of Australia and is a "live fire" zone. Not an ideal place to "reflect and remember," as Phyllis Everill, the daughter of an AATTV member who was killed in action, wishes this memorial would be. But Captain Kerry Gallagher, AATTV Association national president, emphasizes that the placement of the memorial—in the "bush"—is pointed: "It's almost the antithesis of what the training team was. It is a very peaceful place…. It gives quite a degree of peace, particularly to those who've found the journey after Vietnam quite difficult."[3] While the article interested me because of my research, it also was interesting with regard to how the Australians have remembered the war.

Like the United States, the majority of Australia's monuments are located in its self-created capital, Canberra. But (also like the United States) other memorials pop up, like Rocky Creek Memorial Park in Tolga. The Rocky Creek Memorial is rows upon rows of natural rocks with plaques affixed to them, honoring different battalions and wars. Rick and Gloria walked me through the whole park, telling me background information about the Australian military—past and present—as well as the different wars that included Australian troops. From Rick, I got the sense that Australia, though a young country (like the United States), is very proud of its troops, but, most important, they value remembrance, which includes caring about military veterans and creating sites to honor them and their memories.

Of course, the United States does this too. All countries do. But it didn't feel as distant to the culture the way it's become in the United States. Every year, my university's chapter of the Student Veterans of America (SVA)—the University of South Carolina Beaufort (USCB) Sand Shark Veterans (SSV)—puts on an event for Veterans Day (I'm the founder and faculty advisor). It's gotten bigger every year, and we have cake! Veterans Day is the day after the U.S. Marine Corps birthday, and the USMC is usually well represented in SSV. It's a joyful event; Memorial Day is for the tears, but, as my friend Nick Becker once wrote, Veterans Day "should be way more fun…. If you really want to celebrate the warrior caste you should enjoy what we fought for! Celebrate your freedom and party like you might get slayed in a foreign country tomorrow…. Live for a moment as if

Rocky Creek Memorial, Australia (2017).

you stood at the intersection of life and death." Yet, year after year, aside from Savannah's local Veterans Day parade, most people I know use Veterans Day as another day to mark the dead. But it's about those who are alive. Our SSV speakers inevitably explain that fact, in some way, every year—it's a constant lesson. The United States doesn't understand, really, how to celebrate our veterans. Some think parades and medals and pomp and circumstance honor veterans, and I wouldn't rule it out entirely. But, in the United States at least, Memorial Day and Veterans Day have become prime "sales" events instead of holidays; perhaps we could find a more suitable place for Veterans Day, a middle ground between capitalism and pageantry?

Almost every night in Canberra I did the same thing: I spent the morning running around Lake Burley-Griffin, inevitably or eventually ending up at the Australian War Memorial's archives. I got gently kicked out of the archives each evening in time to catch the Last Post ceremony, which is achingly beautiful and includes wreath laying and trumpet playing. It was also sometimes unintentionally comical, as the dome of the War Memorial is one of the local cockatoos' favorite hang-out spots. If you don't teach a cockatoo how to say things, it squawks like any other bird—kind of a shriek, really—and it's distracting. The juxtaposition of the solemn Last Post and a cacophony of cockatoos screeching offered a bit of levity. But because it was winter when I was there, the sun would go down during the Last Post, and I'd shiver my way to the bus stop so that I could hustle over to Bistro Nguyen's in the center of town.

I would sit at my table with my lemongrass chicken and rice, looking over the day's notes and photos. I could never watch my videos of the Last Post in public, though. I don't like to cry in public. Part of it is the bugle; "Taps" dissolves me into a puddle on the floor, even when, like at my grandpa's funeral, it's played over a tape recorder (it didn't help that my second cousin, an army veteran, surprised us all by snapping to attention; that would've made

Last Post at the Australian War Memorial, Canberra (2017).

Grandpa proud). Anyway, the big emotional kicker of the War Memorial's Last Post is the recitation of "The Ode," which has been part of Australian war commemoration services since 1921. "The Ode" is derived from a verse in the World War I poem "For the Fallen," by Laurence Binyon, an Englishman. Everyone around me at the War Memorial said the words by heart (I eventually learned it by the end of the week), always looking soberly into the distance or standing with heads bowed:

> They shall grow not old, as we that are left grow old;
> Age shall not weary them, nor the years condemn.
> At the going down of the sun and in the morning
> We will remember them.
> Lest we forget.[4]

There's an eternal flame in a rectangle pool at the War Memorial, in the internal chamber where the Last Post is held. People stand on either side of the pool and all around the balconies and stairs leading to the antechamber. Even schoolchildren know to be silent and respectful. The poppies beside all the names that run along the memorial walls in the interior blur into a red mass of sadness as the trumpet purrs out one last note into the dusk, and I would think of all the *loss* of war and just splutter into my scarf.

The only reason I ate Italian one night in Canberra was because I thought the people at Bistro Nguyen's got tired of me. I'd arrive early—as soon as they opened for dinner—and order the same thing: lemongrass chicken and a smoothie. At the Propaganda restaurant in Sai Gon, where I'd just come from, this behavior was welcomed; people would smile in recognition when I'd show up with my book and sit by myself. At Bistro Nguyen's, I felt more like eyes were being rolled when I showed up: "Can't she find somewhere else to eat?" After my early dinner, I'd walk to the corner shop down the block and get peanut M&Ms (my travel mainstay—I can go a whole day on a Coke and peanut M&Ms) and another snacky thing, like chocolate milk. Then I'd endure the uphill, windy, quiet, and freezing walk back to my lodging, a dorm at Australian National University. Students were mostly off campus; it was winter break, so the shops and bars near the campus were shuttered. Once in the room, I'd crank the heat and get under the covers at 7:00 p.m.; like a retiree, I was asleep by 9:00. This routine worked well in terms of keeping in touch with my husband and the time difference, and I liked the monkish schedule I kept: wake, run around Lake Burley-Griffin, shower, get lunch and go see a person/go to the War Memorial archive. It was too cold to do much in the evenings, especially for someone who keeps things cheap by walking everywhere.

The early evenings also gave me time to reflect. While watching an old BBC murder mystery one night (Australian television is both exotic and familiar), I found myself getting frustrated with the detective, who persisted in tracing the steps of a likely suspect who was *not* the perpetrator. The detective insisted that tracing the steps of one suspect only led to more questions, which was a good thing; I disagreed. Then I realized that I was taking my frustrations about myself out on the detective. I could trace the steps of the Viet Nam War all over the globe, but I would never actually know it. I could read letter after letter in the archives, but what I was looking *for* (Australian commentary on Americans) wasn't what I ended up looking *at*; instead, I would lament how young the authors of these letters were, or how simple and sweet their wishes to be home with their families became, after reading so many—and here I was, willfully away from my family, in pursuit of something I couldn't grasp. Sometimes it would feel like a stupid thing to be doing:

Who was going to care about this project beyond me, who was the one traipsing around continents to … do what, exactly? Research in archives? Talk to random people?

By the time I reached Australia, I was more familiar with the nuances of "war studies"; I knew representation from Vietnamese voices (and Australian ones) deserved more attention in American books about the war. This chapter's intention was to at least introduce you to people and resources to explore some of these voices further; there's a lot more to learn.

8

1967

My motorbike driver was impressed with how long I stayed in the Vietnamese Women's Museum in Ha Noi; "you must have really liked it," he said with a grin, looking up from his newspaper. Since I'd reserved his services for the better part of the day, he picked our lunch spot. We breezed from the Women's Museum past the Citadel and into a part of town I'd never been to. We crossed a busy road and took what I've been taught to call a "frontage road" into a neighborhood. For $3, I got a bowl of pho with chicken (pho con ga) and a can of Coke. That pho remains the best I've ever had, and I've sampled a lot of it (mark it—June 2015, best pho ever). Constantly tending to the silver vat—it was too large to be a pot—was the proprietor of this "restaurant," a woman with a black-and-white-striped shirt who seemed preoccupied with her own thoughts. She barely spoke to us, and in the background of a photo I have of "the best pho ever," she's looking away, brow furrowed and concentrating.

It's hard to say whether this was really a restaurant—it seemed to serve only pho and a choice of canned beverage (the latter technically purchased from a guy nearby who sold cans from a cooler to whoever wanted a can of soda on the street). My motorbike driver's name was something like Thoung (I didn't ask him to spell it); he was in his 50s, eager to talk, and definitely acquainted with the restaurateur. After wolfing down his pho (my treat), he pulled his motorbike under an umbrella, stretched out across it, pulled his hat over his face, and took a 10-minute snooze while I ate my pho, the chicken in the broth not far removed from the stripped chickens in a bowl nearby. Their waxen bodies looked on as I squeezed a bit of lime into my bowl.

My driver didn't know that I was in the Women's Museum to take pictures of everything for "research purposes." Vietnamese propaganda art—from the old stuff you'll see in museums to the "30th Anniversary of Peace" flags I saw in 2019 in Ha Noi—always includes women. If jubilant patriots are to be displayed, a woman is always part of the picture. Sometimes the woman will hold hands with a child or cradle a baby, but just as often she's part of a farm co-op or gazing defiantly out from under a helmet, weapon slung over her shoulder. Judging by the propaganda depictions, women were a key part of Vietnamese society, equal to men in their love of country and labor. In Vietnamese soap operas, women are as skilled as men in the ways of scheming (isn't that true for all soap operas?) but more likely to, as far as I could understand the plot lines, bring family or friends to reconciliation. (This is less "empirical data" and more "guesswork," as the soap operas aren't dubbed or captioned.)

Back in 2012, I saw the "Sad Woman" memorial near the DMZ. It has always stuck with me in terms of trying to see Vietnamese women's role in society, at least from the

Site of "the best pho ever," Ha Noi, Viet Nam (2015).

perspective of those who erect giant monuments. She inspired more thought than the Lady Buddha of Da Nang, who was pretty impressive. "Sad Woman," with a child at her side, gazes from North Viet Nam toward South Viet Nam from her post on the Ben Hai River (aka the 17th parallel, the imposed line of demarcation between what was once the North and the South). She's flanked by concrete palm fronds, their height imposing a severity on the monument. At the center, "Sad Woman's" face is impassive, gaze direct, and her clothes are rendered heavily, with swirling clouds (a Buddhist symbol that can also be found on statues of Ho Chi Minh) around her. Mr. Anh, my guide for that trip, told me that the "Sad Woman" is looking for the men—sons, husbands, brothers, and so on—who didn't return after the war ended. I've never been clear on whether Sad Woman's penetrating stare is for men who died or men who just didn't come back; Mr. Anh mentioned both, but I wondered how much one interpretation was governmental and another was personal.

The Vietnamese Women's Museum depicted the same type of women embodied in the "Sad Woman": purposeful, sturdy, strong, and mighty. Vietnamese women are resourceful, smart, and brave. They protect the home and hearth; they become doctors and heroes. The museum invokes images of the legendary Trung sisters, Trac and Nhi, who were the leaders of Viet Nam's first independence coup against China in the first century. Read that last bit again—"first century" indicates not only how long Viet Nam has been trying to be an independent nation but also how long women,

War memorial on the southern side of the old DMZ, Viet Nam (2012).

even perhaps mythologized ones, have played crucial roles in Viet Nam's struggle for independence.

When you go to Washington, D.C., you'll inevitably find yourself walking the National Mall with all the famous monuments. There's the Vietnam Veterans Memorial, which is iconic on its own: built into the ground, so that you have to descend to get to it, an ebony slash into the hill with the names of the fallen engraved in stone—it is hard to ignore. You have to pass by the Wall if you're walking from the Washington Monument to the Lincoln Memorial. There are actually three Viet Nam memorials on the Mall (which we did not see on my 5th-grade trip to DC, the first time I ever went there), and they all attempt to interact with each other. If you're like me, it's a bit surprising to realize there are three memorials to one war; we generally only hear about the Wall, and it's interesting to think that a war as polarizing as Viet Nam warranted so much more attention than, say, Korea or even World War II.

As you approach the Vietnam Veterans Memorial (completed with some controversy in 1982), you'll pass the "Three Soldiers" memorial sculpture/statue, unveiled on Veterans Day in 1984. This statue (also referred to as "The Three Servicemen") features the first representation of Latino and Black people at the National Mall. The soldiers face the Wall, their expressions impenetrable, with weapons in hand. To me they look tired. And accurate—the white soldier (in the center, natch) has his vest open to reveal a bare torso and glittering dog tags, while the Black soldier's shirt is unbuttoned halfway down his chest, and his dog tags are less prominent. The Hispanic soldier sports the only hat

Vietnam Veterans Memorials in Washington, D.C., United States (2014).

(not a helmet—more like a fishing hat*) alongside bandoliers across his chest and waist; he hoists a M60 machine gun over his shoulder, while his other hand rests on the white soldier's upper back. The white soldier carries a Colt .45 pistol and the Black soldier an M16A1 rifle. Frederick Hart, the sculptor, made sure that the weapons and uniforms were historically accurate. He thoughtfully included a sweat towel (draped around the neck of the Black soldier), a clear nod to Viet Nam's notorious climate.

It's important to note the inclusion of the Black soldier; 11 percent[1] of those serving in Viet Nam identified as Black, and Viet Nam was the first fully integrated conflict. The civil rights movement naturally trickled into the military, and everything from the regulation of black hair to enduring overt racism got more attention. Wallace Terry's *Bloods: Black Veterans of the Vietnam War—An Oral History* is my go-to book on the subject, but novels like *Matterhorn* touch on the subject of racism (in Karl Marlantes' rendering, tensions come to a head with a tragic fragging† incident), and films like *Same Mud, Same Blood* (an NBC documentary from 1967) and Burns and Novick's *The Vietnam War* (2017) feature Black veterans' voices. From all I've read and watched, racism was harder to take in the United States once you'd served; you had to get along with your fellow soldiers, but citizens didn't share a code of ethics.

There isn't very much written about women of color's experiences in the war at all. In addition, the Montagnards (an ethnic minority from the Central Highlands in Viet Nam who have darker skin than the majority of Vietnamese people) were historically

---

*This light and floppy hat with an adjustable cord under the chin is called a "boonie" hat. If you Google it, you'll go "oh, okay, yeah." They were standard-issue uniform components in the Viet Nam War with the U.S. and Australian armies. It's also called a "giggle hat." Both of those words sound suspect for racist or "dirty humor" undertones, but I couldn't find any evidence of either. The hats are pretty effective for landscaping and outdoor work, per my USMC veteran pal Norman, who wears his to mow and so on in steaming Lowcountry summers. Norman doesn't give bad advice either.

†Military slang for tossing a fragmentation (hence the term) grenade at a fellow soldier or into their quarters.

oppressed in Viet Nam and became great allies to the U.S. Army during the war. After the war, many left Viet Nam. Their war stories are hard to find as well. There are clearly gaps in the overall story of the Viet Nam War if the voices of people of color are marginalized or unheard, which goes double for women of color.

I ran into the Vietnam Women's Memorial by accident while looking for the Korean War Memorial (lone silver soldiers, draped in ponchos, silently midstep in low-growth bushes); it isn't as celebrated or featured as the Wall. The Vietnam Women's Memorial was completed in 1993, so my 5th-grade field trip to DC ("capitol with an 'o,' not like Raleigh, capital with an 'a,'" per Mrs. Fletcher) in 1992 would've missed it. But I went back to the Wall twice, last time in 2014, and it wasn't until that visit that I found the women. I didn't even know to look for them. It's a sculpture, like "The Three Soldiers"—it's not a big piece of art, and it's not only a commemoration of service and sacrifice like the Wall, the World War II Memorial, or even Arlington Cemetery. The Vietnam Women's Memorial is a tribute—a small gesture—to a grander idea of equality.

The Vietnam Women's Memorial is bronze and about 10 feet tall. Glenna Goodacre, a native of Lubbock, Texas, created the piece. Four people are frozen in poses on a round pedestal base, with rock and sandbags supporting a woman who holds a fallen soldier. Another woman (I think a Black woman, but maybe I just want to think that) wears fatigues and a hat like the guy in "The Three Soldiers." She stands to the side of the sitting woman, her hand behind her, on her friend's arm, as she looks up and away, mouth open. She could be looking for a medevac helicopter, or we can muse that she's crying out to a higher power, but it's a tender detail, the face wide, calling to the skies for help. A third woman sits to the left of the sitting woman, also in a hat. She looks downward and downcast.

Of course, in the Viet Nam War, women weren't allowed to serve on the frontlines. Women in the U.S. Armed Services were often nurses, sometimes on a ship docked somewhere in the Pacific, but frequently at a base in the medical platoon. Ms. Goodacre's rendering of women in service, during the Viet Nam War, is pretty accurate with regard to women's roles in the service.

While I am glad that women have been honored for their military service on the National Mall, it does pain me a little to look at the Vietnam Women's Memorial. The focal point of the statue is the woman cradling the fallen soldier. His legs are akimbo, and his eyes are bandaged, as if he's been purposefully blinded in order to see his fate. The gaze of the primary female figure, a nurse, is on him, and she looks upset at his state. Glenna Goodacre wrote, for the Vietnam Women's Memorial website,

> The kneeling figure has been called "the heart and soul" of the piece because so many vets see themselves in her. She stares at any empty helmet, her posture reflecting her despair, frustrations, and all the horrors of war. The soldier's face is half-covered by a bandage, creating an anonymous figure with which veterans can identify. Even though he is wounded, he will live. I want this to be a monument for the living.[2]

Ms. Goodacre's sentiments and pathos are pure; the anonymous center woman is a person "many vets see themselves in," and her posture is explicitly "despair," "frustration," and "horror." I do have to wonder: Is that what most vets think of when they think of the conflict? Many I've spoken to have as many funny stories as they do ones of despair, frustration, and horror.

◄► ◄► ◄►

The kindness of strangers never ceases to amaze me. Stuck in this chapter of the book, I took to Twitter; I wanted more meat on the bones of the "American woman in Viet Nam" narrative. Women (most notably Jane Fonda) visited Viet Nam for entertainment (like USO shows) for the troops, but these stories we know. Women "back home" in the United States, Australia, and New Zealand waited, hoped, studied, worked, protested, and organized. But what of the American women enlisted in Viet Nam? Who were they? I met a few Viet Nam War veterans who'd served in the medical corps in the navy—including a colleague—but life on the boat was limited to the happenings on the boat. I wanted to find out more about the women on the ground. I think I also wanted to know *if* there were many women on the ground—the U.S. military didn't lift the rules on women serving in combat positions until 2015.

I knew more about Vietnamese women. First off, they have a museum (which I doubt is representative of all women in Viet Nam, but so rarely do we get the full story that it's nice to get something, you know?). Most of their stories involve survival; in a communist society, the sexes stand shoulder to shoulder, after all. There are biographies of vicious VC fighters and stories about women who shot down planes. Both the Women's Museum and the Museum of Revolution in Ha Noi hammer home the fact that women volunteered, in droves, to help with the war effort during the American conflict. Books like Nathalie Nguyen's *Memory Is Another Country* (an oral history of Vietnamese women's memories of the war and adjustment to life as refugees in Australia) or *Last Night I Dreamed of Peace: The Diary of Dang Thuy Tran* (a female medic's view from the frontlines) echoed much of what I'd learned in fictional books like Nguyen Phan Que Mai's *The Mountains Sing* (a story of war told from a young female protagonist's point of view) or Duong Thu Huong's *Paradise of the Blind* (a multigenerational story of women surviving the war). I think those works should speak for themselves in telling these stories; I have nothing to add but my support—and my encouragement to you, the reader, to seek these stories out.

But I still needed voices of the women Viet Nam War veterans. Enter the kindness of strangers, in the form of Dr. Justin Brummer. Dr. Brummer, whom I know only through Twitter and email, is the founding editor of the Vietnam War Song Project. He combs record stores around the world looking for obscure and unique songs written about the war, and the collection he's continually building is some serious and important work. After connecting on Twitter, Dr. Brummer sent me a link to the 1969 song "Incoming" by Emily Strange, an American Red Cross Donut Dolly with the 9th Infantry Division and Mobile Riverine Force (1968–1969), and Barbara Hager of the U.S. Army Special Services in Dong Tam, Viet Nam.[3] The duo recorded the song on tape, and Emily, who passed away in 2016 (Barbara in 2017), had sent Dr. Brummer a copy. "Incoming" features acoustic guitar and vocals and is hauntingly pretty. While constructed simply, the chorus has the same darkly sarcastic wit as "I Feel Like I'm Fixin' to Die" by Country Joe and the Fish. The "Incoming" chorus also has a notable detail: no civilian song is going to mention standard-issue essentials like rain ponchos. The particulars in "Incoming" confirm that this is a war song created in the midst of war, where essentials and content are derived from the direct circumstances of these two Viet Nam War women.

Strange and Hager go on to further (kindly) bemoan their decision to go to Viet Nam, using wit to describe their good-hearted motivations. Their plain-spoken rendering of Viet Nam as a fantasy world is only underscored by the repeated warning of danger. The diversions that "Charlie" (shortened slang for Victor-Charlie, which was military code for "VC," meaning Viet Cong) provides are deadly, however. But you wouldn't know it from the clever lyrics or the lilting of the women's voices. They simultaneously convey lightness (via gallows humor) and weariness at the constant sirens and mortar shelling. The final verse's words are chilling: Are we trapped during a mortar shelling or trapped in this war in a general way? Both?

The YouTube version of the song that Dr. Brummer shared with me includes photos of Ms. Strange and Ms. Hager in Viet Nam. They look so young and tan, and their short, military-approved haircuts reveal full heads of shiny hair. There's one photo of the women playing guitar and singing outside among a group of GIs; the ground is sandy and there are palm trees, but the cohort is surrounded by sandbags. It's a bizarre place to have a singalong, but the women do describe Viet Nam as a Peter Pan–esque fantasy land, where the abnormal might be normal. Strange and Hager, through their song "Incoming," offer us a momentary glimpse into the life of an American woman's role in a combat zone in Viet Nam. It's buggy and hot, and there's the constant threat of death. It's a real testament to their talent—and their fortitude—that they could make such a funny song out of their situation of despair, frustration, and horror.

Oh, 1967—the Summer of Love. Lots of big albums came out that year—the Beatles made *Sgt. Pepper*, and bands like Pink Floyd, the Jimi Hendrix Experience, Big Brother and the Holding Company, the Grateful Dead, the Velvet Underground, and the Who released albums featuring what are now staple classic rock songs. Dolly Parton joined Porter Waggoner's band, a venue that would launch her into stardom. One of the first reggae songs, "54–46, That's My Number" by Toots and the Maytals, was released in 1967. In June, the Monterey Pop Festival, the first large-scale outdoor rock music festival of its kind, included performances by Booker T. and the MGs, Otis Redding, Ravi Shankar, the Who, Simon and Garfunkel, Eric Burdon and the Animals, the Byrds, Jefferson Airplane, Big Brother and the Holding Company with Janis Joplin, and Jimi Hendrix. On *The Ed Sullivan Show* in 1967, the Rolling Stones tamed their lyrics ("let's spend the night together" became "let's spend some time together"), but the Doors refused ("*higher*"). The first issue of *Rolling Stone* magazine, featuring John Lennon on the cover, rolled out, and the final episode of the popular television show *The Fugitive* aired on ABC. The first Black justice of the U.S. Supreme Court, Thurgood Marshall, was confirmed, and a former movie star, Ronald Reagan, became governor of California. In Cambodia, the Khmer Rouge took up arms against the Kingdom of Cambodia, beginning the Cambodian Civil War, which the United States would soon exploit.

The number-one song of 1967 (a year famous for the "Summer of Love") was of course a love song, though perhaps not the type of love one might immediately think of; "To Sir with Love" by Lulu is really a father-daughter wedding dance song, an ode to being faithful to the man who changed the narrator's life. Compared to the other music that came out in 1967, "To Sir with Love" sounds outdated. Many different "operations"— Cedar Falls, Deckhouse Five—were undertaken in Viet Nam at the beginning of 1967, but the "Human Be-In" in Golden Gate Park, San Francisco, on January 14, set the stage for the rest of the year. Basically, *a lot* of people gathered together to take acid and listen to groovy tunes, but the United States had never seen anything like the Human Be-In before; it signaled a sea change in U.S. youth culture. In March, a Central Park Be-In followed the example of San Francisco, and soon be-ins began popping up—sometimes as sit-ins, sometimes as bed-ins—all over the world.

In spring, "Love Is Here, and Now You're Gone" became a top hit for the Supremes, in which Diana Ross lamented the loss of love and the burn of heartache. After a week-long cameo by the Beatles' "Penny Lane," the Turtles' "So Happy Together"—the antithesis of heartsick love songs—held the top spot for three weeks in March and April. In the streets, however, being "happy together" meant demonstrating together. Large anti–Viet Nam War protests were held across the United States in 1967. Dr. Martin Luther King, Jr., joined the National Mobilization Committee to End the War in Viet Nam (the MOBE) in New York on April 15, having only spoken out against the war in his speech "Beyond Viet Nam" on April 4. At the end of April, another voice joined the anti-war fray: Muhammad Ali's draft number had been called in late 1966, and he attempted to abstain from fighting in the war on account of his religious beliefs. But because the "Louisville Lip" elaborated, "My conscience won't let me go shoot my brother … or some poor, hungry people in the mud for big powerful America. And shoot them for what? They never called me nigger,"[4] his conscientious objector status was mocked. Stripped of his boxing titles and banned from the sport for three years, Ali spent his new free time with Elijah Muhammad and the Nation of Islam. Racial issues played out in big ways in the political spheres of the world in 1967; in May, Australia passed a referendum to remove language in the country's Constitution that took rights away from Aboriginal people, and the U.S. Supreme Court ruled that laws prohibiting interracial marriages were unconstitutional.

By June, Aretha Franklin's "Respect" ruled the Billboard charts and spoke to the ethos of many movements in the United States—the civil rights movement and women's movement could appreciate the demand for a little respect. The song's message sank deeper in the "Long Hot Summer" of 1967 as Black communities in Detroit (the 12th Street Riots), Milwaukee, and all across America rose up against police brutality, unfair housing legislation, and systemic racism. The Beatles' debut of "All You Need Is Love" on the live, international show *Our World* reached 400 million viewers. The band, resplendent in colorful hippie velvet, made an anthem for those cosseted in the good vibes of the "Summer of Love," while songs like Aretha Franklin's "Respect" kept the fires for change burning.

In Viet Nam, China took a more active role in the combat zone, giving North Viet Nam aid in addition to shooting down a U.S. plane that flew into Chinese airspace; the surviving pilot would be held as a POW until 1973. In Bangkok, Thailand, the Association of Southeast Asian Nations (ASEAN) commenced work on August 8. While I was briefly in Bangkok in 2019, I noticed lots of ASEAN paraphernalia around town that I hadn't seen on my last visit in 2017. The association now includes Viet Nam, Laos, and Cambodia, and it works as a collective for economic and political power.

Political power took center stage in South Viet Nam in September 1967; the South held elections, and Nguyen Van Thieu was elected president. His vice president and running mate had led Viet Nam for the past two years—Nguyen Cao Ky—and wanted to continue doing so with Thieu as a figurehead. The U.S. military doggedly took on battles alongside ARVN troops throughout the fall, though by October, in a news conference, U.S. Secretary of State Dean Rusk pinned the lack of change in Viet Nam on the North Vietnamese, who wouldn't budge at peace talks. Autumn of 1967 marked the moment that Lulu's "To Sir with Love" topped the Billboard charts. The song was the theme to the film *To Sir, With Love*, starring Sidney Poitier as a Black man tasked with teaching unruly white children at an East End London school. The movie is fair enough for a 1960s film, but I find the song boring. Perhaps that's what was needed in 1967—a soft rock–sounding film soundtrack.

The end of 1967 revealed fits and starts at home and abroad. On the *Smothers Brothers* show in September, the Who ransacked their instruments, a move they would make their live performance hallmark. In October, while duetting with Marvin Gaye, singer Tammi Terrell fainted in her partner's arms; she would soon die of a brain tumor at the age of 24. On October 18, students at the University of Wisconsin–Madison protested the presence of Dow Chemical recruiters on campus, resulting in a riot. A few days later, on October 21, anti–Viet Nam War protestors rallied around the Lincoln Memorial and the Pentagon. Notably, Abbie Hoffman (former member of the SNCC and founder of the Youth International Party, or "Yippies") vowed to levitate the Pentagon as Allen Ginsburg intoned Tibetan chants. The building did not rise, but the Johnson administration's attention to the anti-war movement pivoted; Johnson and the "Wise Men" decided to report positive things about the Viet Nam War, which meant squashing unpopular opinions or reports. This meeting on November 2 was immediately followed by the Battle of Dak To on November 3, in which North Vietnamese and U.S. troops suffered many casualties. Tom Hayden, one of central figures of the anti-war movement (he was a Freedom Rider and a member of the MOBE, authored the Port Huron Statement for SDS, was arrested as part of the "Chicago 8" at the 1968 Democratic Convention, etc.), received three U.S. POWs in Phnom Penh, Cambodia.

In mid–November, President Johnson declared that progress—measured by the number of enemy dead versus the number of American dead—was happening in Viet Nam. General William Westmoreland echoed those statements, but Secretary of Defense Robert McNamara did not. McNamara, having held on to his post despite opposition to the administration's bombing of North Viet Nam, resigned; Johnson, tired of McNamara's dissent, had all but frozen him out of top discussions by that point anyway. And Johnson had more to worry about: Senator Eugene McCarthy, a smooth talker from Minnesota, would be challenging Johnson on the Democratic ticket. Many young Americans cut their long hippie hair in order to get "clean for Eugene" as they mobilized door-to-door campaigns; the senator had a much stronger anti-war stance than President Johnson, which would be even more appealing after Tet in March 1968. The last hits of 1967—the Monkees' "Daydream Believer" and the Beatles' "Hello, Goodbye"—let the year end on positive note, musically speaking, and Jimi Hendrix had just released his *Axis, Bold as Love* album, priming musicians all over the world to raise the bar for guitar virtuosity for decades to come.

◁▷ ◁▷ ◁▷

Whenever someone in my family is talking about one of the inevitable parts of aging—colonoscopies, pre-cancerous mole removals, blood pressure medicine—I sing the first line of the Rolling Stones' "Mother's Little Helper" (1966). It usually gets a laugh.

The Rolling Stones are one of many Viet Nam War–era bands that have always been part of my life. As with the Beatles, the Grateful Dead, Jimi Hendrix, and Led Zeppelin (and many, many more), I can't remember a world without them. My parents, freshmen in high school in 1969, bonded over music, and they owned and played records often. The record player was a sacred space; I wasn't allowed to use it until I was about 10 or 12 years old (and I still messed a needle up, to my father's dismay). As a young child, I remember marveling at the covers of the albums while sitting on the floor listening to the music. Because I heard these songs when I was little, they left an impression on me, and my feeling toward them is still pretty innocent; I thought (and still smile thinking) that Robert Plant was trying to sneeze in the bridge of "Whole Lotta Love."

Bands like the Rolling Stones also bridged my childhood into my teenage years, and they're still planning a tour as I write this in summer 2020; the Rolling Stones have been a reliable constant. I remember rolling coins with my mom as a child (that's how my parents bought their concert T-shirts back then) and thinking the Stones' "Steel Wheels" shirt was slick; I like the cheeky, somewhat subversive mouth logo the band used. Seeing Mick Jagger strutting around in the "Start Me Up" video on MTV was funny. I laughed at radio DJs making jokes about Keith Richards outliving a nuclear blast ("I saw a bright light and I thought it was time to go on"). The band's "bad boys of rock" image (usually contrasted against the Beatles) was completely lost on me. Madonna was the controversial pop star of my era.

But as I look back at the band, and particularly "Mother's Little Helper," I can see clues to what life was like for women in the 1960s. The perils of uppers and downers were clearly outlined in Jacqueline Susann's novel *Valley of the Dolls* (which, like "Mother's Little Helper," came out in 1966). I didn't really like the book, which I'd read in my teens because a celebrity mentioned reading it, and I thought that celebrity was the bee's knees. The three women protagonists' narratives start out with so much promise, and then they get all torn down—one even dies—by the end of the book. In the wake of their destruction were uppers for being perky (and staying skinny), along with downers when you needed sleep and your happy hour cocktail wouldn't cut through the residuals of the uppers. Episodes of *E! True Hollywood Stories* informed me that Judy Garland (my beloved Dorothy) was also a victim of barbiturate and stimulant abuse; it makes me so sad to know my Gram was one of the thousands of women who, in 1950s and 1960s America (and I guess the United Kingdom?), relied on pills to get her through the dull reality of being the dutiful housewife.

Maybe women enjoyed aspects of this sort of life; I wouldn't know, because that life never appealed to me. It got in my head pretty early that I could be anything and that it was perfectly reasonable to forgo being a stay-at-home mom in favor of chasing something else. "Mother's Little Helper" might've been part of planting that seed. The narrator in the song, the mother, is having trouble coping with the new reality of adulthood in a postwar Western world. The kids aren't the same as they used to be, and the mother needs help holding it together. The socially acceptable thing to do, even if she's not physically ill, is to take medicine. The subduing of the woman—just calm down; take this pill, even though you're not really sick; you just can't bear reality—feels so sad, as well as somewhat familiar. Even now, in the 21st century, you can see traces of this thinking; if women don't fall neatly into social constructs, the social judgment is fierce. In a 2019 interview with *CBS Sunday Morning*, singer-songwriter Taylor Swift noted the survival of this trend: "A man does something, it's 'strategic'; a woman does the same thing, it's 'calculated.' A man is allowed to 'react'; a woman can only 'over-react.'"[5]

The Every-mom in "Mother's Little Helper" also doesn't care much about housekeeping and takes advantage of social advancements—frozen food, instant meals—in order to get through the day, along with her pills. She further laments that men contribute to her general feelings of malaise. As the lyrics progress, so does the mother's dosage; she takes more pills. By the end of the song, life's too hard and an overdose is the finale.

What a grim way to live. If "Mother's Little Helper" is a true description of life in the early years of the Viet Nam War, then it is no wonder the women's movement reared up strong during that era. What young woman, watching her mother "up and down" her day in the name of domestic perfection, would want the same fate?

Feminism in the Viet Nam War era is now called "second-wave feminism," which purportedly lasted until the 1980s, when a "third wave" came through. In 1962, Betty Friedan's *Feminine Mystique* came out, revealing that housewives clocking 55-hour work weeks weren't happy with their lot in life, contrary to popular belief. Furthermore, women in the 1960s, if employed, were usually in nurturing-centered professions, like nursing or teaching, and were woefully underpaid in comparison to their male counterparts. And finally—and most important—the birth-control pill came out in 1960. Suddenly a woman could be in charge of when and if she had children, rather than having her sex life dictated entirely by a man's ability to use a prophylactic or ye olde "pull out" method.

The women's rights movement had an active presence and agenda in the 1960s. Groups like the Women Strike for Peace and the National Organization for Women (NOW), formed in the 1960s, simultaneously protested the war and pushed for an Equal Rights Amendment (which still hasn't passed). It's always been a bit difficult for me to teach students about the varying "movements" and groups that mingled together in the 1960s. It's important to note that the "counter-culture" movement began with the Beat poets—Jack Kerouac, Allen Ginsburg, William S. Burroughs—in the 1950s. That eventually split into a continued "counter-culture" movement, which included demonstrating for civil rights and women's rights, though it did not always mean "hippies"; the flower children were banging a totally different drum than the more organized anti-war movement. But, like in a Venn diagram, the different "movements" sometimes overlapped.

Folk singer Pete Seeger, for example, was long an activist for equal rights and marched in civil rights demonstrations. His performance of the song "Waist Deep in the Big Muddy" in 1967 on *The Smothers Brothers Comedy Hour* was initially censored by the Johnson administration for its perceived anti–Johnson and anti-war stance. Never mind that the song is set in 1942; President Johnson knew who the song's "fool"[6] was. Seeger wasn't a hippie—he certainly didn't look like one on the *Smothers Brothers* broadcast, with his librarian sweater—but he was part of the larger counter-culture movement that protested oppression and injustice. Seeger, along with trailblazers like Joan Baez and Arlo Guthrie, honed folk music into a tool for several movements in the 1960s, perhaps the most notably in the adaptation of "We Shall Overcome," a Black slave song that filtered through workers' rights unions in the 1940s and was reshaped for those marching for equality and/or against the Viet Nam War.

The civil rights movement also dovetailed with the women's rights movement; many leadership roles in the Black Panthers were held by women, and some members went on to scholarly careers, like Angela Davis, who wrote books like *Women, Race, and Class* (1980) and *Blues Legacies and Black Feminism* (1999). The trailblazing these women did, under the auspices of "second-wave feminism" (for those who keep track of such things), still reverberates with women's issues today. If not for Betty Friedan or Gloria Steinem (or, for that matter, Janis Joplin or Aretha Franklin), feminism in the 21st century wouldn't have the force it holds. The parallels can be crazy at times; the Moratorium to End the War in Viet Nam in 1969 was the largest U.S. protest until it was surpassed by the 2017 Women's March, which was then surpassed by the Black Lives Matter/George Floyd marches in 2020.

Thanks to the work of the women in the 1960s, the voices of women today are amplified. Without them, I would not have had the option to pursue a career instead of my "MRS degree." Because of them, I can choose to not have a child, whether by birth control or termination of a pregnancy. Due to their work, women today have *choices* that women of the 1960s never dreamed of; it wasn't until 1974 that a woman could have her own line of credit! Women start at a disadvantage, historically. I like to think of women of the 1960s as a variation of Viet Nam's "Sad Woman" and the heroic medics in the U.S. Vietnam Women's Memorial—determined, strong, and working within the existing limitations to make a difference that would eventually break through those barriers.

9

1968

I don't have any photos of my trip to the My Lai massacre site. Or, rather, I *believe* my photos from five years ago might still exist on a dead, shattered phone that I have in a bag somewhere.

The My Lai massacre occurred on March 16, 1968. Between 350 and 500 innocent, unarmed civilians were brutally murdered by U.S. troops, most of them under the command of Captain Ernest Medina, in Charlie Company. Charlie Company had suffered some difficult losses prior to the incident, and many of the men were tired, hungry, angry, and ready to kill in the name of avenging their fallen brothers. The soldiers had been told to expect some action, but instead they created their own form of it. There weren't many men around the village, and the women and children were moving around because it was a market day. The image most associated with the event is a photo of a Vietnamese woman being held from behind, her face a combination of sorrow and disgust and anger, clutching a dark cloth to her abdomen. My guide to the My Lai site, Thanh, was the first person to explain to me that she'd been raped, and she was trying to hold her skirt together.

The energy of the My Lai massacre site, I firmly believe, channeled tragic juju into my Motorola. It is a grim place to "visit" when you have alternatives like a beach where people bring you food and beverages and offer to massage you (Hoi An), but I wanted to see the controversial "Pinkville" (the name the U.S. military had given the area) and observe how such an atrocity could even be rendered into a tourist "attraction." To get to My Lai, I needed a guide, and I picked one who would take me around in an "authentic army jeep" because, well, why not get the real experience? (Pro tip: Army jeeps are not very fun long-term vehicles to ride in. If you need more luxury—like shocks or air conditioning—pick a bus tour.) My guide and I were born about three years apart, but his childhood memories are a lot different from mine. I grew up collecting glass bottles for change at gas stations; he grew up fishing spent metal shell casings from the war out of swollen creeks for change.

Thanh proved an excellent host, and he explained everything to me that I could possibly ask him about, which was nearly everything we passed. He taught me about "model villages" (villages that get awards—which might be signage or money—from the government for being "good" in some vague way) and explained the nuances of the area's geography and history. He took far more joy in showing me sugarcane juice (perfection on a hot day) on the side of the road than the My Lai site.

At My Lai, Thanh was visibly bored. So was the jeep driver, who noodled around on his phone and smoked a cigarette outside of the vehicle. The outside of the site has

109

concrete molds of footprints, which I don't need a photo to remember, as well as a diorama of structures that would've been in the village and photos (with far more context) taken of dead or raped villagers. Thanh wandered around, talking to the minder on site—they obviously knew each other, and we were the only guests at the site for the entirety of my visit—while I watched a video in which an American veteran who'd been on the scene in 1968 reconciled with a Vietnamese man who'd been a child living in the village during the massacre. It is *hard* to watch. You feel absolutely terrible, because the Vietnamese man is still angry and the American veteran is so sad, and there's all this brutality and loss of life, and there's no way to reconcile it. Sniffling and quiet, I followed Thanh outside to the main area, and, seeing a frail tree as a symbol of hope, I stopped to take a photo. Barely four feet from the ground, my phone slipped out of my sweating hands and shattered on the paving stones, buzzing like a cicada. Furthermore, until we were able to find a hardware guy in a nearby town to disconnect the internal wires, the phone's temperature began to climb (in the 98-degree heat), and I was afraid it might melt into the seat of the "real American jeep" I was touring in.

The My Lai massacre wasn't the only one of its kind in the Viet Nam War or many other wars. Helicopter pilot Hugh Thompson is credited as a hero of the massacre, stopping soldiers from killing more civilians and also ferrying victims away from the site. Lieutenant William Calley became the scapegoat for the crimes perpetrated at My Lai, as many of his fellow soldiers were out of the military by the time the trial began in 1970. This brief episode of brutality launched many songs, a film, and even a play in the United States; Calley is alternately seen as a victim or a beast, but he's most often portrayed as a man who simply followed bad orders. I don't understand where people's consciousness goes when they're faced with these moral dilemmas. Surely, even in your early 20s, you're wise enough to know that war won't be won by destroying a village and killing innocent people? Certainly, even though you'd face some sort of punishment for disobeying orders, your higher moral compass would kick in and tell you you're doing the wrong thing, right? I still cannot empathize with some of the first-person U.S. troop accounts I've read about My Lai, but I do retain some level of compassion for the soldiers. I also hold space for the victims, because the My Lai massacre was beyond a war crime—it was a crime against humanity.

◁▷ ◁▷ ◁▷

Instead of staying in the larger city of Da Nang to get to My Lai, I chose to go to Hoi An (a UNESCO World Heritage Site). Family friends had been to that part of Viet Nam before for vacation, and the photos were gorgeous—plus, I hadn't seen that part of Viet Nam yet. It's a great location for getting to some good war-based sites, *and* there's a beach. And lots to eat and do! Let's go!

Hoi An has become one of my favorite places in Viet Nam. I spent a week there, using it as a base to go to places like the My Lai massacre site and My Son. My first (and only) blind massage experience happened in Hoi An; my masseuse had lost his sight due to Agent Orange in the Viet Nam War—he giggled a lot, and it wasn't very good. There are lots of nongovernmental organization (NGO) shops and businesses to check out, many privately funded by other countries. Because Hoi An was close to a lot of bombing, many people working with the NGOs have physical or mental disabilities from direct damage or UXO damage or were disabled by the poison of Agent Orange. The chemical defoliant (named after its orange barrels) was really good at getting leaves and debris out of the way so that the United States could better bomb the hidden trails of the North Vietnamese troops. It was also really good at getting into the soil and water systems of the area, as well as traveling through the air; these latter traits account for its reputation for making anyone—both soldiers and civilians, as well as their children and grandchildren—sick, disabled, or dead. Aside from birth deformities, like two-headed fetuses displayed at the War Remnants Museum in Sai Gon, Agent Orange can cause a host of problems in humans, ranging from Down syndrome to diabetes. Physical deformities, like blindness or uneven limbs, are some of the lesser side effects of Agent Orange. This is why Hoi An—and many other places in Viet Nam that were heavily bombed—counts many disabled people as citizens and hosts scores of NGOs aimed at helping those hurt by the toxin cope with its aftermath.

Hoi An is one of my favorite spots because it is a beautiful place, with rivers and beaches surrounding lush farms. My itinerary included a lounge on a beach (where people seem to emerge out of nowhere to bring you food, drink, trinkets, and massages) where I (unknowingly) swam among giant jellyfish. The people bringing you menus on the beach are often women, and despite the heat, they're usually in long sleeves and pants in an attempt to preserve their skin from the sun. I biked a good bit in Hoi An; though the hotel bikes were on the shabby side, they worked, and if you aren't in a hurry (which Hoi An requires you not to be, by tropical climate alone), then a gimpy bike won't get in your way. My favorite memory of Hoi An is from a research venture gone wrong: biking among the rice paddies, findings ducks and pigs at intervals, enjoying the quiet scenery. Feeling free and warm and—at that point—even (gastrointestinal-wise) good, it was a moment of unfettered enjoyment, not "part of my research agenda" but an experience of the country that was pure and pleasurable, in the simplest of ways.

I wouldn't have had that experience had something not gone wrong: I was supposed to visit an organic farm that was trying to be sustainable and unique in ways that lots of businesses in Hoi An aspire to be. I went to the service entrance, to shorten the story, and held court for about an hour with two Vietnamese teenagers who, once they'd practiced their English with me and introduced me to some recently hatched baby geese, loped off to find something more fun to do. I ended up biking around the perimeter of the farm.

The first night I was in Hoi An, I walked the opposite direction of the town, down a dimly lit street, and happened upon a restaurant. Hungry, I decided not to be picky. I was the only non–Vietnamese person there, and the owner, seeing me take a photo of my food (chicken and rice), insisted on making "something special" in front of me (and my camera) on his small charcoal grill. At this point in the story, people usually jump in, expecting me to say my grill-master friend cooked something exotic and strange, like a cockroach. Some people get icky and racist, suggesting dog or cat (for the record, I've never seen dog on any Asian menu). I can reliably say the meat was poultry and delicious, and it ruined my (admittedly extremely sensitive) stomach. The next day, after a night fraught with terrors of the bowels, I woke up at 5:00 a.m. to take a tour of My Son, an ancient Cham ruins site that was bombed by the United States during the war.

After I scared the hotel owner awake from his cot by the check-in desk, he opened the door for me so I could get in a van with other sleepy tourists. Our guide was relatively quiet until about 7:00 a.m., when we were closer to the ruins and more awake. The Cham people (the same folks who made Angkor Wat in Cambodia) were central to Hinduism, and Cham ruins dating back to 4 AD can be found all over Viet Nam. The ruins themselves—and the giant B-52 crater and pock marks all over the site from U.S. bombing and bullets—were interesting, but the bugs ignoring my DEET-covered self were harder to ignore. Furthermore, my guide was young, maybe 21. He was nice but much less interested in answering my war and culture questions and more into discussing his plans to study abroad with some of the other group members, who were Australian and American college-age kids. As a college professor, I could've chimed in, but I instead kept quiet. My stomach was still suffering from the night before, and the toilets we'd been offered were squat and fetid. Also, the guide's obvious favoritism regarding "Western" education was hard to understand. What was so bad about where he was? Why was the West so appealing to him when he had just given us a tour of its past bombing the mess out of his country's history? I gazed out at a little hamlet with a water buffalo meandering in a field, the sunlight catching in his coat and making him seem shiny. The minibus hit a bump as it moved onto a slicker, newly paved road, and I clutched my midsection. I didn't care about much now except for getting off the bus.

As soon as I was dropped off, in the blistering 95-degree heat at the edge of the old town, I booked it to a lovely looking restaurant that had just opened for the morning, replete with canvas umbrellas and cushioned rattan chairs. I ordered two banana lassies (yogurt and banana smoothies—excellent for the gut), a large water, and a toasted baguette with butter and jam. I then informed my waitress that I was leaving my hat and book at the table while I darted toward the bathroom. She looked at me as if I'd lost my mind and didn't trust me. I didn't fret none; a blessed "Western" toilet greeted me, and when I returned to my seat, I pounded the lassies and asked for one more. The waitress still looked at me curiously. You don't have to tip in Viet Nam, but it seems appreciated. I try to follow local rules when I travel, but I tend to tip (or at least round up the bill) wherever I am. On this occasion I doubled the bill out of gratitude. My stomach was safe now, thanks to the endless banana lassie supply. And the bread—good ol' plain bread. The saving grace breakfast lassies, baguette, and large tip cost me $15 and were worth every penny.

After my belated breakfast, the sun rose high and hot. I decided it was a good time for a nap. Not trusting my stomach—and back in the days of picking up a ride off the corner—I paid a guy the equivalent of $10 to take me back to my hotel (a ten-minute walk from the restaurant). I lay directly under the fan in my room, thinking of the bombed-out Citadel I'd seen a few years prior in Hue, wondering how much damage the United States had really done, overall, to the country—so much physically, but also mentally.

I went to Belgrade, Serbia, in 2010 for a conference, where damaged buildings from UN bombs still stood, mostly in ruins and home to feral dogs. The young people I'd spoken to in Belgrade dismissed the relics of the Yugoslavian Civil War (for which the Serbs were largely blamed) as things the government couldn't afford to fix; the older people I spoke to saw the rubble as monuments to the war. Perhaps that's why the young My Son tour guide wanted to leave; he may not have wanted to be among the ruins of the past, perhaps preferring to go somewhere that had long put its wartime past behind it.

The old quarter of Hoi An is nice, but it was too packed with tourists for me to fully enjoy it. The town's ancient wooden Japanese covered bridge quaked under the weight of foreign visitors; I am glad I went to Hoi An before the advent of the selfie stick, or it would've been unbearable (and less economical for Hoi An, where locals charged $1 to take your picture back in 2015 by hanging around strategic photo op areas; they do that in Rio as well). The same stuff that was on sale all over Viet Nam was there, but some extra things were available, such as the opportunity to put a votive candle in a paper lantern, which you then let go in the river with your "special wish" (mine got stuck on a stick in the river), or just buying a colorful lantern (remember that you might need an adapter to turn this product on at home, and you also have to pack this fragile purchase). I drifted into the open market, where all sorts of chintz were available—I got a $2 elephant-themed anklet that broke in a week from a very pushy saleslady.

While enjoying arguably one of the best meals I've ever had in my life (I can't remember the name, but there was pork involved, in a bowl, with rice—really narrows it down, doesn't it?), I watched a rat run across the deck where I was having my meal. Another white woman, very blonde and tan and also eating alone, wiggled her eyebrows at me as the rat skittered past us before going back to work on her laptop. I looked over the riverside scene, where a children's show was taking place among the various markets, restaurant portico seating, and folks mingling around. It was tranquil, beautiful, and softly lit by lanterns—a far cry from the events that had happened in this town only three decades before I sat and ate my pork-rice delight.

◁▷ ◁▷ ◁▷

January 1968 was a hellish month in Viet Nam. On January 21, the Battle of Khe Sanh began; President Johnson, determined not to let the site fall, ordered more troops to be pumped into the location. The Marines trapped on the base fought under fire from the North Vietnamese People's Army of Viet Nam (PAVN) as well as the U.S. Air Force, which rained down tons of bombs to defend Khe Sanh from above in Operation Niagara. Finally, in March, U.S. troops broke through the defensive wall the PAVN troops held around the perimeter of the base; afterward, the Americans, deeming the location ultimately unimportant, dismantled the base they'd fought so hard to keep. I've been to Khe Sanh—it's hard to get to and out in the middle of nowhere. The kerfuffle over Khe Sanh is often depicted as a distraction; North Vietnamese and Viet Cong forces were moving all around Viet Nam in early 1968 in preparation for January's Tet Offensive, which took the United States by surprise.

In the Billboard charts, the Beatles' "Hello, Goodbye" was knocked out of the top spot by "Judy in the Sky (with Glasses)" by John Fred and the Playboys. The Beatles' "Hey Jude" would be the number-one song of 1968, a leap year. In mid–January, Johnny Cash played his legendary Folsom Prison show, instigating a trend of "outlaw country" that continues (in a less authentic fashion) to this day. Something else from 1968 that's still going is America's fraught relationship with North Korea, which seized the "spying" USS *Pueblo* and built an entire anti–U.S. propaganda campaign from the ship's capture.

On January 30, the Tet Offensive began, splintering off into skirmishes across South Viet Nam, with some of the most notorious fighting in Hue, where shootouts occurred door-to-door. America's taste for blood spilled onto the television screen on February 1, when Viet Cong soldier Nguyen Van Lem was shot, point blank in the head, by Police Chief Nguyen Ngoc Loan. In the footage, Lem falls into the street, blood spurting out of his temple, as the police chief goes back to the cigarette he was smoking. A photograph of the cold-blooded kill won photographer Eddie Adams a Pulitzer Prize, but the video turned a lot of Americans off the Viet Nam War.

Perhaps the violence at home and abroad carried Paul Mauriat's instrumental "Love Is Blue" to the top of the Billboard charts for five weeks in February and early March. Orchestral and lush, the song's serene sounds stand in sharp contrast to the events of February, including civil rights protests in Orangeburg, South Carolina, the University of Madison–Wisconsin, and the University of North Carolina at Chapel Hill (or sim-ply "Chapel Hill," as my native North Carolinian/ACC-raised self wants to write). Three massacres—the Phong Nhi, Phong Nhat, and Ha My—also occurred in February, each involving soldiers from the Republic of Korea Marine Corps and the murder of innocent civilians. On February 24, the Tet Offensive halted, and a battered ARVN retook the stra-tegic city of Hue.

Early on in my research career, a very naïve me contacted Dr. Christina Schwen-kel, professor of anthropology at the University of California, Riverside, asking for advice on "talking to people near Hue" about the Viet Nam War. Dr. Schwenkel kindly guided me to read more; a few months after the Battle of Hue, which left 40 percent of the city destroyed and over 5,000 missing or killed, mass graves began to be found on the out-skirts of the city.[1] PAVN and VC forces had infiltrated the city ahead of the battle, dis-tributing literature encouraging the citizens of the imperial city to rise up and join their North Vietnamese brethren in the fight. The people did not rise up, and many of those found in the mass graves—often with hands restrained by wire or similarly cruel addi-tions to the gunshot wounds that killed them—are suspected to be people identified as enemies to the Communist Party. People around Hue thus were left particularly trau-matized by the war and likely unwilling to talk about anything that might be construed as negative to the party. Even the Vietnamese subjects in Ken Burns and Lynn Novick's 2017 documentary *The Vietnam War* express trepidation in speaking about what is now known as the "Massacre of Hue," one of the more brutal instances of Vietnamese fighting their fellow Vietnamese.

In March 1968, President Johnson announced a partial halt to the bombing of North Viet Nam in an attempt to begin peace negotiations; while the United States counted the Tet Offensive as a victory, the way the Vietnamese took the Americans off guard dimin-ished American confidence in the war. North Viet Nam insisted that bombing in the North cease before any peace talks could occur, and Johnson finally capitulated. In the political sphere, the president was struggling. He barely won against Senator McCarthy in the New Hampshire Democratic primary, and then Bobby Kennedy, younger brother of the still-golden JFK, announced his bid for president, seeking the Democratic nomi-nation. By the end of the month, Johnson would announce that he was no longer seeking reelection. A Laotian civil war had broken out (containing some proxy warfare from Viet Nam), and Howard University held a historic sit-in that protested the Reserve Officer Training Corps program and the Viet Nam War, as well as the lack of Afro-centric curric-ulum material. Protests against the war in France and England were also held in March, just as Otis Redding's "Sittin' on the Dock of the Bay" hit number one in the pop charts. Otis Redding is my favorite male vocalist of all time, and he recorded this timeless, beau-tiful song only days before he died in a plane crash. The song laments feelings of power-lessness and homelessness, which spoke to the American public's general unmooring by the Tet Offensive and civil unrest.

While "Sittin' on the Dock of the Bay" has a wistful quality to it, it is also a blues song (save for the whistling at the end, maybe). And America got the blues in April. On April 3, in Memphis, Tennessee, Dr. Martin Luther King, Jr., gave his last speech at the Mem-phis Mason Temple. If you look it up on YouTube, you can hear the rainstorm that thun-ders in the background, in addition to seeing the sweat on King's face amid the packed crowd. Often referred to as "The Mountaintop Speech," King ended his oration with these now-famous lines:

We've got some difficult days ahead. But it really doesn't matter with me now. Because I've been to the mountaintop.... I've seen the promised land. I may not get there with you. But I want you to know tonight, that we, as a people, will get to the promised land. And I'm happy tonight. I'm not worried about anything. I'm not fearing any man. Mine eyes have seen the glory of the coming of the Lord.[2]

The next day, April 4, 1968, Dr. King was shot on the balcony of the Lorraine Motel in Memphis. The nation went into a state of disarray. President Johnson called for a national day of mourning, but the shock waves of the event continued to ripple through the country. At a televised concert the next day at the Boston Garden, James Brown held police off the stage as kids rushed it; he understood the kids were not all right and needed some space to vent their complicated feelings in the wake of King's assassination. The following day, April 6, a shootout between the Black Panthers and the Oakland, California, police erupted.

One of music's most talented singer-songwriters, Nina Simone, dedicated her first-ever performance of the song "Why? (The King of Love Is Dead)," written by Gene Taylor, to Dr. King at the Westbury Music Fair on April 7. The song was partially released on the album *Nuff Said* (1968), and it is extremely moving; again, you can find it on YouTube. Perplexingly, as the nation mourned Dr. King, Bobby Goldsboro's "Honey" took the top spot in the charts. The song, a simpering ode to a missing sweetheart known only as "honey," is infuriatingly bad. I can't figure out whether the song is about a lover or a daughter, to be frank, but its outright infantilization of the woman as the subject of the song is annoying, especially considering its timing; couldn't the American public have picked a more suitable song for this mourning period? By the end of the month, the Civil Rights Act of 1968 was signed into law, and students at Columbia University took over a building in protest of the Viet Nam War.

In May 1968, while the country still reeled from the death of Dr. King, communist forces in Viet Nam launched Soviet rockets at 119 cities, and peace talks began in Paris. On May 17, the Catonsville Nine burned draft cards with napalm at the Selective Service Office in Catonsville, Maryland; two members of the group were Catholic clergy, and photos of them, in clerics' clothing while watching the cards burn outside in a small pyre, sparked more conversations regarding the ethics of the war among Christian leaders. On June 5, at the Ambassador Hotel in Los Angeles, Bobby Kennedy was shot during a campaign event, and the murder was captured on live television. The deaths of two Kennedys in the space of five years rattled the American public, and when added to the assassination of Dr. King, Americans had to ask themselves how they had become a country where leaders were shot in broad daylight, in cold blood. Even if people didn't agree with their politics, the brutal nature of these deaths only served to amplify the violence broadcast into American homes from Southeast Asia.

By June, after Herb Alpert made a brief appearance at the top of the pop music charts, Simon and Garfunkel took the top spot again with "Mrs. Robinson," a song that would later in the year gain more popularity due to its featured presence in the film *The Graduate*. "Mrs. Robinson," a catchy, folksy song, also contained lyrics that lamented perhaps simpler times gone by and Americana heroes like baseball legend Joe DiMaggio. Mrs. Robinson, the song's subject, is at a sanitarium—a fitting place for someone who was fine looking back but had trouble looking forward. (If the song is entirely about the Mrs. Robinson character in *The Graduate*, then it's an even darker tune about a troubled woman, miscast and outcast in suburbia.) Finally, a great irony of 1968 is that in July, a young man named Saddam Hussein took up a position in the Iraq Revolutionary Council; he would appear as a major global player—and American target—in about 30 years.

The summer of 1968 was quite different from the Summer of Love in 1967; in place of be-ins, police and protesters came to blows in Chicago outside the 1968 Democratic National Convention, which settled on Vice President Hubert Humphrey as its nominee. Abbie Hoffman and the Yippies were involved in the Chicago protests that August, which were denounced as disruptive and un–American by the mainstream media. In July, James Anderson, Jr., became the first Black U.S. Marine to receive the Medal of Honor (MOH, posthumously) for heroism in Viet Nam. Later in the year, U.S. Army Major General Keith Ware, a World War II MOH recipient, was killed in a helicopter crash in Viet Nam; he posthumously received the Distinguished Service Cross. In Viet Nam that July, South Viet Nam's Truong Dinh Dzu's call for a coalition government earned him five years of hard labor, proving the South Vietnamese government was just as intolerant of alternatives to war as the North. The Doors' slinky seduction "Hello, I Love You" and the Rascals' brass-filled ode to unity, "People Got to Be Free," dominated the summer charts, the latter urging folks across the world to get on a freedom train and learn to love one another. The song's lyrics provided a soothing balm to the uproar of the summer, but the calls for unity would ultimately remain unheeded in 1968; there was more work to do.

In September, members of New York Radical Women crashed the Miss America Pageant in Atlantic City, New Jersey, protesting the pageant's exploitation of women. It was one of the biggest feminist demonstrations to date, and it highlighted the sexism in American culture. Fighting against accepted norms, Arthur Ashe won the first U.S. Open of the "Open Era" (meaning that Grand Slam pros could now play amateurs), earning the distinction of being the first Black male to win the title. In Mexico, as the country geared up for the Summer Olympics, the Tlatelolco massacre occurred, where a student demonstration at La Plaza de las Tres Culturas ended in over 300 dead. The Mexican government hastened to cover up the event, presenting a united front as the Games officially opened 10 days later. On October 16, on the winners' podium for the Olympic men's 200-meter event, Black athletes Tommie Smith and John Carlos raised their fists in Black Power salutes. Australian Peter Norman, in second place, wore (like Carlos and Smith) a silver Olympic Project for Human Rights badge and stood quietly supportive on the world stage. The United States was furious; in the 2008 film *Salute*, Carlos and Smith detailed the blacklisting and backlash they faced back home. Their gold and bronze medals and Olympic accomplishments were deemed worthless in light of their subversive and anti-patriotic behavior at the games. Echoes of this "shut up and play" mentality still reverberate today for professional athletes, especially in the wake of the Black Lives Matter movement; it can be disturbing to see how little changes in American history despite the brave acts of athletes like Carlos and Smith.

What was and wasn't acceptable patriotism remained a hot topic in American popular culture as 1968 moved into the fall season. On October 7, during Game 5 of the 1968 World Series, blind folk singer José Feliciano sang a slowed-down, Latin-tinged rendition of "The Star-Spangled Banner." If you look up a recording of the performance, you can hear the "boos" of the crowd, even though Feliciano's version of the song is quite beautiful, sincere, and easier to sing than the traditional version. Feliciano (later known as the genius behind the American Christmas staple "Feliz Navidad") would be plagued by death threats after his performance, as well as calls to check his citizenship (American citizen via Puerto Rico) and his blindness—some Americans were convinced the artist wore sunglasses out of disrespect. In Puerto Rico that year, Luis A. Ferré became the first governor of Puerto Rico. The island had several men vying for the position, which could wield some power against the mainland; the issue of the U.S. Navy having used Puerto Rico's island of Vieques for bombing practice (since the 1940s) did little to gain favor from Puerto Ricans regarding the Viet Nam War.

From the end of September through the end of November, the Beatles' "Hey Jude" reigned supreme on the pop charts; its call, essentially, to make lemonade from lemons was a lyrical bandage on a bleeding nation. That October, troop numbers in Viet Nam reached 540,000. Paradoxically, the U.S. Department of Defense sent 24,000 troops back to Viet Nam for involuntary, additional tours. In November, Richard Nixon, who had pledged to leave American politics so that he wouldn't be "kicked around" only four years prior, became the president-elect of the United States. Also, in November, Yale University decided that women were allowed to study in its hallowed halls (tardy, but I'll take it). In that same week, the United States began quietly bombing Laos, which hosted parts of the strategic Ho Chi Minh trail.

In one of 1968's most notable music upsets, on November 17, Diana Ross and the Supremes replaced the Beatles' "Hey Jude" in the top Billboard spot with "Love Child"; this would be the last of five turnovers at number one between the Supremes and the Beatles during the 1960s. The Beatles, who released their famous "White Album" at the end of November, were on their way toward breaking up. "Hey Jude," a song Paul McCartney wrote for Julian Lennon, John Lennon's oldest (and largely neglected) son, is made more touching in its message of seeking to comfort a child. The world—especially the United States—could have used some comforting in late 1968. By the end of the year, rock juggernauts Led Zeppelin made their U.S. debut in Denver, and Marvin Gaye's super-pop-mega-hit (I really like the song) "I Heard It Through the Grapevine" was climbing the charts. While Gaye's song details rumors of a love about to end, it also symbolically alluded to the national identity that the United States was trying to hold on to.

◁▷ ◁▷ ◁▷

In U.S. Viet Nam War history, the Tet Offensive in January 1968 is usually referred to as "the turning point of the war," though there are several compelling arguments to the contrary. Nevertheless, 1968 was one of the most terrifying years of the war, as well as a terrible year in U.S. history. The My Lai massacre happened in March 1968. Ho Chi Minh died on September 2, forever martyred in Viet Nam. President Johnson announced he would not seek reelection, instead focusing on the problems at home and abroad, leading to Richard Nixon winning the presidential election in November. The battles of Khe Sanh (January) and Hamburger Hill (May) and the end of Operation Rolling Thunder (November) marked purposeful shifts in U.S. military involvement in Viet Nam. Dr. Martin Luther King, Jr., and Robert Kennedy were assassinated in April and June, respectively. There were a host of events that kept Americans trapped in a perpetual place of tragedy; even the Democratic convention, a normally staid affair, was the site of rioting and police clashes in August.

Historian Michael Beschloss, in the 2004 documentary *Decisions That Shook the World*, tells a story about Lyndon Baines Johnson, fresh off Nixon's inauguration on January 20, 1969: After Nixon was sworn in and Johnson hopped on the plane to take him back to Texas, he whipped out a pack of cigarettes. He lit up, to the surprise of his daughter. Four years later—January 22, 1973—Johnson died of a massive heart attack. An interview 10 days prior to his death quoted him telling Walter Cronkite that he felt it did his heart good to smoke; better for the heart "to smoke than to be nervous."[3] Moral of the story—stay quit, my fellow former smokers!

But I identify with that story: Johnson had been through a hellish couple of years, so what better time to restart smoking? In times of great crisis, the Marlboro Man seems like the only thing that understands you. Johnson couldn't fight the smokes anymore. He took his habit back up with gusto, along with eating, gaining over 20 pounds in a year. If we have empathy, we see these breakdowns of willpower as hallmarks of an unhappy man. I mean, I've always seen Johnson as a kind of bully—what my granddaddy might call a sonofabitch—but I also feel sorry for him. Not having lived through his governance, I can only proclaim this judgment from the jaded eyes of a historian, looking over facts and transcripts; listening to interviews, speeches, and tapes; and cobbling together a man who was, at his most basic level, a Texas do-gooder.

Johnson's presidential career suffered because of the anti-war movement; the constant presence of protesters at the White House made him worry for his family's safety, and the pressure of the anti-war movement pushed him to make weak decisions regarding Viet Nam. Indeed, historian Melvin Small believes that "As Johnson came to make his decision to deescalate and quit the presidency in late March of 1968, he probably did so in anticipation of a respite from incessant criticism and recurrent harassment" from the anti-war movement.[4] While the taunts that Johnson endured during his presidency were at times unnecessary and cruel, these taunts came from a patriotism not unlike that which Johnson advocated. The anti-war protest movement represented the emerging voice of a different sort of patriotism, one that was not greater or lesser than the one which blossomed under the Cold War, but one that was new and curious, dissatisfied, angry, and impassioned all at once.

President Lyndon Johnson, rarely regarded as a sympathetic character with respect to his role as an architect of the Viet Nam War, agreed with the pro-war songwriters in that he believed in a form of patriotism that placed America on a pedestal. Johnson bought into the myth that viewed America as a beacon of light and hope for the rest of the world. He was not significantly more hawkish or dovish than his advisors, and, during the war, "the President was increasingly concerned about the situation in Vietnam. [He] was more confident of what *Americans* could do."[5] What Americans could do, however, was blame the war on Johnson, who inherited the problem and made it worse, in the eyes of many citizens. Domestic policies aside—the Voting Rights and Civil Rights Acts, for example—Johnson's foreign policy didn't hold up to the test of the American public.

Ultimately, President Johnson could not escape the brutality of war, even from his cushioned and protected view at 1600 Pennsylvania Avenue. The bombs dropped on Viet Nam, Laos, and Cambodia in 1968 left unexploded ordnance that is still a public danger in those countries over 50 years after the fact. Chemical weapons, like Agent Orange, likewise took a multigenerational toll on all those involved in the war in Southeast Asia. Johnson also did not anticipate a violent, persistent war at home that encompassed demonstrations not only against the president's leadership but also opposing any person who spoke out too loudly for the civil rights movement, the Black Power movement, and the women's movement. The assassinations of Dr. King and Bobby Kennedy hammered home the fact that Americans weren't safe from each other, a chilling side effect of a country living through the legacy of an increasingly unpopular and complicated war.

While modern-day Viet Nam has done some innovative things with relics of war—making memorials and museums or reworking American bases and airports into Vietnamese domestic and military outposts—the violence of 1968 is still something that both Americans and Vietnamese people have difficulty talking about. Furthermore, global anti-war and anti-establishment protests dotted the landscape of 1968—at times, it seemed like 1968 was a raging fire that could not, despite the best efforts of those in power and protest, be put out.

10

1969

My friend Ted was telling me a story about a man named Danny Dietz, who died in a Special Operations mission in Iraq. The story involved Danny being memorialized by a bit of freeway and a statue. Ted was taking a photo of a friend with the statue when an angry man emerged, asking them what they were doing. Turned out it was Danny's dad, and he warmed to Ted and his friend; Danny's dad was a medic in Viet Nam.

But the story brought up some other things; if the American government came up to you and said, "Tell you what: you graduate high school and join the military, get trained to be the best of the best of our personnel weaponry specialists, and go get killed—then we'll name a bit of freeway in Denver after you," would you go? Danny got a posthumous medal, as did the rest of his dead friends. The tragic mistake in Danny's story was that his group passed a shepherd on the way to their mission and didn't kill him.

Like many civilians, I am woefully naïve about the rules of war and untrained in the art of fearing or suspecting danger from everyone you might encounter. My conversation with Ted edged around the outcome for Danny and his company had they shot the shepherd/messenger/scout. Would Danny still be alive?

I don't make those conjectures; they get on my nerves. A lot of Viet Nam scholarship involves (mostly men) going on about topics like "What if McGovern had won the election?" or "What if JFK hadn't been shot?" To me, questions like these are a waste of time, because JFK *was* shot, and McGovern *was not* elected president. Also, Danny and company *did not* shoot the shepherd.

To be conversational, I asked, "Couldn't they have just taken the shepherd hostage?"

Ted: "No! You don't want him and his sheep dragging behind you! You're on a mission."

I made a joke about not accounting for the sheep, but it was interesting to see the embedded processes of mission, danger, compromised position, and so on come instantly as good sense into Ted's (USAF Viet Nam veteran) head. For my part, I'm sad about the shepherd. He was probably just trying to get by when the Taliban came along and said, "Be a lookout or we'll kill your family." Or maybe he hated Americans for no reason (we could invent one, like the United States bombed his uncle's house or something— it wouldn't be too implausible) and ratted them out because he liked murder or money. Who knows? It's the point of view, though, that needs considering.

Do we ever feel sorry for the Vietnamese? When we watch footage of Sai Gon in the 1960s, we see pale, tall Euro-looking dudes perusing shops alongside 1960s chic Vietnamese women; do we ever wonder what that woman's life was like, living in a place where the pale people could bust into her house whenever and do whatever they wanted, really? Ted was telling me about a search that included a pointless dig in Baghdad due to a misread metal detector, and I was left thinking about the poor Iraqi guy who got a hole dug in his yard for no reason. I realize empathy like that can be dangerous—I might lose you as a reader, in some cases—but if I'm going to wonder about something, it seems more productive to wonder what it's like to live in a world occupied by people who don't look like you, talk like you, eat like you, or even like you that much.

◁▷ ◁▷ ◁▷

Looking back at 1969's popular music charts, the Viet Nam War can be found—referenced indirectly or directly—in most of the top 100 songs of the year. Kenny Rogers and the First Edition's "Ruby, Don't Take Your Love to Town" is told from the point of view of a disabled Viet Nam War veteran, and the Youngbloods' "Get Together" implored listeners to get together and love each other despite—or maybe *in* spite of—our differences.

First, an acknowledgment: the saccharine "Sugar Sugar" by the Archies (a fake cartoon band) was the number-one song of 1969. This fact reminds us that adolescent girls are often what drives pop album charts and that happy songs trend upward in times of national difficulty, which is why this book's methodology includes songs that did not reach the top slot but did chart; if I stuck to only number ones, my ears might ooze pop music syrup.

The year 1969 did not start with a teenybopper beat. It began with a Richard Nixon presidency. Mere weeks before the inauguration, Christmas Eve of 1968 brought the iconic "Earthrise" photo from Apollo 8. In Nixon's inauguration speech, he reflected that the scientific marvel allowed Americans to "shar[e] the glory of man's first sight of the world as God sees it, as a single sphere reflecting light in the darkness." Beautiful as this image may be, Nixon's statement reeks of famous American beliefs that the United States acts like "beacon of light" and "city on a hill" for the rest of the world to look up to. These ideologies, for the better part of the 1960s, seemed outdated in light of unrest at home and war abroad. Nixon emphasized *peace* several times in his speech, intoning, "For the first time, because the people of the world want peace, and the leaders of the world are afraid of war, the times are on the side of peace."[1] Nixon's "fear of war" resulted in Operation Menu and a Hail Mary attempt at Vietnamization in the coming years, as well as numerous secret talks and sly plots; his attempts to end the war in Viet Nam were devious and Machiavellian. But after his inauguration, 1969 didn't look too bleak—nor did it sound that way.

Charting at #51 on the Billboard Top 100, Sammy Davis, Jr.'s cover of "I Gotta Be Me" from the Broadway musical *Golden Rainbow* appears innocuous enough at first. The song remained in the top 40 in 1969 for 11 weeks, and Davis notoriously sang "I Gotta Be Me" at the same 1972 Republican National Convention where he famously (and controversially) endorsed Nixon with a hug. As a child in the 1980s, all I knew of Sammy Davis, Jr., was that he wore gold sunglasses and smoked a lot. Little did I know that Davis was a talented dancer and singer who served in the army, where he was bullied because of his race. My friend Jim (a poet, Viet Nam veteran, and pop culture virtuoso) scoffed that Davis was an "Eisenhower puppet," but what he meant was that Sammy's music wasn't the hip thing for the Viet Nam War generation. "I Gotta Be Me," lyrically, is an American dream song—fame and fortune are just beyond the singer's grasp. It also asserts American ideas of individualism and pioneer spirit. Though not always seen as a civil rights pioneer (his embrace of Nixon at the Republican National Convention angered fans who saw the president as bigoted), Sammy Davis, Jr., was a trailblazer and remains a legend on the global entertainment stage.

Another legendary trailblazer hit the charts in 1969. Recorded in February and released on vinyl in July, Johnny Cash's *Live from San Quentin* single "A Boy Named Sue" shares themes of American manliness and individualism similar to those featured in Sammy Davis, Jr.'s rendition of "I Gotta Be Me." Adapted from a Shel Silverstein poem, "A Boy Named Sue" held the third spot in the Billboard Top 10 for three weeks. News of Nixon's nefarious ways had yet to be revealed, but Cash's reputation as an "outlaw" was far more palatable than Nixon's. What's curious about "A Boy Named Sue" is the reconciliation at the end; the song tells the story of a boy whose father walked out on his family but bequeathed his son the name "Sue" before his exit. Sue manifests anger toward his father and makes it his mission to find him. When he does, he famously declares, "My name is Sue, how do you do?"[2] and engages in a fight with his father in a bar, rolling around on the filthy floor. Then his dad comes clean about why he named his son Sue: a fatherless kid would need a sissy name to help him develop thicker skin, because his father wouldn't be there to do it. After this confession, the son, Sue, throws down his gun, choked up, and the estranged father and son embrace. While there is a fight in "A Boy Named Sue," the vendetta resolves somewhat peacefully. If even the "Man in Black" sang songs about reconciliation, could that mean that 1969 was a year to be heralded for peace? The Paris Peace Talks began in 1969, and Nixon made promises to withdrawal troops from Viet Nam throughout the year. Hope was in the air.

An infamous three days of "peace and music" in August 1969 underscored this hope. At the Woodstock Festival, Jimi Hendrix played a blistering, lyric-less version of the "Star-Spangled Banner" that drew ample criticism along with awe. While Hendrix had played live versions of the national anthem before, this rendition gained public attention. On the *Dick Cavett Show* in 1969, Hendrix answered the host's query on why he played the anthem "in such an unorthodox way" by gently demurring, "[My version] isn't unorthodox, I thought it was beautiful. But there you go."[3] Cavett tried to stick up for Hendrix on the show, noting Hendrix's service in the 101st Airborne, but Hendrix continued to receive negative attention for his "beautiful" anthem. Many music critics likened sounds in Hendrix's anthem to real "rockets" and "bombs bursting in air," and still others thought Hendrix was playing to the anti-war movement. It is true that Hendrix "openly condemned that American soldiers were deploying napalm against civilians in Vietnam … 'The world is nothing but a big gimmick, isn't it? Napalm bombs, people getting burned up on TV.'"[4]

The reaction to Hendrix's performance at Woodstock that morning was quiet and visceral, but when the Academy Award–winning *Woodstock* documentary showed the entire nation his national anthem, "reactions were immediate and wildly divided." Some loved the performance, viewing it as a patriotic commentary on the nation's polarized political climate. One critic from the *New York Post* celebrated, "You finally heard what that song was about, that you can love your country, but hate the government."[5] While the "moral" outcome of the performance would be bandied about into 1970, Hendrix's take on the national anthem ultimately bolstered his guitar-god status in the rock 'n' roll pantheon.

Rock critic Greil Marcus wrote that Hendrix's masterful performance is "so complex, with so many different layers of disgust and celebration and alienation and engagement, there's really no way to just characterize it as a protest against the war…. It's certainly that.

But he's also saying, 'I'm a citizen of this country, too.'"[6] Hendrix struggled with his racial identity; "blacks ... dismissed him as a musical Uncle Tom: a black man playing white man's music.... Hendrix also was frustrated by legions of white fans who only saw him as a racial stereotype—a hypersexual black man who was high all the time—instead of a serious musician."[7] In Viet Nam, racial difficulties heated up; the summer of 1969 marked the highest number of "fragging" incidents[8] to date in Viet Nam, and many of these events stemmed from racial inequality and simmering tempers on active duty.

Near the end of 1969, the United States transitioned, culturally speaking; the feel-good vibes of the 1960s were giving way to more war, more inter-U.S. conflict, and more cultural turmoil. The protest movement, infiltrated by Nixon spies, fractured; vocal government officials got louder as they moved away from "hawk" and toward "dove," though many citizens' anti-war protests retreated into simple frustration over the war. The United States (and, arguably, many soldiers fighting in Viet Nam) was experiencing battle fatigue. The Viet Nam War and its many offshoots saturated American culture, and the end of 1969 appeared to be a death knell for 1960s optimism.

In November and December 1969, Creedence Clearwater Revival's "Fortunate Son" (aka "the song featured on every Vietnam miniseries") gained the top spot in the Billboard charts. While the Mets won the World Series in October, the first Vietnam War Moratorium convened on October 15, making waves as the largest display of public dissent in U.S. history.[9] Nixon responded with his infamous "silent majority speech" on November 3, but a second Moratorium March on Washington convened a week later, in which protesters surrounded the White House and sang the Beatles' "Give Peace a Chance" to Nixon, who sat in the White House listening. This unprecedented anti-war protest occurred in the wake of CCR's new number-one song.

"Fortunate Son," however overplayed, remains a staple of any anti–Viet Nam War songbook. It takes up a theme that has spanned anti-war songs throughout history—how those with wealth and privilege get out of the fighting (aka the dirty business of war)—and demonstrates pride in being an average American. The snarling, loud refrain of "Fortunate Son," as well as the jarring, explosive guitar of Hendrix, is the antithesis of Nixon's suggestion in his inauguration speech that Americans needed to lower their voices to achieve peace. This wish would not be fulfilled.

Released in 1969 in the midst of a huge "comeback" tour (the group hadn't toured in three years), the Rolling Stones' *Let It Bleed* featured hits like "Gimme Shelter" and "You Can't Always Get What You Want." The blues-influenced album temporarily knocked *Abbey Road* off the UK charts and opened at number three in the United States in December 1969. Like "Fortunate Son," the Stones' "Gimme Shelter" can often be found in documentaries and films set in the 1960s. The song's guiding force is menace, but it ultimately fades out into lauding love over violence.

Guitarist Keith Richards told an interviewer that the "germ of the idea [for "Gimme Shelter" was] people running about and looking for shelter" and mostly inspired by Richards looking out the window during a London rainstorm.[10] But both Richards and vocalist Mick Jagger note that the band "went further into it" because of the "very rough, very violent era," and disturbing images of the war, like "pillage and burning," influenced the song's "moody" outlook "about the world closing in on you a bit."[11] The apocalyptic message of the song, in conjunction with the turbulence of the end of 1969, came to a head on Thursday, December 4, at the "west coast equivalent of Woodstock"—the Altamont Festival. Performers like the Rolling Stones, Grateful Dead, Santana, and Jefferson Airplane were slated to play under the watchful eyes of the Hells Angels at California's Altamont Speedway—the choice of security was ill informed at best, with the bulk of the Hells Angels being rather ideologically opposed to most of the audience members. While Jefferson Airplane played, a scuffle broke out that left a member of group injured, and the bands started to leave. Undeterred, the Rolling Stones went on, but during their set,

> a 21-year-old Hells Angel named Alan Passaro stabbed a gun-wielding 18-year-old named Meredith Hunter to death just 20 feet in front of the stage where Mick Jagger was performing "Under My Thumb." Unaware of what had just occurred, the Rolling Stones completed their set without further incident, bringing an end to a tumultuous day that also saw three accidental deaths and four live births.[12]

The disturbing footage from Altamont could only be topped by more destructive footage from the war. The end of 1969, at least sonically, marked a transition from "peace and love" to apathy, frustration, anger, and conflict. As the war plowed on and more bombs were dropped, still more unrest and turbulence would follow; the My Lai massacre story broke that November, a domino that would eventually lead to the Kent State shootings in 1970. With regard to the Viet Nam War, both hawks and doves were running for shelter across the globe, afraid their "very life" would "fade away."

America's conflicting feelings regarding ideas like race, national identity, and patriotism can be heard (as well as seen) in music from the tumultuous year of 1969. While Sammy Davis, Jr.'s "I Gotta Be Me" remains a Broadway showpiece, it also remarks on U.S. national identity in 1969; individualism, whether right or wrong, triumphed, and success was still seen as a goal that could be achieved through diligent hard work. The war, sadly, did not reflect that idea, as the Nixon administration scrambled to clean up America's excess through stalled secret talks in Indochina. The hardnosed gravitas of "A Boy Named Sue" was *not* absent from the Americans fighting in Viet Nam, but, as the song explains, vengeance can be turned with a different point of view, and many soldiers were questioning U.S. involvement in the war.

Stateside and worldwide, the shaggy-haired anti-war protesters were admonished for not having toughness or grit, but those traits are required to stand up for an unpopular belief, especially toward one's government. The creative defiance of Jimi Hendrix's "Star-Spangled Banner" is both awe inspiring and haunting, and the treatment he endured after performing the song underscored issues of race that were only magnified in American culture. The gate-crashing "Fortunate Son" further emphasized the public's growing disdain for the Nixon administration and the U.S. government in general. The events at Altamont, set against the backdrop of threats, placed the Rolling Stones in the unenviable role of ringmasters for the evils of rock 'n' roll and the wraiths of future doom.

◇ ◇ ◇

Not all musicians shared the "hippie" aesthetic of the Viet Nam War era in the United States. Activist and anti-war artists emphasized an insatiable cultural desire to push the country toward a peaceful exit from the Viet Nam War through heightened social awareness and social experimentation. But many American songwriters, artists, filmmakers, and television personalities pushed for an agenda that stood by whatever decision U.S. leaders made in Viet Nam, no matter how controversial or morally unsound. Several singers and songwriters supported a more hawkish view of American patriotism through song lyrics that expressed overt contempt for draft dodgers, protesters, hippies, and anyone who attacked the previously established norms of the United States' national identity when at war. Dutifully following the blueprint of previous pro-war songs, the Viet Nam War–era songs focused on the bravery of the soldiers fighting to liberate a country from evil. These new "Yankee Doodles" were usually represented by musicians whose public personas identified them with the American cultural trope of the cavalier patriot, an iconic idea that leaned heavily on historical representations of outlaws who defied critics with headstrong and confident dedication to their principles to "take the law in [their] hands."

The majority of pro–Viet Nam War songs came from the country music scene, including Merle Haggard's "Fightin' Side of Me" (1970) and "Okie from Muskogee" (1969), as well as Johnny Wright's "Hello Vietnam" (1965). Even Johnny Cash composed the patriotic (but not necessarily pro-war) "Ballad of Ira Hayes," which utilized country music's use of plain-spoken narratives about traditional American cultural values. Sergeant Barry Sadler's "Battle of the Green Berets" (1966) is one of the few songs representing a soldier rather than a blue-collar cowboy. Sadler exploited the expected cultural tropes of the brave soldier in public performances, but, instead of a cowboy hat, Sadler sang in full uniform on television. Pro–Viet Nam War music was country music, most often associated with rural and blue-collar Americans; in this way, it was a contrast with folk and rock music, which is often identified with members of the counter-culture movements, flower children, and hippies. Country musicians attacked the ideologies espoused by the counter-culture, which, to them, meant any type of cultural activity that they disagreed with. Draft dodging, long hair, communist sympathies, and anything less than steadfast loyalty to the United States was roundly vilified.

Rarely did pro–Viet Nam War songs offer any more of a "solution" to the problems the war caused than anti-war songs did, though pro-war songs often preferred to keep the United States the way it (never) was instead of changing. The America and sense of patriotism behind pro–Viet Nam War songs echoes current political and social debates; lately, America has been accused of losing the morals, values, and traditions that it manifested in the late 1940s and 1950s. The idyllic America of *Leave It to Beaver* remains a dream deferred from the 1960s to today, and yet songs written in favor of the Viet Nam War— and in favor of wars today—continue a dialogue of aggressive and fervent allegiance to a vision of America that was permanently altered by the anti-war movement.

Pro–Viet Nam War songs matched the anger and passion of the anti-war songs as the Viet Nam War progressed, and country musicians enjoyed a larger audience than rock and folk musicians at the time. The generally clean genre (though there were several "outlaw" artists, like Johnny Cash and Merle Haggard) was the lucky beneficiary of several popular nationally syndicated radio and television shows in the United States. Variety shows that featured musical performances, like *The Grand Ole Opry*, *Hee Haw*, *The Porter Wagoner Show*, and *The Jimmy Dean Show*, caught America's attention during the 1960s, and many of the songs crossed the genres of both popular and country music. Country music about the Viet Nam War was less politically critical than its rock and folk counterparts, but it did make statements that reinforced patriotic and political ideologies embraced by conservatives and hawks:

> By the mid–1960s, when the Vietnam War became a critical issue, country music had begun to reach a wider audience with its almost unanimous pro-war message, thus making it an important part of the musical dialogue that debated the legitimacy of the war. This was in large part a reaction to the rising tide of dissent against the war. Until "agitators and hippies started

stirring things up," country performers mostly refrained from putting political views in their music…. If a country song touched on anything political, it usually contained a sanguine view.[13]

The soft politics of country music allowed artists to criticize those who were "stirring things up" in the United States.

One of the more vocal critics of the "agitators" was country star Merle Haggard, whose songs "Fightin' Side of Me" and "Okie from Muskogee" featured patriotic sentiments that reinforced the political rhetoric coming out of both the Johnson and the Nixon White Houses. One veteran, whose service dates are unknown, suggests that Haggard's "distinctly patriotic music played well in Vietnam, where troops regarded it as 'their kind of music' because they agreed with the message, especially the denunciation of war protestors in 'The Fightin' Side of Me.'"[14] In "Fightin' Side of Me," the song's narrator dismisses those "gripin' 'bout the way things ought to be" and declares that these naysayers are "running down [his] way of life." This declaration likely resonated with many returning veterans, who generally came from blue-collar backgrounds in which angry, cavalier forms of patriotism strongly responded to anti-war sentiments. "Fightin' Side of Me" gives a lyrical ultimatum to these undesirable dissenters: "If you don't love it, leave it." This phrase underscores the way that many Americans felt about the anti-war protesters. As Haggard sings:

> Runnin' down the way of life,
> Our fightin' men have fought and died to keep.
> If you don't love it, leave it:
> Let this song I'm singin' be a warnin'.
> If you're runnin' down my country, man,
> You're walkin' on the fightin' side of me.[15]

These lyrics stress that dissent will not be tolerated and could result in a physically violent altercation. The narrator explicitly "warns" the anti-war faction that pro-war folks will fight those who disagree with them.

One can surmise that Haggard's song revolves around an underlying rage "against war protestors," and the narrator "worries that if criticism of the war continues unabated, American democracy may be doomed."[16] The reiteration of the pro–Viet Nam War themes such as the domino theory, anger at protestors, and the "warning" that questioning the rationale behind the Viet Nam War would bring on "the fightin' side" of those who support the war no doubt boosted the morale of troops listening in Viet Nam (i.e., "in country"). The overall message of the song promotes retaliation against any war sentiment that did not align itself with the established patriotic ideology of the United States. Historian Lee Andresen points out that the main "flaw in the reasoning behind this song is that it never does explain how suppressing freedom of speech will preserve freedom,"[17] but reasoning doesn't appear to have been an essential part of most pro-war songs, which often relied more heavily on emotional appeals.

Haggard promoted this sentimental pro-war support a year before the release of "Fightin' Side of Me" in his middle-America paean "Okie from Muskogee." The earlier song takes a less aggressive stance against dissent concerning the Viet Nam War, instead perpetuating the political ideology and patriotism that Presidents Johnson and Nixon, as well as pro-war hawks, deemed valuable. The opening lyrics of "Okie from Muskogee" depict a small, idyllic American town where people live simply, freely. The good folks of Muskogee proudly display the American flag at the courthouse, and they don't do drugs, grow long hair, or disrespect their elders. The citizens of Muskogee, it appears, would disapprove of, for example, the long-haired students who publicly displayed the aforementioned behaviors while briefly taking over buildings at Columbia University in 1968. On the contrary, "Muskogee, Oklahoma, USA" is a place where more conservative folk can party, and the narrator takes comfort in the knowledge that this town has not been polluted by liberals, hippies, or any other bums from the counter-culture. The lyrics make it clear that the counter-culture has no place in Muskogee, even though they use slang from the era that contains double, more "liberal hippie" connotations. Merle Haggard would eventually play "Okie from Muskogee" on *The Smothers Brothers Comedy Hour* in 1969 and refused to let Senator George McGovern's 1970 campaign use the song, claiming it was satirical in nature and actually not a commentary on contemporary culture.

Haggard would not permit a politician to co-opt his art; though a "pro–American" artist, Haggard was an *artist* whose musical career spanned several decades. Allowing his song to be used in a senatorial campaign would have changed his work in a fundamental way. The song might have become more associated with McGovern's liberal agenda than Haggard's pro–American sentiments in cultural memory. However, Lee Andresen, who unpacks various meanings of the song against interviews Haggard gave in his book *Battle Notes: Music of the Vietnam War*, disagrees:

> Those who have decided to further their education at Muskogee appear to be a smug and condescending lot, secure in their knowledge that their political parochialism makes them perfect citizens. However, it seems that they occupy a fantasy world. Haggard says that this song was done tongue in cheek, but he sounds dead serious in other songs he recorded about similar issues.[18]

It is easy to dismiss the "Okies" as relics occupying a fantasy America, a country untouched and unruffled by the cultural changes and political turmoil of the 1960s and early 1970s. Many Americans genuinely longed for a reality that closely matched the typical middle-America Muskogee that Haggard depicted, a place frozen in time and devoid of constant societal clashes. It represented paradise for average American citizens frightened by the violent changes they saw in their country. The innocent occupants of Muskogee were not that far removed from the majority of Americans, who identified with Haggard's vision of America and rejected as well as resisted the one offered by the anti-war movement.

Numerous pro–Viet Nam War songs came out of the country music genre, and most of them echoed the theme of righteous anger against protestors, hippies, anti-war dissenters, and those who did not sufficiently fear the specter of communism.

> [Nashville] dutifully parroted the government rationale with songs.... Dave Dudley's "What We're Fighting For" [features] a dreadfully homesick soldier [who] feels that keeping communism from our shores makes his time in Vietnam well spent. This GI is so troubled by the fact that his mother's letters describe protests against the war that he urges her to "tell them what we're fighting for!"[19]

Real or imagined, soldiers' anger that their work and sacrifices in Viet Nam were not being taken seriously boils over in Pat Boone's "Wish You Were Here, Buddy" (1966), which "condemns war protestors as well as the then-Cassius Clay (now Muhammad Ali) for avoiding the draft" and features a narrator "incense[d] that not only is the man he calls sarcastically 'buddy' safe at home, he is also engaging in campus antiwar rallies."[20]

The anger in Boone's lyrics resonated with many Americans, including soldiers serving in Viet Nam. While Country Joe and the Fish's 1969 anti-war song "I Feel Like I'm Fixin' to Die" would ask why the United States was in Viet Nam in an exasperated and acerbic way, many soldiers were truly confused regarding why they were in Viet Nam while their friends weren't or why they were even soldiers in the Viet Nam War in the first place. The best answer, according to Johnson, Nixon, and pro–Viet Nam War songwriters, was to stop North Viet Nam from spreading communism to the citizens of South Viet Nam; many soldiers wholly accepted this argument. They had to believe in *something* to keep going. Historian Christian G. Appy notes in his book *Working Class War: American Combat Soldiers in Vietnam*:

> Most enlisted men found the war itself to be without point or purpose. Those who generally accepted America's right to intervene in Vietnam were most disturbed by the absence of meaningful measurements of military success, a clear definition of victory.[21]

It was hard to define "success" in the combat zones of Viet Nam, and many firsthand accounts of the war report flagging morale as the war dragged on with no clear signs of victory. With all the rhetoric coming out of Washington, as well as the pro-war songs declaring, as Johnny Wright sang, "we must stop communism in [Viet Nam] or freedom will start slipping though our hands,"[22] soldiers felt they had little choice but to believe that communism was the evil they fought to defeat.

Through the sentimental use of patriotic fervor and overt emotional manipulation, pro–Viet Nam War songs exploited America's fears of communist threats to its freedom. In this way, the songs promoted the aggressive war agenda put forth by the U.S. government. While the pro-war songs do have some artistic merit, their heavy reliance on tropes of past war songs and their bellicose, intolerant position regarding social change and protesters undermine their aesthetic merit; these songs only perpetuate what was written before. Still, one must conclude that writers of pro–Viet Nam War songs meant what they said. But the pro–Viet Nam War citizens failed to realize that their patriotic beliefs had *already* been compromised by the United States' war in Viet Nam. The war may have been promoted as having the noble goal of stopping a communist threat, but flouting the Geneva Accords of 1954 and not allowing the Vietnamese to vote in 1956 showed the United States exhibiting communist behaviors. How can a country say it is spreading democracy when it rejects a country's right to democratic election? President Lyndon Johnson and his secretary of defense, Robert McNamara, ultimately saw their political aspirations collapse due to their decisions regarding the Viet Nam War, and musicians who penned pro–Viet Nam War anthems are rarely remembered in contemporary cultural and historical accounts of the war. The pro–Viet Nam War hawks did not "lose" their battle for Viet Nam any more than the anti–Viet Nam War doves "lost" their battle against the war, but both parties played an undeniable role in shaping the future of America at war.

Merle Haggard no doubt has a protégé in Toby Keith, who wrote a knee-jerk reaction song to the 9/11 attacks and the subsequent war in Iraq. And while anti–Viet Nam War songwriters might see their ideals reflected in albums released by Green Day and Pearl Jam at the beginning of the 21st century, it seems clear that one must always choose a side in war. The U.S. government undoubtedly prefers its citizens to side with its wartime policies and decisions, and many Americans will align themselves with those actions without question. The pro-war folks may have to fight a little harder to disseminate their beliefs among those who do not share them. However, if Robert McNamara (or Merle Haggard, who later opposed the Iraq War) serves as an example, it is possible to adopt different political beliefs or change one's mind about American decisions regarding foreign wars. Patriotism and American national and cultural values continue to fluctuate. If grand ideas can change and morph over time, it is easy to believe that an individual citizen could begin to question the traditional norms of war—both after the war and while in the midst of it—and still remain a patriotic American. The anti-war movement loved America too, but not like the hawkish "love it or leave it" perspective prevalent during the Viet Nam War. The protestors' patriotism differed from that of Johnson or McNamara, but both forms of patriotism expressed a genuine concern for the future of the United States. Pro–Viet Nam War patriotic music and lyrics pushed a familiar American cultural agenda.

◁▷ ◁▷ ◁▷

The looming cloud of war no longer hangs over Viet Nam. In Sai Gon, you can wait in line with buses of tourists and school groups to visit the Reunification Palace (formerly Independence Palace) and see which mustard-colored chair Henry Kissinger, President Nixon's forbidding-German-accented secretary of state, sat in during peace negotiations. Lots of posters and photos detailing which myriad dignitaries visited the palace dot the walls, but the place has the wide, expansive character of a dull office building; even the helicopter pad on the roof doesn't lend it much excitement. There's a tank outside, a replica of the one that crashed through the gates during "the fall of Sai Gon" on April 30, 1975. Children are permitted to climb on it a little, but not adults. It's a popular photography spot.

The park surrounding the palace proved more interesting to me, as the palace, like many places in Viet Nam, relied more on fans than air conditioning to keep things cool. I stood next to an oscillating fan while looking around the old "war room," which looked like something straight out of a 1950s film, complete with old rotary phones in weird pastel colors. The war effectively ended on April 30, and reunification (hence the new name of the site) of the North and South became the next objective.

A few blocks away from the Reunification Palace stands the guarded space where the U.S. Embassy once was, roughly. Rory Kennedy's 2014 film *Last Days in Vietnam* tells the story of the United States' fabled evacuation of the embassy in 1975 far better than I could, but to wit: The 1973 Paris Peace Accords resulted in a ceasefire and removal of U.S. troops from Viet Nam, but about 6,000 noncombatant troops and military personnel remained.[23] As the Northern forces advanced toward Sai Gon, Ambassador Graham Martin (a fellow North Carolinian) dug his heels in, waiting until the last possible moment to leave, rather dramatically, via helicopter. The tank crashed the gates of the palace around 10:30 in the morning, though the embassy was only done evacuating people about three hours prior. It's a sordid, messy tale that underscores the United States' perpetual underestimation of the Vietnamese.

Today the embassy is gone (there is one, in another part of town), and the land contains the U.S. General Consulate building. When I started to take a photograph of the site, a Vietnamese guard quickly waved me away and then stood watching me as I crept across the street. I furtively snapped a quick shot while pretending to look at my phone for directions, but all I got was the fence surrounding the area. The guard and I exchanged a wave from across the street as I went to Propaganda Café (again) for lunch. He couldn't have been more than 20 years old; I wondered if he even knew he was guarding the scene of America's clumsy exit from the "American War," but then I realized I was the one who thought there was "something" beyond the gates. Sai Gon (now Ho Chi Minh City), with a light rail in progress and Starbucks on the corner, had obviously decided there wasn't anything worth seeing at that site.

Because the Vietnamese won the war, and it took place in their country, they get to tell the story of the conflict the way they want. Furthermore, Viet Nam has largely moved beyond the past; every time I visit, something's changed. When my friend Ted advised that I get a SIM card or a Vietnamese phone on my most recent visit to Ha Noi, I scoffed. He argued that things had gone digital, but, true to form, I had to learn things the hard way. Stepping out of boxing class on my second morning in the city, I looked down to the corner of the street, expecting to hear the rousing calls of "motorbike, motorbike, where you go?" greet me as they always had. No such luck. Fleeced by a taxi twenty minutes later (I could see the meter was rigged, but I was too tired and sweaty to argue over, essentially, five dollars), I turned on my portable Wi-Fi device and downloaded the Grab app—essentially the Uber and Uber Eats for Viet Nam, but you get the transportation choice of a motorbike or a car—chastised and begrudgingly accepting that Ha Noi had entered the digital age. What new Viet Nam had I stumbled into?

Walking through the rabbit warren of the Old Quarter on a different day, I watched a woman pluck black feathers off a bird on a butcher table next to women haggling over produce; while the Grab app might've changed how tourists and natives get around, there were still some things that remained the same. To further test my theory, I revisited the Viet Nam Museum of Revolution. The first time I'd visited, I'd noticed two things. The first was an exhaustive exhibit on the ground floor detailing global protest against the American War, which, while extremely educational, seemed to invoke a particular message: look how unpopular this war was, look how bad it was, look how everyone knew what a terrible idea it was *except* the "American imperialists" and their "puppet government" in Sai Gon. The second was the near entire absence of a decade in Vietnamese history—the 1980s. While the Vietnamese History Museum (across the street, and dedicated more to art and culture than war, but that's in the name) spans centuries of history, the Museum of Revolution focuses on the various countries that have invaded Viet Nam and attempted to make it their own. The French, the British, and the Japanese are the first offenders by reason of the Indochina wars and the First and Second World Wars.

The French earned the "most despised" superlative in Vietnamese history, as the descriptive placards in the museum are written in Vietnamese, French, and English. The French also stayed in Viet Nam, trying to run things, far longer than the Americans. This information is all detailed on the top floor of the museum (you begin by going upstairs in a beautiful old building, with expansive windows and polished wood floors that sharply contrast against bamboo paneling and portable air conditioners). The American War begins on the second floor; you must physically go *down* to see the effects of this conflict. The atrocities against the Vietnamese people at the hands of the United States and its allies are detailed a little less enthusiastically than at the War Remnants Museum in Sai Gon, but that is likely due to the heavy-handed message the government likes to portray when it comes to the South.

After the liberation of Hue, Da Nang, Hai Phong, and the like in 1975, the museum dedicates a whole wall to the rebuilding of Viet Nam. The room prior to this part of the story, as of 2019, includes a display devoted to anti-war baubles and trinkets, like mugs and pins, underscoring global support of peace in Viet Nam. The Sai Gon government's "violation" of the Geneva Accords in 1975 interrupts this narrative of progress, forcing the North to go south to liberate its people from the "puppets" once again. Just as I'd seen in 2012, however, the 1980s remain conspicuously absent. There are two direct mentions of the decade: a bridge built with Soviet assistance and a bridge built by Vietnamese engineers, both in 1985. Above examples of ration books and other ephemera, a photo is captioned "Inhabitants stood in line to purchase good and foodstuff by their ration tickets in the subsidized period prior 1986 [*sic*]." Some books are on display, noted as "Some National Assembly laws passed during 1988–1990 period." Two newspapers published "from 1986–1990" can be found, but then, all of a sudden, we're in 1992. In the next room you see a smattering of gifts given to Ho Chi Minh (who died in 1969, making this part of the museum a bit anachronistic), and you're done. Well, not entirely; the global anti-war exhibit I'd seen in 2012 has been replaced by "Ho Chi Minh: Portrait of a Great Man." More on him later—and he's very interesting and quite inspiring—but what happened in Viet Nam in the 1980s besides bridge building, food rations, laws, and newspapers?

Perhaps, since there's no revolution to speak of, it doesn't make sense to include this period in the museum. But simply leaving out nearly an entire decade of history doesn't mean there is no history to speak of—quite the opposite, but that's why it's not there. War history museums in Viet Nam take great pains to emphasize the forced labor and appalling treatment the Vietnamese faced during the country's various occupations and invasions, but it will not tell on itself in a public way. I have no interest in belittling or discounting the suffering of the Vietnamese under French and American occupation—the facts are indisputable. Survivor accounts and military testimony of the atrocities of the My Lai massacre, the notorious photo of an American tank dragging a Vietnamese corpse behind it, the infamous and horrifying photo of a young girl running naked and burning from U.S. bombs, and U.S. veterans' own accounts of how they treated enemy corpses (removing ears was popular) and villages (lighting up thatched roofs with Zippos) stand as testament. But why won't Viet Nam address what it did to its own people? What of the "reeducation" camps, where anyone remotely involved with the United States went to repent for their sins against the government?

These omissions reminded me of the turmoil of 1969, long past but still present. Fifty years later, it's the United States with detainment camps it refuses to apologize for or explain, despite wide protests. Fifty years on, Viet Nam detains foreign citizens (of Vietnamese heritage) for smuggling anti-government propaganda into the country. A family friend born in Viet Nam in the late 1960s fears returning, and my mother asks me what, exactly, would this woman, who was maybe 10 years old when she left, have to be afraid of in Viet Nam?

Seated at an outside table at my hotel bar—a safe enough place to have a drink, I reasoned—I looked around to see what San Juan, Puerto Rico, might look like in the evening. For that trip in 2012, I'd chosen a hotel that I don't think exists anymore; I now stay at "the old Quality Inn" (now the Wave Hotel Condado; if your cab driver is confused, use the former name) when I visit San Juan. Back then, however, I was on a graduate student budget and happy to stay, cheaply, outside the main tourist drag. The conference I was in San Juan for was held at a bigger, Hilton-like behemoth hotel with escalators, ocean views, and outrageously priced (bad) food. My hotel was across the street from a veterinary office and next to an old church that I stared at in the mornings while smoking the required six feet away from the hotel door.

I'd only been in Puerto Rico for 24 hours when the bartender/waiters at my 2012, post–Maria, nameless hotel happily chatted with me and a daughter-mother duo at the table nearby. When we all learned the daughter was on a pre–study abroad celebration trip, the bartender insisted we all have a specialty drink, the name of which translates as "little fuck." As we sipped, the waiters enlightened us regarding the Puerto Rican "free month" in which folks could brew their own, homemade, recipe-passed-through-generations rum. Despite my prudent drinking, my glass never seemed to empty—such diligent waiters!—so when I got up to go the bathroom and the room pitched, I decided to switch to water. One "little fuck" was enough.

"Dimensions of Empire and Resistance" (aka the conference theme) ended up being a complete wash; I was perturbed that maybe three people attended my panel, as I'd expected prospective employers to at least stick their heads in the room to see whether I was interesting. I didn't understand the academic "game" at that point, so I bunked off after day two to actually learn more about Puerto Rico. The next evening, sticking to my trusty Bud Light, I struck up a conversation with the friendly wait staff (two guys). The bartender asked me why I was in town, and I told him, "To talk about Roy Brown." I'd said this to a cab driver that morning, and he'd nearly run off the road in excitement; he effusively insisted that I call Mr. Brown (I demurred because I didn't have his number, though the cab driver offered to look it up for me). The bartender reacted similarly: "Oh my God! You should call him! Really? How do you know who he is?"

The explanation is kind of embarrassing: I wanted to go to a conference in Puerto Rico and figured I'd have better luck getting in if I presented on a Puerto Rican artist. A quick Google search later, and I was in a rabbit hole of *nueva cancion* (new songs, roughly), a folk-Caribbean hybrid music genre. Roy Brown Ramírez emerged as the most interesting and applicable figure, at least to me—he made an album in 1969 called *Yo Protesto!* that has become one of my favorite finds. His Spanish is clear enough for me to translate with my rudimentary skills, and a track from *Yo Protesto!* ("Yo no se qual es la verdad") was even played at my wedding by a skilled guitarist.

Yo Protesto! features melodic Spanish guitar playing instead of the folksy harmonies (CSNY, the Grateful Dead, Bob Dylan, Pete Seeger, etc.) or amped rock (Country Joe and the Fish, the Animals, the Rolling Stones, Jefferson Airplane, etc.) that most anti–Viet Nam War American musicians performed during the Viet Nam War era. What bonded me with the (cute—I should admit that he was cute) bartender was our off-the-cuff duet of the refrain from the album's first track, "Monón": "Fire, fire, fire / the world is on fire! / Fire, fire / Yankees want fire!"[24] Mr. Bartender showed me his arms—goosebumps. "You see this?" he asked, pointing to the raised hair on his arm. "I can't believe I'm singing this with a white ... with an American."

You can't get this kind of experience from a conference; I sincerely hope this anecdote persuades any budding scholars reading this book to follow my "bad" academic example—it's much more fun than the conference cash-bar-mixer crap.

I didn't have time to remind my new friend that he was an American, like me (FYI: Puerto Rico is part of the United States), because he again pushed me to call Mr. Brown, making me wonder whether things worked a little differently in San Juan than anywhere else. I've never heard another derivation of this argument elsewhere: "Oh, you're in London writing about Mick Jagger? You should call him." Mr. Bartender elaborated that he grew up listening to Roy Brown; his spooked reaction to our singing was due to the song's past. In Puerto Rico, "Monón" was the adopted battle cry of Puerto Rico university protesters in the 1970s—against the Viet Nam War, of course, but also against the unfair treatment Puerto Rico endured (and arguably still endures—check out Nelson Antonio Denis' *War Against All Puerto Ricans* if you want to know more). So I emailed Roy Brown, who replied! He appreciated the gesture but was too busy watching his *turbanido* (little tornado) of a grandson to sit for a rehash of the past with a starry-eyed grad student.

The songs on *Yo Protesto!* carry a strong theme of resistance against a complex imperial power. Brown's lyrics suggest this enemy is as destructive in Puerto Rico as it is in Viet Nam. Exploring his lyrics reveals a new perspective on the United States during the Viet Nam War era. "Monón" also admonishes a metaphorical United States as ticking time bomb of evil. Much like the shadowy figures in Bob Dylan's "Masters of War" (1963), the oppressor in "Monón" is careless and heartless regarding the havoc he wreaks around the world. In the song "No Me Sulfuro Mas," the one who must be stopped (the United States) is identified as the enemy of not only Puerto Rico but also all those who suffer under its oppressive actions. And, far from the hippie messages of peace and love from the 1960s, Brown's lyrics for the song "Páco Marquez" seethe with violent intention against an oppressive United States. The album encourages the people of Puerto Rico to rise against their captor, the United States.

Brown is not unique in challenging the United States through song lyrics—three years before visiting Puerto Rico, I studied abroad in Panama and wrote about Rubén Blades and Willy Colón's "Tiburon," a song with thinly veiled anti–American sentiment. "Tiburon" means "shark" in Spanish, and the United States was the sleeping, watching, menacing shark. But Puerto Rico has a different relationship with the United States than Panama. Puerto Ricans, for example, can be conscripted into military service. Despite the racial strife that dominated the Viet Nam War era in the United States, all "races" of the country appeared in the U.S. armed forces during the conflict. The hastily and purposefully timed 1917 Jones-Shafroth Act allowed the United States to draft Puerto Ricans into World War I, and Puerto Ricans have consistently served in every U.S. conflict and in its armed forces since. Like every other American "group," Puerto Ricans made a large contribution to the Viet Nam War. An estimated 48,000 Puerto Ricans served in the armed forces during the conflict, and hundreds of Puerto Ricans died in the Viet Nam War, either killed in action or taken as prisoners of war.[25] Many Puerto Rican soldiers returned to the United States with anti–American sentiments and anger that would stoke the fires of Puerto Rican protests against the war in Viet Nam and in favor of their country's independence. Furthermore, the Young Lords (a pro–Puerto Rican independence group) staged several demonstrations for equality in 1969.

Similar to the Black Viet Nam War experience, the Hispanic Viet Nam journey was often one of the "other." George Mariscal chronicles the Chicano American experience of the Viet Nam War in his book *Aztlán and Viet Nam: Chicano and Chicana Experiences of the War*, interspersing literature from and about the war with historical and cultural accounts, such as Mexican American veterans' war memories. Mariscal asserts that Latin Americans, despite their large contribution to many U.S. war efforts, are left out of the larger dialogue about the war:

Two of the surnames that appear most often on the wall of the Viet Nam [*sic*] Memorial in Washington D.C., are Johnson and Rodriguez. These two names tell us something about the composition of the U.S. military during the war, especially the combat units ... histories of the war and cultural representations of the war have yet to hear the voice of "Rodriguez."[26]

I asked my friend Frank Gutierrez about all of this; Frank is a Mexican American Viet Nam War veteran, as well as an outstanding public citizen in his native Lubbock, Texas. He's taken me around town, and he does some amazing outreach to fellow veterans. Frank joked that "the Puerto Ricans were *mean*" but quickly cited the achievements of Puerto Ricans in Viet Nam, such as Captain Humbert "Rocky" Versace, a Medal of Honor recipient from Puerto Rico. Another Viet Nam veteran friend knew of "Rocky" by reputation; this guy is a big deal.

What's unfortunate, from the Puerto Rican perspective, is that many Hispanic veterans feel they're passed over for accolades in favor of their Caucasian counterparts. Years ago, in February 2014, President Barack Obama announced that he would award the Medal of Honor, retroactively, to nineteen "discrimination victims," seventeen of whom are classified as "Hispanic." It is worth noting that, even in 2014, Jesse Erevia (the son of one Hispanic recipient, Santiago J. Erevia) remarked that his family "wondered why [Santiago] didn't receive [the award] the first time and thought it may have been because of his name."[27] Tensions between the Latin American community and the U.S. government have sadly been a predictable object of consternation in U.S. history for the majority of the country's past and present. It's worth mentioning, just in case you find yourself singing with a fellow American who might not identify or see themselves as such.

11

1970

I like to remind my students, when I'm teaching classes on the Viet Nam War, that we dropped more ordnance on Viet Nam (and Laos and Cambodia) in one year than we did during the *entirety* of World War II. Starting in 1964, in Operations Barrel Roll and Steel Tiger, the United States engaged Laos in air warfare and bombed the ever-living mess out of the tiny, land-locked country of two million inhabitants. The target was the Ho Chi Minh Trail, but for a country the size of the United Kingdom, everything is close to everything else. Unexploded ordnance (UXO) riddled the countryside, especially the northern panhandle that bordered North Viet Nam.

Whenever anyone asks me something along the lines of "you've traveled to many places, what are your favorites?" the first place I name is usually Luang Prabang, in Laos. Some people just say "Laos," though the full title of the country is "The Lao People's Democratic Republic." Swaddled by China, Myanmar, Viet Nam, and Cambodia, Laos is tiny. The language is a lot like Thai, and lettering in Laotian looks like Thai script (I've heard that Thai people can read it). Due to its status as Southeast Asia's only land-locked country, as well as its size, lots of Laos' neighbors like to take advantage of Laos, especially China. Agriculture drives the Laotian economy, and most people living in Laos have links to some agrarian kin. As in Viet Nam, the French occupied Laos for the better part of a century, and civil strife continues in various forms—Laos is unapologetically communist and has some human rights issues (think random "disappearances" under sketchy circumstances, ethnic minority cleansing, etc.). But it is also unapologetically beautiful.

Situated alongside the Mekong River among jungle-mountain hills, Luang Prabang maintains the UNESCO-deemed historical colonial French architecture as well as its own; outside of Thailand, I have never seen so many "wats" (Buddhist pagodas). The city used to be the royal and capital seat until 1975, when the communist Pathet Lao fighters overthrew both the French influence and the royal family. In a historical sense, Luang Prabang reminds me of a small version of Hue, the former imperial capital of Viet Nam. Traditions—giving alms to the monks, the night market, chanting monks in wats, and so on—continue without fail; the city appeared to be just fine with doing things the way they've been done for centuries, and the Laotian people I met carried themselves with a kind of inner poise and peace that you don't see very often. I'd chalk it up to Buddhism.

While my main goal while in Luang Prabang was to visit its UXO center (which I did), my secondary goal was to get to the turquoise exquisiteness of the Xuang Xi waterfalls. Whenever I want to go somewhere, I set my desktop background on my work computer to a photo of my desired destination; I'm not sure whether doing so helps manifest the wish into a reality, but it certainly works as a good reminder to stay focused. The

Xuang Xi waterfalls stayed on my desktop for over a year, and in person they exceeded expectations. We took a long tuk-tuk ride from our hotel (delightful, had a lotus pond, served the best lemongrass-stuffed pork *ever*) to the drop-off point, which had people hawking souvenirs, food, and the like. After passing a "bear park" (no chained animals, just a few endangered animals representing a larger poaching/Chinese medicine problem), we arrived at the falls. The Xuang Xi falls are a bright cerulean, with hints of green, and they fall in many tiers. The actual falls themselves have competition in the Blue Ridge Mountains I know from my youth, but the levels of bright aqua pools were something brand new. Typical of most natural waterfalls in the mountains, the Xuang Xi waters were quite cold, a fact confirmed as people dipped into the water. Squeals of delight and laughter in more languages than I could count filled the area, where everyone left their stuff on the side and hopped in. My husband made a friend—an older Chinese gentleman—and I have pictures of them both whooping with glee under the main falls. Xuang Xi turns everyone into a child again, and that's why Luang Prabang stays at the top of my "best places to visit" list. That and the lemongrass-stuffed pork.

◁▷ ◁▷ ◁▷

In Cambodia, we watched President Obama eulogize those who were murdered at Emanuel African Methodist Episcopal Church; we were more than an ocean away from our family and friends in Charleston, but I will always know where we were on June 17, 2015.

Our hotel, situated outside the main town and tourist drag of Siem Reap, had a relaxing pool, amazing bathrooms, and delicious food, all of which was about $30 a night. When we walked around the outskirts of town, I tried to find the right adjectives for it. There was a newly built square with a couple of restaurants that jutted up against an old market. The pharmacy sold everything you could want, and we had dinner at an Italian restaurant one night that was really good; other than the Cambodia Landmine Museum, I hadn't looked up much about Siem Reap beyond an obligatory pilgrimage to Angkor Wat. We poked around the ancient complex for a day and a half, starting at sunrise. My stomach, ravaged by traveling and eating new things, remained upset, and the bugs—gnats and mosquitos—that were dawn risers really sucked the awe out of that experience. Immediately after the light spread over the ancient ruins, I found a Coca-Cola and water vendor and sat sulkily on a sticky bench. I'm not a morning person, no matter the amazing wonder of the world.

The Angkor Archaeological Complex did, as a whole, impress me a great deal. We had a lovely guide, Nat, who knew his way around the stories depicted all over the temples. He showed us pocked spots in the walls where ancient weapons had fired during some war or another—the complex is so old and historic; it has witnessed a lot. While I tried to focus on what Nat said about Cambodia and how it got wrangled into the Viet Nam War, the tales of Shiva and Hanuman, hanging out with a variety of Buddhas, moved ahead in the interest lanes of my brain. I loved the faces and the snakes—*nagas*—on the South Gate, as well as the Ta Prohm temple, which Nat said was generally ignored until the 2001 *Tomb Raider* movie. In the mid–1100s, King Jayavarman VII commissioned Ta Prohm as a tribute to Pranjaparamita, a Buddhist deity of wisdom—and also to his mother. I watched hushed Buddhist monks slip through the doorways, entranced; these spots were sacred, not just for their historical value but also for their religious significance. Monks actually live on the Angkor site, keeping the Buddhas' tunics fresh for the visitors. At another temple, Banteay Srei, my husband and I were struck by the unique reddish sandstone that composed the structure, allowing for absurdly detailed reliefs of plants and deities. Like the rest of Siem Reap, the main attraction (Angkor Wat) barely scratched the surface of what there was to see and learn about.

When we walked into town, for instance, we encountered an eight-sided glass display pillar filled with skulls. We were at a commemorative site, near a temple that honored those lost in that part of the city to the Khmer Rouge genocide. The outdoor exhibit nearby detailed the crimes of humanity that the Pol Pot regime inflicted on the Cambodian people, and my husband and I were both quiet and reflective. As we looked at the dates of atrocities that took place, we noticed that my husband's brother and sister were born in that era, and we started looking at people that age we met in Siem Reap—such as our hotel owner, Mr. Nat—with a new sort of interest. What had these people lived through and seen? It was nearly impossible to tell; my husband had remarked on the "Khmer smile," an impenetrable, closed-lipped smile that seemed to invite good cheer but at the same time conveyed the opposite of goodwill. We decided that this smile, which we could see on some folks we met, was part friendly and part "keep out." Some of the giant warrior Brahman statues at Angkor War had that smile—was it an invitation for a fight or an invitation for a cup of tea?

Elizabeth Gilbert once wrote that "Cambodia is hard."[1] She talked about the hard-packed earth, the beaten-down soil, and the people. If you were like me, you knew Cambodia via either the Khmer Rouge/Pol Pot era or the fact that Angelina Jolie adopted a child from there while filming *Tomb Raider*. Starting in the late 1960s, Cambodia suffered a long and painful civil war (oversimplifying, but this book is not about that) that wasn't helped by U.S. bombs and general presence in Southeast Asia. But it continued past the Viet Nam War. Protracted wars don't just mean fighting; they also mean malnutrition, injury, and shorter life spans. I was reliably told that if you're over 40 and Cambodian, it's likely that you have experienced some trauma. I carried that knowledge with me whenever I met someone in Siem Reap. But it was a magical pocket of the world, even if, at times, "hard."

At Angkor Wat, Hindu deities share space with Buddhas, and temples vary in states of amazing ruin and presence. There's a butterfly sanctuary, a really crazy downtown scene, and a circus of "street kids" that is flat out ridiculous (Cirque de Soleil–level talent). I didn't get to spend too much time in Cambodia, but I didn't find it as "hard" as Elizabeth Gilbert. It was dry, and our tour guide told us some things in that furtive, under-the-shoulder way that people living under governments that disparage free speech do. I've seen it in China (regarding Tiananmen Square), Thailand (regarding the king), and Viet Nam. The guide was not the only person, however, to mention the recent drought to us on our visit; even Bill Morse mentioned it in my brief conversation with him at the Cambodia Landmine Museum.

My reason for going to Siem Reap was to speak to Bill, the international project manager at the Cambodia Landmine Museum. During the Viet Nam War, the United States dropped over 2.5 million tons of bombs on Cambodia, the rationale being that the Ho Chi Minh Trail (or Truong Son Trail; see chapter 3) ran through Laos and Cambodia. The UXO left behind is devastating. The Khmer Rouge didn't help; they laid many mines, and then Viet Nam invaded Cambodia. Three decades of war left Cambodia as one of the most heavily mined places in the world. It's getting better, but the stories associated with it can be heavy.

While waiting to talk to Bill (he basically told me via email that he'd be there, but getting an appointment would be tricky), who was deeply engaged in conversation with other visitors, my husband and I (he'd been able to tag along for part of the trip) checked out the Cambodia Landmine Museum. The building is circular, the inside situated around a lotus pond, with a pagoda of different sorts of mines that the Cambodia Landmine Museum Relief Fund (CLMMRF) has cleared. The museum grounds are littered with detonated bomblets, as well as posters featuring the guy behind the efforts, Aki Ra. Mr. Ra was a child soldier with the Khmer Rouge, and he founded the museum and fund in order to take on bigger de-mining projects. According to the posters in the museum, Ra's underlying mission has been to "make [his] country safe for [his] people."

This mission manifested in several ways. Aki Ra and the CLMMRF helped establish the Cambodian Self Help Demining NGO in 2008, an "all Khmer" organization "comprised of ex-child soldiers, widows, mothers, fathers, villagers and university graduates" dedicated to "[clearing] small villages throughout the Kingdom of Cambodia." Ra was awarded a Korean honor, the Manhae Grand Prize for Peace (2012), as well as a CNN Top Hero award (2010) and a commendation for his efforts from the prime minister of Cambodia. His accomplishments and tireless work toward de-mining Cambodia are well documented throughout the museum, from newspaper clippings to Ra's own experiences with the Khmer Rouge. One museum photograph's caption reads, "Near Ban Taprick, 1981: A Khmer Rouge supply line across the Thai border. In 1980, I followed a guerrilla unit until a high-ranking militia arrested me and held me captive for several hours. I saved this film and never showed my face again in that zone." Guerrilla war, taking captives, the *waiting*—these are the parts of war that are hard to convey to those who haven't taken part in them. I'm a civilian; I've never been as afraid as anything described in that photo caption. And I'm grateful not to be. To be a veteran of a war and go back to

Collected UXO at Cambodia Landmine Museum, Siem Reap (2015).

the combat sites after the war to *help* has to be a very difficult thing to do. Such acts convey elements of atonement, but also bravery. It's hard to heal oneself of the wounds of war, especially on the battleground. Americans usually go back home after our wars; what happens when you keep living where the wars were fought?

While the caption is not about the Viet Nam War, you can't deny that's a helluva caption—and it's just one of *many* stories like it in the museum. I was most struck by pictures drawn by children maimed by mines, depicting themselves (often without an arm or a leg) as sports champions. I think anyone—I'd argue mostly men, since those sports actually pay—has once upon a time dreamed of being a sports star. But coming from a country ravaged by war—and having a body ravaged by war's legacy—doesn't make the odds of achieving that dream very favorable. I was heartened by these child artists' ability to dream and be resilient, but a picture of a one-armed soccer player stuck with me. While the kids could imagine their lives differently, I was imagining a different past, one in which people weren't so careless about brutally covering their countries with explosives that lived longer than the wars they represented.

When I finally got to talk to Bill Morse, the museum was about to close up for the day. Instead of sticking to my prepared script on de-mining efforts, we talked about the people with whom Bill worked. The staff was mostly young people, beaming with that inner light that only earnest youth will bestow; they did educational outreach as well as land surveying, detonation, reporting, and building communications around Cambodia to create a database. But we also just talked about Cambodia. We laughed over Cambodian idiosyncrasies, like getting a steady shipment of a specific type of food (this is the type of conversation that Americans inevitably fall into). We mostly talked about the kids; Bill told me a lot of different stories about young people, injured by a mine, who'd gone on to do amazing things despite their injuries. These are things we don't have to worry about in the United States. We have school shootings (to which we're nearly immune), but letting your kid play in your yard is rarely a life-altering hazard.

Child's drawing at Cambodia Landmine Museum, Siem Reap (2015).

UXO Lao, which we'd visited prior to our time in Cambodia, was similar to the Cambodian Landmine Museum and Project RENEW (see conclusion). The entryways in all these locations are "decorated" with shells and shrapnel. Various exhibits explain what you're looking at (for example, a rusted piece of an exploded cluster bomb next to an intact one). These artifacts are usually accompanied by a photo of someone injured by weapon on display (severe burns and/or losses of limbs, ears, eyes). There are always maps on the walls, indicating where UXO had been found, how it was disposed of, and usually (because of the types of governments in Southeast Asia) a token lauding of whatever government relief was made, as well as donations and global partnerships. In Laos, Cambodia, and Viet Nam, the U.S. government does offer a few million dollars for de-mining, which always feels like a poor pittance: here, let's have someone poorer than you clean up the destruction you made. At UXO Lao, visitors could watch a 45-minute-long documentary, which detailed the success of outreach and public education. There were three or four main "characters" (real people) who'd survived a UXO explosion, and they spoke soberly of things like "think before you pick up a piece of metal." One young girl had been preparing an area in a woodland clearing to make a fire; one minute she was working, and the next she lost an eye and an arm. She asked viewers not to play in areas that are rarely used. While the film ended on an upbeat note of progress, the pervasive fear of the dangers of the environment in the film couldn't be avoided.

Entryway to UXO Lao Visitors Center, Luang Prabang, Laos (2015).

Like UXO Lao, the Cambodian Landmine Museum made efforts to educate visitors on the global spread of UXO. (Just Google "UXO world map"—see what I mean? It boggles the mind.) In fact, every continent except North America and Australia has UXO in its soil. Bombs dropped over a century ago still pose risk to people. If nothing else, the Cambodian Landmine Museum will turn you off to war quick, but it's easy to adopt an anti-war stance when you see all the damage war can do.

◁▷ ◁▷ ◁▷

Musically, 1970 began with the hit "Raindrops Keep Fallin' on My Head" by B.J. Thomas. The song wouldn't be out of place in a Disney film, as it extolls the virtues of positivity against less-than-ideal circumstances (rain). Happiness is inevitable in this tune; the rainstorm is temporary. The metaphorical rainstorm of the 1960s would not be defined by inevitable happiness, but rather hard-earned dissent. The deaths of Jimi Hendrix and Janis Joplin, both of drug overdoses at the age of 27, shook many in the music world; the breakup of the Beatles in April would also be a blow. The Jackson 5 got their first number-one hit in 1970, "I Want You Back," at the end of January, and an eponymous album by the band Black Sabbath (now recognized as the first heavy metal album) was released in mid–February. Other firsts, not necessarily in music, also happened in 1970. A historic meeting of the leaders of the divided East and West Germany would occur in March, as well as the first Earth Day, the first Pride Parade (and the Stonewall Riot), and Glastonbury Festival celebrations. In addition, Anna Mae Hayes and Elizabeth P. Hoisington would be the first women to gain the distinguished rank of brigadier general in the U.S. Army.

In mid–February, the "Chicago Seven" were found not guilty of inciting a riot at the 1968 Democratic Convention, which was a victory for the anti-war and anti–Nixon crowds. The U.S. military did not have many victories in 1970, at least in terms of public opinion. General Creighton Abrams, who'd assumed control of U.S. MACV in 1968 after General Westmoreland's departure, began to vigorously push President Nixon's Vietnamization policy, which was designed to get ARVN units doing more work so that U.S. troops could withdraw. In March, however, the military was in the headlines for My Lai; the U.S. Army charged 14 officers with suppressing information.

As these events unfolded, Simon and Garfunkel released *Bridge Over Troubled Water*, their last album together. The title track, featuring mostly Art Garfunkel on vocals along with a sparse piano, held the number-one spot for six weeks. It is my least favorite Simon and Garfunkel song (it's too melodramatic, and I don't like Art's voice alone), but I can see how the song's promise of hope and friendship resonated with an American public still reeling from a decade of turmoil. The Beatles broke up on April 10, and their single "Let It Be" ousted Simon and Garfunkel from the Billboard number-one spot. "Let It Be," another piano-heavy song, stood out as a sort of koan to time past, the wisdom of the words "let it be" serving as guidance for those struggling to figure out how to navigate the first year of a new decade. In the White House, President Nixon preferred Johnny Cash to the pop charts, inviting the Man in Black to perform at the Executive Mansion.

At the end of April, as the Jackson 5's "ABC" hit the top of the charts, the United States invaded Cambodia, a neutral territory, expanding the war and angering many Americans. Across the nation, protests against the war flared up—most notably on May 4, when the Ohio National Guard fired on "protestors," killing four college students on the Kent State campus. Two of the victims had zero ties to the anti-war movement; they had simply been walking to class. Five days later, nearly 100,000 people descended on Washington to protest the Cambodian incursion. President Nixon, famous for dismissing anyone who demonstrated against him as a "bum," fumed. The Guess Who's first hit, "American Woman," topped the charts in May; its transparent anti-war lyrics are hard to miss. Ironically, in July, the band would play at the White House for the president and the visiting Prince of Wales at Nixon's invitation, but "American Woman" was stricken from the set list. The Senate, wary of the growing anti–Viet Nam War protests and the widening war in Cambodia and Laos, repealed the 1964 Gulf of Tonkin Resolution on June 24, and two days later U.S. troops withdrew from Cambodia. Hoping to soothe any hurt feelings, Bob Hope hosted Honor America Day on July 4, 1970, in an increasingly divided America.

Though the sleepy soft rock of the Carpenters' "(They Long to Be) Close to You" dominated the airwaves in early summer, Edwin Starr's guttural "War" hit the top of the charts by August. The song is brash and loud, and its repeated choral question—"War? What is it good for? / Absolutely nothin' / Say it again!"[2]—held the ear of the American public. On August 24, Viet Nam War protestors bombed Sterling Hall at the University of Wisconsin–Madison, and an international manhunt ensued. On August 26, New York's famed Fifth Avenue hosted the Women's Strike for Equality, which was equal parts celebration (the 50th anniversary of the passage of the 19th Amendment to the Constitution, giving women the right to vote) and protest (organizer Betty Friedan hoped the strike would call attention to unequal domestic labor[3]). At least 50,000 women attended the event, which was largely peaceful. A few days later, in East Los Angeles, the Chicano Moratorium March against the Viet Nam War was held, but police resistance to the event sparked a riot that killed three people. The Chicano community had a specific reason for its anger, as "Mexican Americans drafted to fight in the Vietnam war were dying at twice the rate of their white compatriots."[4] Furthermore, like Black Americans, Native Americans, and Puerto Rican Americans, Mexican Americans were subject to racism and unfair abuse.

In October, as the Khmer Republic identified itself as a legitimate governing body (thus heightening the Cambodian Civil War), President Nixon announced that the United States would withdraw 40,000 American troops from Viet Nam by Christmas. The Jackson 5 scored their fourth hit of 1970, "I'll Be There," in the fall, and things looked to be calming down in Viet Nam. A Civil War relic—the *Hunley*, a Confederate submarine—was discovered near Charleston, South Carolina, in October, by 22-year-old Dr. E. Lee Spence. At the end of the month, a horrific monsoon hit Viet Nam, stalling the war as hundreds of people were killed and left homeless by the flooding. Journalist James P. Sterba wrote in the *New York Times*, "The war is quieter when it rains."[5] The quiet might have contributed to MACV's November announcement that it could report its lowest weekly death toll (of American soldiers) in five years.

By mid–November, the My Lai massacre trial began, with Lieutenant William Calley as the primary suspect (or scapegoat). Lieutenant Calley did not act alone, but because of the time between the event (1968) and the trial (1970), several members of Charlie Company were no longer enlisted and therefore no longer under the jurisdiction of the military courts. Captain Ernest Medina, who had been in charge of Charlie Company, would eventually be acquitted of any wrongdoing, but Calley would not escape unscathed.

As the year wound down, President Nixon requested $155 million from Congress to aid Cambodia; the Nixon administration did not want North Viet Nam and the Khmer Rouge to overthrow Cambodia's government, preferring to work with Cambodian premier Lon Nol over the communist Khmers and North Vietnamese. While George Harrison's "My Sweet Lord" would be the last number-one hit of 1970 (and the first number-one song by an ex-Beatle), the second-to-last top hit of 1970, Smokey Robinson and the Miracles' "Tears of a Clown," topped the charts for two brief weeks. I thought "Tears of a Clown" was an earlier, Motown hit; it sounds like one. It's also the song I always use when trying to describe, to students or whoever will listen, the perfect pop song. The lyrics of "Tears of a Clown" are so very sad, but the music is so very happy, with whooshing saxophones and trilling keyboards, buoyed by Smokey Robinson's high tenor. The juxtaposition of the happy and sad in "Tears of a Clown" matched the mood of 1970 well; even if the outer appearance of the world was one that was calming down, inside there was still a great amount of pain to address.

◁▷ ◁▷ ◁▷

The 1970 shootings at Kent State University in Kent, Ohio, proved a violent disruption in the anti–Viet Nam War movement; it mobilized the anti-war protestors who had fallen silent after President Nixon's and the conservative Republican Party's victory in the 1968 election. Ohio governor James Rhodes, fearing that the protest against the United States' decision to bomb Cambodia, scheduled for May 4, 1970, would turn violent, called in the National Guard. He declared a state of emergency in the state, specifically targeting Kent State, where days of rebellious and angry behavior had persisted since Nixon's April 30 announcement of his "Cambodian Incursion."[6] The National Guard, for reasons still not clearly known, opened fire on students at about 12:22 p.m.; four were killed and twelve wounded. None of the victims have ever been linked to violent or criminal behavior, and two of the victims had no prior involvement in any sort of protest activities—Sandra Scheuer and William Schroeder were simply walking to class. The clash between nervous soldiers and angry protesters served as a violent reminder that the "second dimension," or a more ideal society (as portrayed in anti-war protest songs), was fleeting; the establishment—the government, the schools—could not and would not tolerate much more dissention.

Crosby, Stills, Nash and Young (CSNY) recorded "Ohio" on May 21, 1970, as a protest to the Kent State killings. The photos of "Kent State Massacre" in *Life* magazine deeply affected songwriter Neil Young. He later wrote in the liner notes of the band's album *Decade*:

> It's still hard to believe I had to write this song. It's ironic that I capitalized on the death of these American students. Probably the most important lesson ever learned at an American place of learning. David Crosby cried after this take.[7]

Crosby clearly weeps as the song fades out; he repeatedly howls a refrain of questions, and his voice breaks because of its intensity. Crosby's battered vocals echo the voices of many battle-weary protesters of the era; as veterans returned and various protest marches—especially in the civil rights movement—turned violent, people became angry, confused, and embittered at the protracted Viet Nam War. The United States was imploding as it wearied of infighting as well as seemingly unending international squabbles.

The militant, four-four marching beat that introduces and sustains "Ohio" is not accidental; "Ohio" is CSNY's call to arms. At a press conference the day before the shootings, Governor Rhodes, exasperated with the anti-war demonstrators, shouted, "They're the worst type of people that we harbor in America. I think that we're up against the strongest, well-trained, militant, revolutionary group that has ever assembled in America."[8] Rhodes' comments encouraged an "us against them" mentality in America, and his fear of the "militant revolutionary group" is evident in his comments. The Kent State shootings, along with Rhodes' brusque remarks, spawned a domino effect of university protests and closings, spurring national debate as to what role the government should take in protests and what was lawful in situations similar to Kent State's, as well an in-depth discussion as to where America was headed. "Ohio" met Governor Rhodes' vitriol with a scathing comment on his handling of a peaceful protest, increasing the "us against them" mentality that Rhodes had already fostered among his constituents.

The first words of "Ohio" immediately place the listener in a sonic tone of militant threat; the lyrics are at once a warning and a relief—the movement is finally able to act on its own. Even though a threat (Nixon and his bombing campaign in Cambodia) is coming, those who hold the idea of peace in Indochina are left alone after their moment with the soldiers. An alternate reading of these lyrics invites a similar understanding of the anti-war mindset of the time; both the tin soldiers and Nixon did come, and the anti-war movement is left alone to regroup and repair. However, the lyrics continue with the sounds of drums, metaphorically read as the bombing campaign that inspired the protest at Kent State. The Kent State shootings occurred in early May—the song hints that an even worse battle, heralded by the beating of war drums, is on its way. The confrontation of these issues brings the song to a head: perhaps finding a friend dead on a college campus sidewalk will force the listener to acknowledge the fissures in society, making people realize that the war was not going well and that action, on their part, should be taken.

"Ohio" was recorded on May 21, 1970 (17 days after the Kent State murders) and released three weeks later, in mid–June, with the companion single or "B-side" titled "Find the Cost of Freedom." The band rushed to release the single so as to add to its emotional potency: the lines referred to fresh memories of an unprecedented and horrific event in American history. Considering the timing of the song's release, the lyrics would have resonated with a still-stunned American public—or at least those who heard the song. Bill Halverson, the recording engineer for "Ohio," remembers it as a divisive and censored recording:

> I do recall that AM wouldn't play it and it was very controversial that AM wouldn't play it and FM, the underground, all the FM stations started playing it … and it got up in the 30s [of the Billboard chart] or so just with FM play and at that point FM was pretty underground and AM was the deal. But they tried to ban it.[9]

Obviously, the song struck a nerve with some and found an eager audience with others. Neil Young biographer Jimmy McDonough wrote that the ten lines of "Ohio" captured "the fear, frustration, and anger felt by the youth across the country and set it to a lumbering D-modal death march that hammered home the dread."[10] Most of the older generation no doubt felt that these young people, in some way, got what they deserved, but the majority of youth in the nation were frightened, if not appalled.

Young intended the lyrics to focus the public's attention on the Pulitzer-winning photo, published in *Life,* of the aftermath of the massacre. A young woman (Mary Ann Vecchio), her arms outstretched and a look of anguish on her face, looks directly at the camera; a body (Jeffrey Miller, dead) lies in front of her with blood seeping from the head. This image jarred the public when it appeared in the papers, but Young's direct reference to it in the "Ohio" lyrics only added fuel to the fire for those angered by the events at Kent State. Viewing the photographs of the Kent State shootings while listening to "Ohio" results in extraordinary audience reactions; the combination of the song's disjointed narrative and the photojournalism remains a potent reminder of the horrors that occur when war comes "home." The song's lyrics echo a united ethos of the protest movement: citizens running away from the situation—of the war, of the government's oppressive tactics toward anti-war protestors—even though they know it's wrong, was unthinkable. The anti–Viet Nam War movement valued accountability, but the government refused to take responsibility for the carnage it was causing in the war *and* its own backyard.

The nation's youth found it difficult to digest the undeniable knowledge that America's own government had authorized the cold-blooded murder of four innocent people on a college campus. CSNY member Graham Nash defended the band's release of the song, describing it as an aural promise of devotion to social activism: "We are going back to keep awareness alive in the minds of all students … to be vigilant and ready to stand and be counted … and to make sure that the powers of the politicians do not take precedent over the right of lawful protest."[11] The band's defiant attitude manifested itself in the song's lyrics. Young boldly mentioned then President Nixon by name in the song, and he did not fear possible repercussions of challenging the president so publicly. His and the band's anger was so strong that it could not be repressed by any threat of government intervention, and those who felt a kinship with the song only bolstered the movement.[12] "Ohio" was the last bombastic anti–Viet Nam War protest song that signaled the waning of an era, rather than its triumphant resurgence.

No one wrote a song about the shootings at Jackson State in Mississippi on May 14, 1970. Students were angered over a rumor that Charles Evers, brother to slain civil rights activist Medgar Evers, had been killed, and someone set fire to a dumpster. Tensions between Black and white residents escalated, and rocks were thrown at the police, who lost their cool and opened fire. Two people were killed. The Jackson State shootings aren't as dramatic as the Kent State shooting because there wasn't anyone there to take photographs. Even if an anti-war demonstration were planned at Jackson State, would the governor call in the National Guard on Black students, or just let the police handle it? The Jackson State shootings serve as a micro-example of the larger problem of discrimination and segregation that permeated the United States, especially in the South. The civil rights movement—and the anti–Viet Nam War movement—still had some work to do.

One of the highlights of my trip to Luang Prabang, Laos, was volunteering at Big Brother Mouse, an English conversation and literacy nonprofit. It was there, sitting with my husband and a group of young men, that I learned what life might be like for the average Laotian in the 21st century. The majority of the boys we met—young to teen—were able to come to Big Brother Mouse because they were also Buddhist monks. That's how many poorer male children earn an education—through the Buddhist temples. Taking vows of poverty, shaving their heads, and enduring a demanding schedule of prayers, the boys seemed to think these things were a fair trade for free education and meals. One morning my husband and I woke up very early to participate in the Alms Ceremony. Each day, at the break of dawn, monks from nearby pagodas walk the street that runs through the main drag in Luang Prabang silently, baskets in hand to receive food or money for their daily meals. It is a humbling experience for several reasons, not the least of which is knowing that one of these saffron-robed young men might be someone who's just trying to help his family by getting an education. The lack of entitlement would stun an American student, who expects their K–12 experience to be competitive, free, and perfunctory.

I don't know what women get to do for their education, or even whether they get one if they're poor in Laos. I didn't meet any young women at any pagodas or at Big Brother

Mouse, but I did see some wandering the street markets at night, selling flavored ice drinks. Women made things—there were lovely textiles, jewelry, and hand-painted lanterns for sale. The market got crowded relatively early in the evening, giving my husband and me time to look around the city on the way back to our hotel. It's a modest but beautiful place, and I could hear gleeful shouts of children as they tottered home from the market. We had dinner that night at a nice Italian restaurant that was tucked into a colonial French building by the riverside; jazz played and wine glasses clinked, oblivious to the history of the structure of street, which looked more like Provence than Prabang.

When we arrived back at our hotel, the dusky pink lotus flowers in the pond in the center of the hotel buildings were open, glowing from the lights that lined the dock near the pond. The lotus flower is emblematic of purity despite struggle. Lotuses grow in the mud, but they always blossom into a clean, beautiful flower. Even in Jiujiang, the white lotuses in the city's artificial pond looked healthy, in spite of the trash that people cast into the water.

Lotus flowers are also a symbol of Viet Nam and Buddhism. The Buddha emerged from enlightenment on a lotus. Luang Prabang emanated a Buddhist-infused sense of peace, but it also hid some of the hardships that went into creating that sense of peace. As we wandered from wat (temple) to wat, staring into the eyes of one impassive Buddha statue after another, I began to think that the ethos of acceptance and impermanence—two of the primary tenets of Buddhism—didn't play a larger role in the Laotian, Cambodian, or Vietnamese perspective on the Viet Nam War. The American attitude of rushing and fixing and doing was held in check in the soft light of Luang Prabang on its way to bed; instead, the temples and Buddhas and monks and lotuses seemed to say "*slow down*." I sat on the deck of our hotel the next morning, watching the lotus flowers fold back into the mud as I smoked a cigarette, contemplating how many times nations rise and fall, in and out of muck, only to rebloom, hopefully, beautifully.

12

1971

Driving through Viet Nam is not like driving through America. The roads are fine, and some of the ones closer to the cities are the same multi-lane highways you would find anywhere. What's different is the signage and the clusters of cities by the roadside. You move out of town, and no one really bothers with your car or who's in it—no one's looking at you; they're crossing the street or walking somewhere. The only "idle" people I ever saw in Viet Nam were older people, who would get up early in the morning, sit outside, and watch the world go by, talking to passing people, before retreating inside at the first sign of heat and for breakfast, I assumed.

Aside from buses between cities and the occasional private car (and the beloved motorbike), I've often traveled in a tour van or bus, which are markedly different. It always felt like you weren't meant to stop in just any town or divert from the path of a tour; maybe this was for the best, I've thought. I had to use the bathroom once, unscheduled (my stomach was rejecting some really good food), and there aren't convenience stores or fast-food places off the interstate. The Vietnamese maintain a healthy curbside food service industry (stop for the sugarcane juice), but this means someone's set up a grill under an umbrella, not a whole restaurant.

But back to emergency stops in Viet Nam: There are truck stops, with clean bathrooms and the equivalent of a Subway/Sbarro combo and a foodstuffs store, and they're widely dispersed. Where my hosts, who were gracious and kind, decided to stop was the equivalent of a backroad southern trucker store. The smell of oil and gas, mixed with the heat off the asphalt and the unrelenting sun, made me woozier. I clutched my bag as I was pointed toward the back of what appeared to be an open-air garage, with various people working on commercial shipping trucks. As in Europe, Asian vehicles are often smaller than what we see in the United States, but the equivalent would be a tractor-trailer. Some men (there were no women whom I could see) gave me a passing glance as I hurried past. I found my sanitary salvation: a hut with three sides and a door you could close *as long as you could hold it shut*, facing a field. And my least favorite thing—the squat toilet. Not all of them are gross, and it's not that hard to use, but should you be in a particularly uncomfortable state…. I held my breath and thanked myself for always bringing my own tissue when I go out, which doubles as toilet paper while traveling.

Viet Nam offers visitors so much in exchange for so little. I watched lanterns drift down rivers, saw freshly baked baguettes served by the roadside, and witnessed beautiful acts of spiritual reverence. On every road trip it was guaranteed that you would see, between the motorbikes, cars, and diesel trucks, a dogged cyclist. On a side tour to Tam Coc, outside of Ha Noi, our tour group was taken by boat down the Ngo Dong River via men and women who rowed the boats with their feet (like pedaling a bicycle), their upper bodies covered by long sleeves. While it was easy to play "spot the tourists" on a tourist excursion, peeking into people's everyday lives was more fun to do. Resorts were popping up in the Ninh Binh area, with giant photos of (often white and blonde) tourists gazing over the emerald karsts in the river draped over "coming soon" advertisements. That also meant seeing workers, often talking on the side of the road or using what we'd call rudimentary tools (the "two buckets on a stick" method is strange to me, who grew up with tractors at hand) to work on new stucco buildings. As we went down the river, random livestock appeared on the banks, often accompanied by a person absently wandering the riverside with them. I caught glimpses of small family picnics and pagodas tucked into the limestone rocks, and I was lulled into happiness by the lapping of the water against our boat.

As we turned around after passing under another fascinating cave-like archway on the river, we were steered into a Vietnamese hustle: a fleet of people selling hats, snacks, and beverages. Bumping into our boat with hers, one merchant woman poked my arm with a bottle of orange soda. "For her," she said, pointing at our oarswoman. I happily obliged but didn't partake myself (I've traveled enough to know not to get something to drink if your next toilet stop is unknown), though I did spring for a can of Pringles. And that's the happy accident—the collateral side-splurge, if you like—of war: your country and culture leave remnants (Pringles) for you to enjoy while you relax (sit on a boat) courtesy of the labor of someone much poorer than you (the boat rowers), and you are hustled to give that person more (the merchants), but it's still far from being a huge burden on your resources (the total cost of the trip, for two people, including tips and food and whatnot, was $80). Not knowing quite what to do with my mixed feelings of pleasure and guilt, I began to sing silly, made-up songs to my husband. Our boat captain, feet firmly pushing her oars onward, ignored me, a tiny smile on her lips. I vowed to learn a Vietnamese song before I returned, if only to make people laugh— then I'd actually contribute to the experience instead of simply *having* it.

Ngo Dong River near Tam Coc, Viet Nam (2019).

⋄⟩ ⋄⟩ ⋄⟩

The Stolpersteine Project, begun by German artist Gunter Demnig, consists of inlaying small stones into the sidewalks outside the homes of (mostly Jewish) people who were driven out during the Holocaust. We've seen the "stumbling stones" in Amsterdam, but, as part of an Airbnb trip, we also saw them in Berlin. Our virtual tour took us on a sort of "healing from tragedy" tour of the city, showing us various monuments or areas dedicated to remembering the Holocaust. The host was particularly interested in memory, or how memorials that we (the virtual group of Americans, an Australian, a German, and a Canadian) may have seen may have struck us. Since I write about that sort of thing, a little, in this book, and have done some "memory research," I didn't talk much. I offered that I found the similarities between the military cemetery in Dien Bien Phu and Arlington National Cemetery striking, but what really came to mind was *the buttons*.

Let me situate the buttons clearly: In Pulitzer Prize–winning author Viet Thanh Nguyen's book on the Viet Nam War, *Nothing Ever Dies*, he writes that war inevitably makes memory out of things that would otherwise have no value: "If the heroic people's collective humanity is only a façade, then it is no surprise that the nation's revolutionary industry of memory also gives life to things that are not human.... Some of the most memorable characters of war were thus not people, but weapons like the M-16 and the AK-47."[1] It's important that Dr. Nguyen mentions the weapons—which, as he and I both wrote about, one can fire for $1 at the Cu Chi tunnels site—because that's one of the first things we identify with war. Tanks. Planes. Bombers. Battleships. And guns—all the guns we can come up with! We like our toys, especially here in the United States. Another thing that pairs well with weapons is uniforms—my first memory of seeing a U.S. Marine Corps dress uniform is from an old commercial in which a festooned but stern Marine breaks protocol to take a little girl's Christmas list. Or she gives him a piece of chocolate. Anyway, I noticed the hat (which looked just like my grandpa's USMC hat) and the silver glint of the bayonet on the benevolent Marine's gun. They go together. And at just about any war memorial museum—it doesn't matter where or for what war or when—they will have uniforms on display, usually donated if the war was recent enough. But what puzzles me are the buttons.

Viet Nam history and war museums, perhaps more than any others I've ever visited, have a "more is better" approach to curating what items help tell stories. An Australian exhibit on the Viet Nam War at the War Memorial in Canberra, for example, includes one uniform (modeled on a dummy) next to some interactive exhibits with video and sound, old photographs with long captions, labeled weaponry, and maybe a few medals. The story of the war continues to be told in this manner, as it does in most U.S. Viet Nam War museums. But in Viet Nam, they throw everything in. If someone special touched something, it's an artifact: Ho Chi Minh's chipped teacup, his fountain pen, the wooden desk he wrote on, and his white outfit (so tiny!); General Giap's canteen and shoe polish tin (empty); Le Duc Tho's notepad and cigarette lighter; the chair Henry Kissinger sat in during the peace talks, accompanied a photo of him in it—*in this exact spot*. All of this is on display, in Viet Nam, in addition to what you'd see in the aforementioned Western museums. No relic that could possibly conjure memory—carefully crafted, approved by the state memory—was left unturned.

And then the buttons. Buttons from the French, buttons from the Japanese. Buttons from the ARVN, the Americans, the Australians, the North. It perplexed me every time—even in the air defense museum, there were buttons from the uniform of a brave pilot. I have an active imagination, but I don't have the ability to derive so many stories from

looking at buttons. Perhaps it's just a matter of aesthetics, or curation, this insistence on
including all, but then I think of the "shoe room" in Auschwitz—is it not the point to
include everything? We were directed to forget nothing, not even the tiniest detail of a
worn brass button.

Politics in the Viet Nam War era should have been a primer for the chaos of the
Trump administration. The media (which has arguably become more problematic when
forced to monetize headlines in a 24-hour news cycle) was beginning to bloom during
the war. Daniel Ellsberg's release of the Pentagon Papers has been heralded as an act of
good citizenship in the rearview mirror of history, but at the time (1971) Ellsberg was
seen by many as a traitor. In *New York Times v. United States*, the Supreme Court ultimately (6–3) agreed that the publication of the Pentagon Papers, originally titled the
"Report of the Office of the Secretary of Defense Vietnam Task Force," did *not* harm U.S.
national security interests.

What the Pentagon Papers did harm was the reputation of the White House. Presidents Kennedy and Johnson and many in their administrations were outed as corrupt
and fraudulent with regard to what they had told the American people about Viet Nam
versus what was actually happening. President Richard Nixon did little to restore the
White House's reputation, famously swearing he was not a "crook" shortly before ducking
out of the presidency in a resignation dogged by the threat of impeachment.

One of the problems revealed in the Pentagon Papers was the Kennedy and Johnson administrations' reliance on numbers. Robert McNamara, secretary of defense under
both Johnson and Kennedy, attempted to "quantify" the war in ways that made it appear
more winnable. But a high enemy body count does not a victory make. The Tet Offensive of 1968 definitely hurt the VC and NVA more than the United States and its allies in
terms of personnel lost. But the surprise attack did a lot of damage to American morale—
at home and abroad—and revealed holes in the ARVN and U.S. defenses.

In a conversation with White House Chief of Staff H.R. "Bob" Haldeman and
National Security Advisor Henry Kissinger in 1971, President Nixon asserted that girls
don't swear. Haldeman volunteered that women in 1971 did, indeed, swear, prompting
Nixon to reply:

> Oh, they do now? But, nevertheless, it removes something from them.... We all swear. But you
> show me a girl that swears and I'll show you an awful unattractive person.... I mean, all femi-
> ninity is gone. And none of the smart girls do swear, incidentally.[2]

With all due respect to President Nixon, the idea that smart girls don't swear is, frankly,
bullshit. But his off-the-cuff statement showed how out of touch the president was with
the direction America was moving. To be fair, it could be hard to tell; in 1971, the controversial sitcom *All in the Family* premiered, featuring a bigoted oaf named Archie Bunker
who mirrored the flaws of American culture back at viewers. The same year, Walt Disney World, representing a far more wholesome brand of family entertainment, opened
in Orlando, Florida. The National Women's Political Caucus (NWPC) was founded in
July, five days after the ratification of the 26th Amendment, which lowered the voting age
from 21 to 18. The push for the amendment stemmed from the draft, as it was unfair that

someone could be considered old enough to fight for their country (and, in several states, drink) but not old enough to vote. The voice of America's youth was thus amplified, changing demographics of elections from 1971 on. The year 1971 was also when America's War on Drugs began (it's still going), though President Nixon's initial steps focused more on treatment and addiction than any of his predecessors would.

The year also started with a 1970 hit single, the still-popular "My Sweet Lord" by George Harrison. By the time South Vietnamese troops invaded Laos (with American support) in mid–February, the Osmonds' "One Bad Apple" hit the top of the charts. To the untrained ear, this song sounds like a Jackson 5 rip-off (it was originally written for the Jackson 5, who passed on "One Bad Apple" in favor of "ABC"), and the flute trills don't do it any favors. Luckily, Janis Joplin bumped the Osmonds out of the top spot with "Me and Bobby McGee," a bittersweet posthumous chart entrance from the talented but troubled singer. Joplin's Texan-tinged blues performance appeals far more to me than the Osmonds, but the music world in 1971 was full of contradictions of taste. In mid–March, the Allman Brothers Band played a now infamous concert at the Fillmore East, their jam-blues-rock sound miles away from songs like "One Bad Apple" or an earlier 1971 hit, "Knock Three Times" (Dawn); I thought both songs sounded like advertisements and was pleased to find that "One Bad Apple" was the theme song for an Osmonds television show—you can hear the commercialism, if that makes sense. By the end of March, *The Ed Sullivan Show*, the prime venue for acts like the Osmonds, went off the air as the Temptations' "Just My Imagination (Running Away with Me)" topped the charts for a couple of weeks, adding a dose of soul music to the pop charts.

The end of March 1971 was a time for courtroom drama; in LA, serial weirdo Charles Manson and three members of his pseudo-cult were sentenced to life in prison for multiple homicides, including the murder of actress Sharon Tate. U.S. Army Lieutenant William Calley was also sentenced to life in prison for his role in the 1968 My Lai massacre. Despite being charged with 22 murders, Calley would later have his sentence reduced to a little over three years' house arrest. An up-and-coming Georgia governor, Jimmy Carter, who (like many other U.S. leaders) felt the judgment against Calley was too harsh, declared an "American Fighting Man's Day" following the My Lai verdict, meant to defend the American military from those who might want to "cheapen and shame the reputation of American servicemen."[3] Carter, like many historians, writers, and Viet Nam veterans I've spoken to about My Lai, considered Calley a scapegoat for a larger offense and his behavior atypical of U.S. officers in Viet Nam. Calley stayed quiet until 2009, when he made his first and only public comments on the My Lai massacre:

> There is not a day that goes by that I do not feel remorse for what happened that day in My Lai. I feel remorse for the Vietnamese who were killed, for their families, for the American soldiers involved and their families. I am very sorry.[4]

Calley would be immortalized in songs like "The Battle Hymn of Lt. Calley" (1971, Terry Nelson and C Company), "Set Lt. Calley Free" (1969, Big Bill Johnson), and "Hang On, Bill" (1971, Rick Riddle), among many others. The refrain "Calley was just doing his job" comes up a lot when reading or talking to people about the My Lai trial, and I agree that Lieutenant Calley shouldn't have been the only person blamed for the event. However, I don't agree Calley deserved to be "let free."

In April, in Viet Nam, a bomb exploded at a CBC Band concert in Sai Gon, killing an American GI and a 14-year-old girl. The CBC Band (a brother-sister duo whose name came from the bar where they started out and whose repertoire mainly featured West-ern rock music) now resides in Texas; in 2011, they played a reunion concert for Viet Nam veterans in Houston.[5] While the CBC Band recovered from their uniquely war-zone music incident, Veterans Stadium opened in Philadelphia, and "Joy to the World" (by Three Dog Night) held on to its number-one spot in the Billboard charts for six weeks in April and May, making it the number-one song of 1971. While a little hokey (in that spe-cial 1970s way), "Joy to the World" broadcast some much-needed residual hippie energy from the late 1960s.

On May 3, on the one-year anniversary of the U.S. invasion of Cambodia, the 1971 May Day Protests began in Washington, D.C. The goal of the protests was to shut down federal business, per the demands of the "Mayday Tribe," a "more militant segment of the U.S. anti-war movement." The War Resisters League, the People's Coalition for Peace and Justice, and the Yippies all joined in; they believed that the familiar protest marches would need to be ramped up (aka become more violent) in 1971 to get the government's attention. The Vietnam Veterans Against the War had been protesting in the weeks prior to no avail; the May Day Protests were thus organized to be disruptive. The May Day Pro-tests were organized around twenty-one key roadblocks, where demonstrators "were told to block the roads nonviolently using stalled vehicles, jury rigged barricades, or their bodies." But Nixon's Washington was ready, with 10,000 police, federal troops, and the National Guard in place to meet the protestors. The result was a massive, multi-day series of arrests, with over 7,000 people arrested on May 1 and 6,000 more arrested over the next few days.[6] Public response was somewhat sympathetic, and many in Washington felt the president had been too heavy-handed in his reaction to the protestors, many of whom did little more than exercise their civil rights.

In June 1971, singer-songwriter Carole King scored her first solo success with her album *Tapestry*. King had coauthored or written over 200 hit songs in the United States and United Kingdom, but her dual single "It's Too Late/I Feel the Earth Move" put her own voice in the spotlight. Her five-week number-one streak was broken by "Indian Res-ervation (The Lament of the Cherokee Reservation Indian)" by the Raiders, marking one of the only times the Native American story—of forced living on reservations and rac-ist treatment and a rallying cry that the Cherokee Nation would return—made it into the Top 40.

In mid–June, the *New York Times* began to publish what would be dubbed "The Pen-tagon Papers." The massive top-secret Department of Defense report had been part of Robert McNamara's study of military involvement in Viet Nam, and Daniel Ellsberg (a retired USMC officer, Harvard graduate, and analyst for the RAND Corporation) passed portions of the report on to journalist Neil Sheehan after concluding that the American people had a right to know the report's contents. The public did not know, for example, that the Kennedy administration had a hand in the coup to overthrow South Vietnam-ese president Ngo Dinh Diem or how the Johnson administration had failed to report how much it had widened the war. Ellsberg approached likeminded doves like Senators William Fulbright and George McGovern about publishing the papers, but their lack of interest led Ellsberg to try other means; Ellsberg had initially been in favor of the war, but he changed his mind after years spent involved in compiling the report and in the war.

President Nixon, who wasn't mentioned in the Pentagon Papers, initially ignored the situation, as nothing in the report hurt his reputation. Eventually, however, Nixon decided that what Daniel Ellsberg did was espionage. When questioned about his motives for, essentially, stealing classified documents and distributing them, Ellsberg stood his ground: "I felt that as an American citizen, as a responsible citizen, I could no longer cooperate in concealing this information from the American public.... I am prepared to answer to all the consequences of this decision."[7] Ellsberg was ultimately not arrested for espionage, and the Pentagon Papers would not be made available to the public in their entirety until 2011. Furthermore, in 2013, when National Security Agency employee Edward Snowden engaged in a significant leak of classified intelligence, his defense would echo Ellsberg's in terms of "informing the public"[8] of information concealed by the American government. Snowden, however, resides in Moscow, Russia, at the time of this writing, with a figurative bounty on his head courtesy of the American government.

In July, the rock music world suffered another casualty: Jim Morrison, aged 27 and lead singer of the Doors, was found dead in a bathtub in Paris. His death occurred only nine short months after those of Jimi Hendrix and Janis Joplin, making Morrison a member of the "27 Club," a grim grouping of musicians who died at age 27 (more recent members include Kurt Cobain and Amy Winehouse). The Fillmore East in New York City had just closed at the end of June, with the list of final concert performers including the Beach Boys, Mountain, and the Allman Brothers Band; the Allman Brothers would lose lead guitarist and band leader Duane Allman, at age 24, to a motorcycle accident in October. The Fillmore West, in San Francisco, would also close in July, hosting Santana, the Grateful Dead, and Creedence Clearwater Revival for its final show. Another hit, "You've Got a Friend," from Carole King's *Tapestry* album, would be the last number-one song of July. This version of "You've Got a Friend" was sung by King's collaborator, singer-songwriter James Taylor. His version would also spend time on the "Easy Listening" charts. The song is harmless enough, though I personally prefer King's version and Taylor's later work.

One of the most important events in July 1971 was Gloria Steinem's "Address to the Women of America" at the inaugural National Women's Political Caucus (NWPC) event on July 10. A year before founding *Ms.* magazine, Steinem's address called for a revolution against gender inequality. The speech was also important because it recognized "intersectional issues of racism and class" along with the NWPC's feminist agenda. Steinem called out "sex and race" as a means of "organizing human beings into superior and inferior groups" that perpetuated a system of "cheap labor."[9] While the speech was heralded as ground-breaking, what's upsetting is how familiar it sounds today, nearly 50 years later, in the context of the COVID-19 pandemic, when "essential labor" has fallen disproportionately on people of color and women; conversations about education and health care—fields heavy with female workers—also dovetail with the underlying messages in Steinem's speech. Clearly, the United States still has progress to make regarding issues of women, race, and labor.

The last few months of 1971 proved busy. Race riots in Camden, New Jersey, broke out in August, fueled by the racist beating to death of a Puerto Rican man. The Who's album *Who's Next* was released in mid–August, taking the band to new levels of success. New York's legendary Madison Square Garden hosted George Harrison and Ravi Shankar's "Concert for Bangladesh," a benefit show for refugees displaced by genocide as a result of the Bangladesh Liberation War. I have seen the DVD of the show several times, and what always stands out to me is Eric Clapton's performance (and the giant rock of cocaine visible in his nostril). In Italy, progressive-rock band Pink Floyd recorded a live album at the Pompeii Amphitheater. Rod Stewart's first chart-topping hits, "Maggie May" and "Reason to Believe," dominated October, only to be ousted in November by "Gypsies,

Tramps, and Thieves" from Cher (her first solo hit after breaking up with Sonny Bono) and the "Theme from *Shaft*" by Isaac Hayes (contributing a little wah-wah sound to 1971; Hayes would become the first Black man to win an Academy Award for Best Original Song for the tune in 1972). Elton John released "Your Song" at the end of October, while Led Zeppelin released its fourth eponymous album, colloquially titled *Led Zeppelin IV*, in early November. *IV* would go on to be one of the best-selling albums of 1972 (and one of the best albums to come out of the 1970s, in my opinion, but I'm heavily biased toward Led Zeppelin). In the world of television, CBS cancelled *The Beverly Hillbillies*, *Green Acres*, and *Hee Haw*, all of which would forever live in infamy once the cable network Nickelodeon incorporated them into its "Nick at Nite" lineup in the late 1980s, which is when I remember watching the shows—*The Beverly Hillbillies* was my favorite.

In Viet Nam, things looked like they were winding down. On August 18, Australia and New Zealand announced their intentions to withdraw troops from the war, and, by the end of October, the total number of American troops in Viet Nam dropped to a record low of 196,700. On November 12, President Nixon declared February 1972 a deadline for further U.S. troop withdrawal, requesting the removal of 45,000 troops by the first of the month. Due to stalled peace talks, however, the Nixon administration resumed bombing North Viet Nam in December. The president had planned a historic visit to China for 1972; perhaps he could talk the communists. In a heated conversation with Henry Kissinger on April 6, 1971, Nixon revealed that he was impatient for progress:

> Well, things better start to happen or—you know, I'm—you probably don't believe me, but I can perfectly turn, I'm capable, that is—even on my own, even Haldeman wouldn't know—I'm perfectly capable of turning right awful hard. I never have in my life. But if I found out there was no other way—in other words, hell, if you think Cambodia had flower children fighting, we'll bomb the goddamn North like it's never been bombed…. We'll start doing it, and we'll bomb those bastards, and then let the American people—let this country go up in flames.[10]

President Nixon was not interested in anything the anti-war movement had to say, nor was he interested in the wishes of North Viet Nam; he simply wanted the Viet Nam War to end, preferably in a victorious way ("peace with honor") on *his* watch so he could claim the victory. His threats that he was "capable of turning right awful hard" would prove empty, but it doesn't bode well for a country's morale if its president is willing to let "the American people [and/or] this country go up in flames."

I have only had the privilege of knowing President Richard Milhouse Nixon from history books and films, and he's always portrayed as a very smart but very paranoid man; his "Tricky Dick" nickname lives up to the hype as well. America in 1971 had to bank on him, however, to end the war in Viet Nam. Everyone was tiring of the constant infighting and the relentless news of the war—when would any of it end?

While I'm hesitant to judge a man, I have no problem judging songs about him. The sanctimonious "Battle Hymn of Lt. Calley" shamelessly reiterates tired tropes of pro–Viet Nam War songs, and it peaked at #37 on the Billboard charts, meaning the record did move units, no matter how irritating the song might be. The "scapegoat" (or "hero," depending on one's perspective) of the My Lai massacre undergoes an American mythological reworking: Lieutenant William Calley's story begins with the formulaic opening of a fairy tale.

Set to the melody of "The Battle Hymn of the Republic," the "Battle Hymn of Lt. Calley" juxtaposes the listener's previous experience with "Battle Hymn" with a new American story. According to the song, Lieutenant Calley dutifully pretended, as a child, to be a soldier until he was old enough to become one, just as American mythology prefers. Calley's games of war became a graphic reality in Viet Nam, where he witnessed a lawless frontier and slain brothers in arms. Those in power did not recognize his sacrifice, instead recrafting him as a villain for his service in Viet Nam.

Lieutenant Calley, in song, berates the anti-war protesters, denouncing them for aiding the enemy and not supporting the war effort in Viet Nam. Through his narrative, *they* (the protestors) remain the ones to blame in the chorus, which originally came from 1861. The "Glory, glory, hallelujah; Glory! Glory! Hallelujah, our God is marching on!" refrain from "Battle Hymn of the Republic" is nearly identical to that in "The Battle Hymn of Lt. Calley," except "our God" is replaced with "we" in 1971. In fact, God does not receive a mention at all in "The Battle Hymn of Lt. Calley"; the song's true deity, as revealed by close examination of the lyrics, is American cultural identity. In 1971, God becomes a military officer. Painted as brave (yet weary) defenders of freedom and democracy, the soldiers in this song have no respect for those who "were sounding a retreat" from the war.

American mythology reworks the anti-war narrative from Lieutenant Calley's perspective; the idea of America turning tail and abandoning its duty in war gets blamed on popular anti-war protest cries of "stop the war in Viet Nam" and "give peace a chance" (neither of which really denotes defeat). The "Battle Hymn of the Republic" remains a victorious song in American cultural history—the Brooklyn Tabernacle Choir performed the song at the 2013 presidential inauguration—and its original message still represents irrepressible freedom granted by God ("[God] has sounded forth the trumpet that shall never call retreat"). Furthermore, the song's biblical allusions and links to the Civil War secure its place in America's canon of patriotic songs. "Battle Hymn of Lt. Calley" is formulaic in its intentions and delivery. But an awful lot of people liked it in 1971, and they probably still do. The song helped reconcile the violence Americans had seen on their televisions for nearly 10 years and, for some citizens, fortified their sagging national pride.

13

1972

The Hoa Lo Prison is a "can't miss" tourist attraction in Ha Noi. The white text "Maison Centrale" over the black, arched entry to the prison signals that this site is a relic from the French-occupation era. It got the nickname "Ha Noi Hilton" when American POWs were kept in the prison during the United States' time in Viet Nam, but it was originally a torture chamber the French inflicted upon Vietnamese dissidents. The prison, in its current iteration, is about a fifth the size of what it used to be. The French built it over a preexisting neighborhood, displacing people who'd occupied the area for centuries, so in the 1990s most of the prison was razed in favor of creating Vietnamese homes and businesses. The waxen dummies you find in every Vietnamese history exhibit are here, chained in a row in a dark dungeon. Open a black door, and you'll find the stiff concrete "bed" where General Giap's wife perished; she'd been locked up for fraternizing with those radical freedom fighters. The museum encourages visitors to think of her horrible death as a primary motivator for Giap to fight tirelessly for Vietnamese independence. I'm romantic enough to buy into the story.

At the Ha Noi Hilton in 2019, there was a new display amid the usual stuff I'd seen before in 2012. There was a series of colorful banners illustrating the long fight for independence, as well as a set of banners highlighting humanitarian work done in Ha Noi. One of the humanitarian banners featured Chuck Searcy, which was a fun find. It's neat to see someone you had lunch with on a banner touting a new era of healing between the United States and Viet Nam. During our meeting, Chuck, a native of my current home state (Georgia), spoke softly, slowly, and carefully about the different efforts Viet Nam still must make in order to recover from the wounds of the war. Over a vegetarian smorgasbord (I don't know what I ate, but I know it was good), we covered topics ranging from Agent Orange to UXO to current affairs to growing up in the southern United States. He was less interested in talking about the war and more animated when we spoke about current initiatives, and I got the sense that he felt a deep obligation and desire to give back to Viet Nam, a place from which people usually take.

Ted Engelmann introduced me to Chuck, who returned to Viet Nam in 1995 and has managed to stay ever since. Names I'd only read about were real people in his phonebook, and he has dedicated the bulk of his life to helping Viet Nam heal from the "American War." Chuck's links to Project RENEW, which works to rid the countryside of unexploded ordnance (UXO), as well as his connections to various NGOs working with the aftermath of Agent Orange, speak volumes about his character. Over lunch, I asked him about the Chinese involvement in Viet Nam; on my tour with Thanh, we kept passing factories, which Thanh told me were Chinese owned. Trips to Cambodia, Laos, Zambia and

Inside Ho Loa Prison ("Ha Noi Hilton"), Ha Noi, Viet Nam (2019).

Botswana revealed to me a rather surprising presence of Chinese companies beyond the borders of China. Chuck's point of view was enlightening: he saw the Chinese influence (and use of other countries' national resources and labor force) as a nonviolent way of exerting influence all over the world, particularly in Viet Nam. Considering that 2018 was *the first year* that Project RENEW saw no injuries *or* fatalities from UXO, I like to think that Mr. Searcy knows something of what he's talking about. Plus, he's spent over half of his adult life working to help people whom he once fought a war against; his agenda is peace.

Along Hoan Kiem Lake, pillars denoting Ha Noi as a "city of peace" had been erected since my last visit, complete with soothing images of doves and lotus flowers. The aforementioned new exhibit on Ho Chi Minh in the Museum of Revolution begins with a declaration of Uncle Ho's dedication to Viet Nam, but also to peace. One of the first pieces of the exhibit is a portrait of Ho, flanked by two quotes, one from Romet Chandra, president of the World Peace Council:

> Wherever there is fighting for independence and freedom, there is Ho Chi Minh and his flag flying high. Wherever there is fighting for peace and justice, there is Ho Chi Minh and his flag flying high. Wherever people fight for a new world, against poverty, there is Ho Chi Minh with his flag flying high.

The quote isn't dated, and I had never heard of Romet Chandra before—a quick Google search (in Ha Noi) brought only Vietnamese results. The sole piece of information I could find dated Chandra's influence to 1981, when he was noted as an "interlocuter" of "realist socialism" amid the break between China and Viet Nam over debates of "cultural revolution."[1]

While I will leave the biography of Ho Chi Minh to those who have already written comprehensive books about his life, the man is undeniably interesting. He traveled all over the world, under a variety of names, and even visited the United States (notably Boston). He was descended from Chinese lineage, and his writings reflect a globally influenced vision of an independent Viet Nam. He modeled the Vietnamese constitution after the "life, liberty and pursuit of happiness" made famous by the U.S. founding fathers, but he studied abroad and joined socialist parties in Europe. He dressed humbly, in white, and it's said that he did not take on the role of a father or have a family in order to dedicate himself to the cause of Vietnamese independence. In photos, he's usually smoking a cigarette. His clothing, often displayed, indicates how slight he was, and his wispy beard usually frames a slight smile. By all accounts, he was a benevolent, intelligent guy who really wanted his country to be free.

Ho did not want to be embalmed in the manner of Lenin, but he is, and his body can be viewed at the Ho Chi Minh Mausoleum. Knowing that he did not want this sort of "burial," and because I think embalming people is creepy, I've never been and don't plan on going to gaze at a waxen corpse. I have been to the museum dedicated to him in Ha Noi, and it's impressive and artistic, much more akin to the idea of the man that I've formed in my own head.

As I continued wandering through the newer exhibit at the Hoa Lo Prison, which relied heavily on the themes of "unity and peace," I stumbled upon a curiosity: One of the independence banners read, "The brave fire of Southern students and pupils," and it depicted a group of students—all male—clustered around a sign (in Vietnamese, which I can't really read—however, I know one word, *my*, means "American"). The banner further explained, "In the years of resistance war against the United States to save the country, the youth in the South were enthusiastically engaged in the fierce struggle against the terrorists to take back the peace…. These activities not only attracted the elite people to participate in, but also strengthened the revolution [*sic*]." Respectfully, I must disagree with the banner's misleading positivity. Let's agree that there was definitely some anti–American sentiment in the South (also, quickly: Why is it still capitalized? Does the South capitalize the North?). The "students" in the picture don't look too "enthusiastically engaged" in anything but milling around like students do, but since it's obviously a candid photo, maybe they weren't camera ready. It's interesting that America jumps from being an imperialist to a terrorist as well—when did that happen?

It's hard to trust descriptive placards in the Vietnamese museums. While I'm the first person to concede that there are at least two sides to every story, it's hard to buy one version when you know, quite well, a very different viewpoint. For example, below a photo of smiling POWs, the museum notes, "During the war, the national economy was having difficulties but the Vietnamese created the best living conditions they could for the U.S. pilots. They has a stable life during their temporary detention periods [*sic*]." The language of war is almost laughable in this instance—being taken as a "prisoner of war" flips to a "temporary detention period." We all know that "temporary" is highly subjective; the longest "temporary detention" of an American POW (Floyd J. Thompson) was nearly nine years. Mr. Thompson, furthermore, was notably tortured and starved, representing at least one POW whose life wasn't "stable" or in "the best living conditions." Many other POW stories echo Thompson's. I mean, John McCain certainly didn't have a luxury suite at the Ha Noi Hilton. This staged photo of forced smiles is not indicative of Vietnamese benevolence, but rather of propaganda. The only true statement on the placard is the remark about the "difficulties" war placed on the economy—but that's true of nearly every war, in every era.

◁▷ ◁▷ ◁▷

The war in Viet Nam had become largely an "air war" in 1972. This does not mean there were no ground troops, but rather that the war had entered a new phase. In the United States, the anti-war movement had also entered a new phase: subdued. Due to troop withdrawals in 1971 and 1972, and the Nixon administration's focus on "Vietnamization," there was simply less to protest. That didn't mean protests didn't occur; in October, the U.S. naval carrier USS *Kitty Hawk* was the site of an anti-war protest led by over 200 Black sailors. Other, more random acts of civil disobedience also occurred. In April, Viet Nam War veteran Richard McCoy, Jr. (no relation, so far as I know), hijacked a United Airlines jet and demanded a $500,000 ransom for it. In April, the Broadway musical *Hair* celebrated its fourth anniversary with a free concert in Central Park and a dinner at the Four Seasons Hotel. At the fancy hotel, the show's coauthor and several Black Panthers got arrested for disturbing the peace and smoking marijuana. And, of course, that summer one of the most infamous instances of civil or presidential disobedience in United States history happened: the Watergate break-in.

In mid–January 1972, Mr. Shoichi Tokoi, presumed dead, came out of hiding (a bit inadvertently) in Guam. Tokoi was a Japanese soldier who had known since 1952 that World War II was over but had decided to go into hiding in Guam instead of facing disgrace; he spent 28 years in a self-made cave-hovel enclosure, living off the land in solitude. Now he returned to civilian life in Japan, touring the country and writing a memoir of his time alone. Tokoi's story would fuel legends of long-lost American GIs in Viet Nam in the 1980s.

The POW/MIA (prisoners of war/missing in action) issue would remain a prickly one in the 1970s. In 1972, the National League of Families (founded in 1970) approved the iconic black-and-white flag that you've probably seen—at least on vehicles as a sticker, but perhaps flying—as a symbol for raising awareness of POW/MIA soldiers and their families. American POWs from the Viet Nam War would not be released until 1973, so the league forewent copyrighting the flag, allowing the image to be shared and duplicated as fast as people wanted, which underwrote the league's mission to get POWs returned.

The year kicked off with Melanie's "Brand New Key," the last number-one hit of 1971; the song's infectious, rolling lyrical delivery always made me think it was an advertisement until I started looking at Viet Nam War–era music. The number-one song of 1972 was Roberta Flack's slow-burning "The First Time I Ever Saw Your Face," which I'd sadly known as a cover song. Upon a second listen, Flack's divine voice cuts deep with emotion, but, sonically, the song makes me want to go to sleep; perhaps this sound was indicative of the public's wish to slow things down in 1972, after the breakneck speeds and hairpin cultural and social turns of the 1960s. Spirits of the 1960s remained, however: Shirley Chisholm, New York's 12th Congressional District representative, put her name in the Democratic Party's presidential candidate hat, becoming the first Black woman (and the first woman) to run for office on the ticket. In April, the Boston Marathon allowed women to compete for the first time, though women had run the race (often unofficially or in disguise) prior to the official decision. Alongside the softer rock of 1972, some 1950s

memories crept into the music scene, notably from Don McLean's "American Pie," a tribute to the memories of Buddy Holly, Ritchie Valens, and the Big Bopper, killed in 1959.
The song stayed at number one in the pop charts from mid–January to February, playing in the background during Ireland's Bloody Sunday (when the British army killed civil
rights demonstrators in Derry, Ireland) and the last draft lottery in the United States.
Those selected in the February 2 draft would not be called to serve in Viet Nam.

In Australia, the end of January saw the beginnings of the Aboriginal Tent Embassy,
which is located right in front of the Australian Parliament House in Canberra; when I
went to Australia in 2017, I stayed so long wandering around the Aboriginal Embassy that
I missed my chance to see the Parliament House—I don't regret it. It's interesting that the
Aboriginal Embassy remains up and running almost 50 years after its establishment.

China welcomed President Nixon on February 21 for a historic eight-day visit. When
I was a child, I had a "Presidents of the USA" coloring book, with each president pictured
with some benign factoid to help children remember who each man was; Nixon had a
panda (impeachment wasn't mentioned). The panda only told so much of the story—
President Nixon's meeting with Mao Tse-Tung was a strong-arm move against North Viet
Nam and a strong-man show to the U.S. public: see the hero Nixon, facing the communist
scourge head on! His visit, which overlapped with the Paris Peace Talks with Viet Nam,
did not impress the North Vietnamese. On February 24, representatives from North Viet
Nam walked out of the meeting in protest of air raids. In March, the North launched an
Easter bombing offensive on Quang Tri, Sai Gon, and Pleiku, resulting in the United
States effectively throwing up its hands and putting peace negotiations on hold. By April,
the United States would be bombing North Viet Nam again.

Spring of 1972 sounded pleasant; Neil Young's "Heart of Gold" (admittedly a bit of a
sleeper, but a classic) and America's "A Horse with No Name" hit number one in March
and April, respectively. Both songs shared earthy, "going back to nature" messages of sim-
plification that had been part of the music scene for a couple of years. My first published
book chapter (back in 2010) was an analysis of the Grateful Dead's *Workingman's Dead*
(I grew up with the Dead and am a fan, but on the tiers of Grateful Dead fandom, I am
in the lower rungs; my husband worked with a guy who could identify songs by year
and venue on the Grateful Dead Live channel on satellite radio, and some of my parents' friends followed the band and exchanged cassette tapes of live shows—my devotion
is not that strong). In 1970, the Grateful Dead had released two albums: *Workingman's
Dead* (June 14) and *American Beauty* (November 1). In my chapter,* I argue that *Workingman's Dead* pays tribute to classic images of Americana and capitalizes on the retreat
into nature that many "hippies" made at the turn of the decade. *American Beauty*, I would
argue, continues the message of *Workingman's Dead*. The Grateful Dead never really were
a Billboard Top 100 band; 1987's single "Touch of Grey" made it to number six, but otherwise the band usually stayed below the radar (which I think suited them just fine). However, the Dead's audio influence, as "Heart of Gold" and "A Horse with No Name" testify,
can be heard all over popular music in the 1960s and 1970s, and they should be recognized for that (and listened to—their live performances are magical, and their *Europe '72*
album, released in November 1972, is a great place to start).

As spring turned into summer, the bombing of North Viet Nam continued, under

*Cf. "'Not Just a Change of Style': Reading *Workingman's Dead* as an American Commentary with Americana Roots," in *The Grateful Dead in Concert: Essays on Live Improvisation* (Jefferson, NC: McFarland),
118–26.

names like Operation Linebacker (military mission names deserve their own book, as they always need to convey some symbol or reference to power, fighting, or destruction). In June, however, ARVN troops achieved a strategic victory in the Battle of An Loc, which had begun in April.[2] Did this success prove that the Vietnamization strategy worked? And even if it did, could images like Nick Ut's Pulitzer Prize–winning photo of a girl running naked with napalm burns (published in June) also show another side of the war? Nixon publicly wondered whether the photograph was faked, which Ut quickly denied.[3] When the truth becomes debatable, you know things are getting bad. Many Americans, angered by revelations in the Pentagon Papers, didn't have much faith in the U.S. government anymore.

While the American public debated the war at home, Mister Show Business (aka Sammy Davis, Jr.) scored the hit "The Candy Man." In February, Davis had guest starred on *All in the Family*, leading to a hilarious episode that exploited protagonist Archie Bunker's bigotry to its full effect (you can find it on YouTube; it's a great "race in the 1970s" discussion prompt in classrooms). I adore Sammy Davis, Jr., but it's ironic that a showman like Davis—who supported Nixon—would have the top hit while another showman, President Nixon, was going down. On June 17, at the Watergate building complex in Washington, D.C., five men were arrested for burglary at the offices of the Democratic National Convention. While the full significance of this incident was not immediately apparent, journalists Bob Woodward and Carl Bernstein of the *Washington Post* eventually began to unravel the knots in the Watergate plot, and President Nixon, after attempting outrageous abuses of power, would eventually resign as president of the United States.

But all was not lost yet. The Democrats (who'd nominated South Dakota senator George McGovern as their presidential candidate) ran on anti-war rhetoric, which gained favor with younger voters, who were now a larger demographic due to the 26th Amendment. Simon and Garfunkel would even reunite for one performance as part of the McGovern campaign. Conservatives stood with Nixon, directing patriotic anger at recent photos of actress Jane Fonda posing on a North Vietnamese anti-aircraft tank. Bill Withers' classic soul single "Lean on Me" climbed to the top of the charts in July, but by the time that the Republican National Convention nominated President Nixon and Vice President Spiro Agnew for reelection, the soft rock elevator music of "Alone Again (Naturally)" by Gilbert O'Sullivan gained the top spot in the Billboard charts. At the start of the fall season, the first episodes of both *The Price Is Right* and *M*A*S*H* aired, and Ted Dabney and Nolan Bushnell founded a company called Atari, Inc.; the rise of the video game would double down on the power of television in the 1970s and 1980s, paving the way for popular home gaming systems like Nintendo and PlayStation.

In early October, Le Duc Tho and Henry Kissinger made headway in the Paris Peace Talks. Kissinger, a week before the 1972 election, declared, "We believe peace is at hand. We believe that an agreement is within sight,"[4] at a news conference. The "peace at hand" statement, plus Nixon's revoking of the draft and, happily, a strong economy, helped hand the election to Nixon, who won in an 18 million vote landslide and became the first Republican to "sweep the south."[5] A week after the election, the United States gave the Long Binh Base to the South Vietnamese military in a powerful move—perhaps the war really was ending! But then peace talks stalled, mostly due to the Nixon administration's decision to exclude South Vietnamese President Thieu from the U.S. agreements with North Viet Nam. Stuck between an ally and an enemy, Nixon gave in to Thieu—and dropped bombs. The "Christmas Bombing" of 1972 was twelve days of the most concentrated bombing in world history.... American planes flew nearly 2,000 sorties and dropped 35,000 tons of bombs against transportation terminals, rail yards, warehouses, barracks, oil tanks, factories, airfields and power plants in the North. In two short weeks, 25 percent of North Vietnam's oil reserves and 80 percent of its electrical capacity were destroyed. The U.S. lost 26 aircraft and 93 air force men.[6]

This move did not win Nixon any new fans in Viet Nam, and it was a costly loss of American lives as well. One of the sticking points of the peace talks—the release of POWs—motivated part of the bombing blitz. Another was the Nixon administration's sheer frustration with the North, which simply would not *give in* to U.S. demands (the North wanted the United States *out* of Viet Nam, but America would only commit to partial withdrawal, for example). But like it or not, the bombing worked out for the United States; peace accords would be signed in January 1973.

The last three musical hits of 1972—"Papa Was a Rollin' Stone" (the Temptations), "I Am Woman" (Helen Reddy), and "Me and Mrs. Jones" (Billy Paul)—varied by message and music styling. "Papa Was a Rolling Stone" is blues funk, while "I Am Woman" was a soft-rock feminist anthem. "Me and Mrs. Jones," a soul song that is more funny than good, detailed an illicit affair—surprising content for a Top 40 hit. Dick Clark's very first *New Year's Rockin' Eve* rang out 1972, featuring Helen Reddy, Al Green, and Three Dog Night. With hopes of moving toward peace in a decades-long conflict, the United States moved cautiously toward 1973.

President Nixon was tired of the Viet Nam War in 1972. In February, after the annual National Prayer Breakfast, Nixon fumed about the war to small audience that included the Reverend Billy Graham. Lamenting his legacy, Nixon claimed the whole thing could have been "flushed down the drain three years ago," with the blame on Kennedy and Johnson. While bemoaning the fact that, if things had gone his way, he'd be "the national hero," Nixon grumped, "Sure, the North Vietnamese would have probably slaughtered and castrated two million South Vietnamese Catholics, but nobody would have cared."[7] It is likely that Nixon's words hold a grain of truth; for all the caterwauling about the Viet Nam War, not many Americans even knew where it was or the history of the country before the United States got involved in the French colonial melee. Furthermore, once the United States was in Viet Nam, it made little effort to get to know the country beyond bomb targets and strategic positions. No one knew the language, and while soldiers were given field guides with some cultural instruction, most were afraid of the Vietnamese people, who could be friend or foe at any given moment.

Nixon did care about getting the POWs back; it sticks in any leader's craw if they know another country is holding their citizens hostage. Raging to Kissinger in April 1972, Nixon promised to "bomb the bejesus" out of North Viet Nam and told Kissinger that morale would be better if soldiers were told, "Boys, here's your chance to be heroes. I want you to knock out everything. These bastards have got your buddies [POWs] up there, and they haven't turned them loose. Now punish them!" While I can get behind this outburst to some extent (yes, let's get our boys and bring 'em home!), the "knock out everything" line feels excessive. Nixon finished his instructions with the chilling "I wouldn't worry about a little slop-over ... knock off a few villages and hamlets,"[8] which only serves to ratchet up a cruelty that—well, perhaps cruelty is required for war, but Nixon's words sound hateful and spiteful, not those of a man who really cares about the country he's mired in war with or the Americans under his leadership. And maybe he doesn't have to.

But what if another nation's leader were recorded saying these things about the United States? Americans would be appalled. I've seen the looks on my students' faces when I show them a clip, from a Dutch documentary on North Korea, in which a North Korean mother sings a "down with the bastard Americans" type of song to her child; my students' faces harden and their posture stiffens—it's an immediate identification of an enemy, without knowing much about that enemy at all. The humanity of war is so often left out of the larger machine of it, and in Nixon's remarks humanity is left out entirely. The "boys" who could have been heroes were people, not tools to stun the enemy. The Vietnamese people were *people*, not just "these little brown people, so far away,"[9] as Nixon rendered them; to the Nixon administration, the Vietnamese were an inferior "other" to the mighty United States and its military-industrial complex. There was no humanity to be saved—only an idea of democracy (of which Nixon, who could be so inhuman, was one of the worst examples).

The humanity argument can go both ways, though; Viet Nam also pushed its "boys" to be "heroes," but not for each other—for a revolution, for independence, for (to be honest) communism. Viet Nam celebrated the "American imperialist" failures, and the Vietnamese were not known as fair fighters or benevolent captors (and some of their leaders' remarks and actions were just as cruel as the comments Nixon made about the Viet Nam War and the Vietnamese people). For every mutilated American corpse in stories of the war, there's a Vietnamese one to be had as well; nobody really wins anything in war. But like the North Korean obsession with the USS *Pueblo*—a tourist attraction designed to show North Korea's cunning might against the American aggressor—some of Viet Nam's representations of the war fall flat. In Ha Noi, for example, the "Historical Vestige" of a crashed American B-52 is simply annoying—yes, the pilot lived, but what does rusting metal rubble in a pond really tell us about the war? Nothing around the site even references the horrors of the Christmas bombing; why is it there?

The spot where a B-52 was famously downed in 1972 is in a family neighborhood, which prompts a moment of queasiness: Why was the United States bombing residential areas of Ha Noi? Or was it residential then? Was there an ammo dump or something here before? Huu Tiep Lake is more like a pond, and the plane's wheel (as well as a brass sign on a concrete pillar) is the only thing that distinguishes it from being a pile of metal in a pond. Across the street, Café B-52 (clever) beckons me to get another gallon of water, as it's June and sweat rolls down my back while I'm standing still. The woman who gets the water for me is pleasant enough but returns to her phone. She's a little older than me and playing what looks like Candy Crush. I stare at the plane and wish I could speak more than a handful of Vietnamese words; I want to ask the Café B-52 lady what she thinks of the plane, of living and working in a neighborhood with a war relic jutting out of an otherwise placid body of water. I wonder whether anyone she knows was part of the story of what happened when the plane went down: a neighborhood man helped the pilot out of the wreckage, saving the pilot's life. But that's the human side of the story—what's left is just a hunk of metal posing as a free tourist attraction or historic landmark.

The human side of the story can be painful, but it can also be illuminating. Back in 2015, when I went to visit the My Lai site, my tour guide Thanh told me a story about earning money from scrap metal left over from the war. When heavy rains fell, he and his friends would go to sandy creek beds to gather spent shell casings that rose to the surface of the soil. They would then sell the metal. Thanh and I were nearly the same age, and, in a strange way, our childhoods mirrored each other. Remembering U.S. culture in the 1980s usually recalls images of MTV, space launches, and Wall Street hedonism. But I remember the decade as a fairly sparse one in terms of economics; there was a recession. Consumerism, restricted to catalogs and physical shopping, had yet to blossom into the massive industry the internet brought later. Thanh's life was far less consumer-based; his money was spent on sugarcane juice (the hands-down best beverage for putting electrolytes back into your body). He described how he interpreted land reform of the 1980s: "A bell rang, you eat breakfast and go to the fields. A bell rings and you eat lunch, then go back to work; a bell rings and you go home and eat dinner." The design of this system echoes anything you might've read about the equalizing goals of communism: everyone who farms does the same thing and receives the same pay, and the land is owned by the state, so your work doesn't get marred by taxes and the clutter of deeds and other such nonsense. But, as Thanh pointed out to me, the bell could ring and people sometimes wouldn't go to work. So, quite quickly, the Vietnamese learned that this method of governance wasn't going to work that well. It should also be mentioned that not all people want to be farmers. Economic change and reform were inevitable, so when Viet Nam opened itself back up to foreign trade in the 1990s, entrepreneurship (which definitely existed before, during, and after the American War) came back in a big, albeit less criminal, way.

14

1973

The Ho Chi Minh Museum in Sai Gon (Ho Chi Minh City) suits the Vietnamese revolutionary. It is humble but bright. The structure is a yellow building, painted pagoda-style with colorful dragons swooping down the roof, but more French in architecture. The museum is flanked by lots of immaculately groomed trees. Some 20th-century additions (like a massive, underused car park) feel forced. As I was combing through my photos, I realized that this was one of the sites I visited during my short "broken phone" era, so I don't have my own photos of my visit.

But I remember the Ho Chi Minh Museum; while only about a 15-minute walk from my hotel, I made several detours. I also had to cross a pretty busy highway, though luckily the off and on ramps weren't very bustling. En route to HCMC's Ho Chi Minh Museum, I went by the Ton Duc Thang Museum—a quaint tribute to the second (after Ho Chi Minh died) and last (because the country unified) president of North Viet Nam. Thang's museum was better ventilated than Ho's, but not nearly as exhaustively researched.

The museum's location is a bit strange and away from a lot of the other sites that the city is known for in the Ben Thanh area. It's also across the river from the Sai Gon Skydeck, a high-rise skyscraper bar and photo-op spot that I have yet to visit, but I hear it's very fun. Most hotels offer vouchers for "$3 happy hour" specials there; I would call it a tourist trap. The Ho Chi Minh Museum is decidedly not, however; the inside of the museum is not as manicured as the outside, and it also doesn't push the same decisive ethos of the Ho Chi Minh Museum in Ha Noi—it's more of a collection of Uncle Ho's life, with copious photos and letters, as well as predictable artifacts (cigarette case, Ho's tiny shirt).

There is always a great deal of emphasis placed on the sacrifices that Ho Chi Minh made in order to lead Viet Nam to independence and freedom. He notably never married (well, there's evidence he did marry, but that's not the story that Viet Nam likes to tell), forsaking a family and instead taking on Viet Nam as a whole as his family. Family is a big deal in Viet Nam and many other Asian cultures; filial piety and ancestor worship only work when you have children. Ho is often pictured with youth—little kids, school children waving flags, teenage soldiers, and so on—as part of Viet Nam's government campaigns. And it always looks as though Ho was never a child himself in museum renderings; his youth is a blip in the overall story. Much about his childhood is blurry and unknown, and while I love Viet Nam, I don't always trust the government to tell me the whole story about him. He is on the money, his face on banners and placards in every city, town, and airport—he is no longer a human being, but rather an icon of freedom, a martyr for the cause of independence and the proverbial "father" of Viet Nam.

What's interesting to me about Ho Chi Minh is how much of the world he saw. He left Viet Nam at some point in 1911 as a chef, under a false name, on a steamship. He was 21. Or 22, 23, or 24—his exact birth year is hazy, as Ho Chi Minh used perhaps 50 pseud-onyms throughout his young adult years. The reasons behind why he left Viet Nam are subjects of Vietnamese folklore: it has been said that his father's refusal to work for the French government inspired him to revolutionize, but perhaps (or also?) his involve-ments, however dubious, with student protests radicalized him. No matter the impetus, we know Ho spent time in the United States, the United Kingdom, Belgium, Switzerland, Germany, Thailand, India, France, Hong Kong, China, and Russia. That's a lot of traveling in an era when boats and trains were the primary means of transport.

Using my own experiences as a template, Ho Chi Minh's worldview would have grown and changed as he saw more of the world. Despite reading his collected writ-ings, I don't really see evidence of that evolution in his thinking. Instead, Ho Chi Minh was a dedicated student of communism, studying in China and Russia, stirring up dust in Hong Kong (which was under British rule at the time), and generally learning about socioeconomics and political movements. He sounds like a pretty smart, rabble-rousing guy, and it's obvious he thought about Viet Nam's predicament thoroughly, even though he spent 30 years away from it. Taking advantage of Japan's invasion of Viet Nam in 1941 (as part of World War II), Ho returned to Viet Nam and started working with the Viet Minh, guerrilla independence fighters who fought the Vichy French and Japanese invad-ers. It was during this time that Ho became involved with the United States' precursor to the CIA, the Office of Strategic Services (OSS). He would later get more involved with the OSS, in addition to receiving treatment for malaria from them, in 1945. This piece of Ho's past always fascinates me: His alliance with the United States during World War II apparently meant little to the United States, and their dismissive treatment of him later reminds me of a soap opera. President Franklin Delano Roosevelt and Ho Chi Minh did communicate, and Roosevelt, preoccupied with World War II, assured Ho he'd get to him after things settled down. But Roosevelt died and Harry S. Truman became president, and Truman simply hated anything communist. Ho's links to Russia and China, in Tru-man's view, meant any line to the White House that Ho might've had was now severed.

Ho spent a considerable amount of time, as part of the Viet Minh, stamping out any political party that he and his cadre deemed unfit for Viet Nam. Trotskyites (communists with a taste for global revolution), for example, were immediately subdued, as Ho Chi Minh wasn't interested in all the workers around the globe rising up; he just wanted the Vietnamese workers to rise up against the French colonial powers, and then the British, and then the United States—anyone having anything to do with suppressing Vietnam-ese freedom (the Ho Chi Minh–style view of it, anyway) were enemies of the Viet Minh.

The better Ho Chi Minh Museum is the one in Ha Noi. It's modern, with interac-tive exhibits and unusual, modern light installations alongside quotes and artistic takes on Ho Chi Minh. A statue of Ho waves, as always, from atop a staircase, benevolent and bearded. Many museums (not limited to those dedicated to Ho) include Ho Chi Minh's clothing. Ho was so tiny, it's absurd. That's the bigger takeaway I have from frequent-ing these sites: How did someone so physically small harness the power to liberate his country from an oppressive colonial regime as well as "American imperialists" (or so the placards read)? Ho Chi Minh's modest, simple, and petite cotton shirts remind me of someone like Olympian gymnast Simone Biles: a pint-sized fighter. Ho was often filmed walking among soldiers in villages, playing with children—perhaps under his simple brown knickers were quads of steel, propelling him ever forward on his singular mission. But I sell him and Biles short; what moves great people to greatness is usually their heart. Ho Chi Minh's heart (in spite of the whole "communist!" thing that Americans are taught to despise) was large and open, full of purpose and an ambition larger than himself. Maybe I've been brainwashed by all the things I've seen and experienced in Viet Nam, where Ho's image is imprinted on everything from the country's currency to signs, but I have a very soft place in my heart for the little man with the big ideas.

I won't ruin the War Remnants Museum for you and tell you everything that's in there. That would be unfair. It's a pleasant walk from my beloved hotel in Sai Gon, and it's a general must-do for most people going to Sai Gon. You definitely see more people at the War Remnants Museum than, say, the Viet Nam Military History Museum or Museum of Revolution in Ha Noi, from all over the world. It's in a sleepy little pocket of town, near Tao Dan Park and the Reunification Palace, and if you still have an appetite after visiting, there's plenty of food to choose from in the surrounding area. The museum became the War Remnants Museum in 1995; it was initially called the "Exhibition House for US and Puppet Crimes" when it opened in 1975, and then it was later upgraded to the "Exhibition House for Crimes of War and Aggression" in 1990. When U.S.–Vietnamese trade relations improved, the museum dropped the "crimes" and "aggression" titles—on the outside, anyway. Inside is a different story.

The museum is on the corner of Nguyen Dien Chieu and Le Quy Don streets, taking up most of the block with its imposing, somewhat communist bloc–style main building as well as an internal compound that houses "tiger cages," U.S. planes and helicopters (like a Huey), and pieces of UXO steering you into the space itself. As an American, it does not feel good walking among tourists taking selfie-stick portraits or family photos amid your country's old machinery; I kept an eye on a family of five (German or

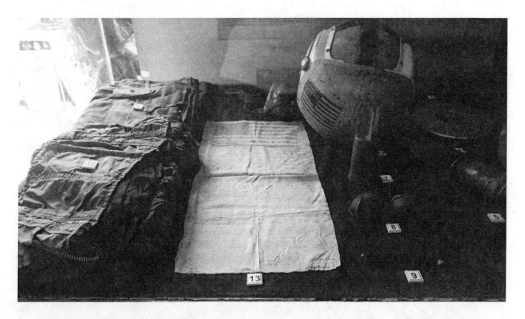

Display of U.S. artifacts, War Remnants Museum, Ho Chi Minh City, Viet Nam (2017).

Austrian) while a man missing half of his left arm tried to talk me into buying a book. I bought his book, and I listened to his broken English story about his wartime experience (he looked too young to be a veteran, but I'm not the best at guessing ages); he was nice, but I could tell this was a rehearsed speech for all the tourists, especially Americans. I didn't want to hide the fact that I was from the United States on any of my visits to any part of Viet Nam, but I sort of did after going through the museum. As I walked in, the family of five laughed heartily, posing for a humorous photo next to a Patton tank. A knee-jerk reaction inside my head muttered coldly, "Yeah, that tank's funny now, wasn't so funny in 1944." I felt defensive. My puerile "fuck you, 'Murica!" attitude would fade as I walked through the museum.

On my first visit to the museum, because of the one-armed man, I skipped over the outdoor torture exhibits (there's also a French guillotine). There are three floors to the museum, and I always opt to start from the top and work my way down. It's a metaphor for what happens to your self-worth, as an American, while going through the museum. On the top floor, scores of photographs depict the American military doing despicable things to the Vietnamese, like tying the still-breathing body of a suspected Viet Cong soldier to the back of a tank and dragging it through the jungle.

I've seen rotating exhibits on worldwide anti-war protest, Japanese photography of "American crimes," and an extended cut of the perils of Agent Orange, which also has a permanent space in the museum. In 2015, the first time I visited, an Agent Orange temporary exhibit occupied the first floor, complementing its fixed counterpart on the second floor. Since I'd started from the top of the museum and worked my way down, I'd gone further and further down the rabbit hole of "war guilt." By the time I reached the atrocities of Agent Orange—birth defects, physical deformities, generational damages—I felt like I was going to throw up from "American" guilt. I wasn't the only "Western"-looking person in the museum, and I know I heard other American accents, but I was in the War Remnants Museum alone. And this museum's ethos is basically: *We finally won against evil*. In the War Remnants' narrative, Americans are "the evil." The guestbooks—strategically placed on each floor—beat me even more into the guilt pit. Here are some examples transcribed from photos I took in 2015:

- "So so awful. Totally evil and unnecessary. I feel proud that I stood against the war in London in the 1970s. I have an American cousin who fought. I wonder how he sleeps at night?" (Thailand)
- "America! Donald Trump! A very dangerous country, intolerant and aggressive. Stay in America and don't touch the beautiful world." (unsigned)
- "Such a crime!—The whole American War in Viet Nam. But Agent Orange remains the worst chemical war crime in the world." (VFP Member, San Francisco)
- "The war makes us no longer human. We forget we bleed the same blood. No one deserves the suffering of war and no one has the right to relentlessly end others lives. May we live in a world without wars." (China)
- "When will Americans ever learn?" (unsigned)
- "I did hate the US. I hate the US. I still hate the US for what they did." (Bangladesh)

It was all so wretched that I skipped through the last part of the museum, which was an homage to the positive relationship between Cuba and Viet Nam.

I was able to hold back my tears until I'd crossed the streets (and past the men hustling transport services: "Hey, motorbike? You need taxi?"), and then tears started to run under my sunglasses. I walked fast with my head down, which made it easier to navigate the walkway's uneven concrete. Within two blocks of the museum, I realized I should probably check my map before plowing through the streets. When I looked up to see where I might duck over and surreptitiously check directions, I saw a man selling puppies out of a box. They were fuzzy, black and gray chow-like mutts. Mr. Puppy Seller was leaning on his motorbike, smoking a cigarette and talking to someone who'd pulled over on a motorbike. I walked over, picked up a puppy, and sobbed into its fur. Passersby looked at me, alarmed, and then quickly looked away. After a few minutes, I put the puppy down, pet its littermates, and waved at Mr. Puppy Seller, who had politely let me cry on his product. He smiled and gestured for me to buy the puppy. I skittered away to my hotel by way of the Circle K that sold Budweiser. Numbing my head with Marlboros and beer at the hotel's cushy outdoor seating area, I emailed my friend Jim, who's a writer, poet, and Viet Nam veteran. He'd been to the museum before, and his reaction had also been to go for the alcohol. And, because I am aware that we all must beware of "white girl tears," let me emphasize that the pain in reading those statements and the sobbing into the puppy were all about the state of the world and how horrible the United States can be perceived, both at home and internationally. I cried because I didn't know how to help.

So, should you, fellow traveler, go to the War Remnants Museum? Yes. My husband met me in Viet Nam two days after my second visit to the museum, and guess where he wanted to go first while in Sai Gon? On that visit, while my husband checked out the tiger cages, I met Richard di San Marzano, who was running a little art store nearby. Finding a captive audience, this delightful British-Italian man talked to me and my husband for an hour, introducing us to the niche world of Vietnamese propaganda art. What interested him, I remember, were the sketches on the backs of the original pieces, indicating the classical art training and individual styles of the artists who were chained to the aesthetic of the state. And he was hilariously witty; he could tell I was feeling low from the museum's heavy content and teased me out of the doldrums. Maybe everyone should go twice; the horrors of war, wave after wave of it, and in relation to your country, are difficult to take. I hear the Hiroshima Peace Memorial Museum in Japan is a pretty rough experience for American visitors too, but so was the Auschwitz-Birkenau Memorial Museum (Poland) for me and everyone else. I cried there and at the Anne Frank House (the Netherlands); war, stripped of nationalism, is simply hell. But I think it's important to go to these places, because, if nothing else, visiting the War Remnants Museum shows us how brutal and gory war is. Losses, not heroics, are the focus of each floor—there are other museums in Viet Nam that glorify those things, but this museum's purpose to remind us why war should be the last resort anywhere.

War wasn't the main thing on Americans' minds in 1973. At the presidential palace in Sai Gon, there are multiple photos of Henry Kissinger talking to various Vietnamese leaders; he is portrayed as an honest diplomat. I have wondered whether anything similar exists at the Hotel Majestic in Paris (not likely). U.S. involvement in Viet Nam "ended" (we would still hang around for another couple of years, but our military forces were no longer engaged in advising or fighting) on January 27 with the signing of the Paris Peace Accords. By early February, the first wave of American POWs was released, and the last U.S. combat soldier left Viet Nam on March 29, 1973.

The United States was moving on from Viet Nam. In August, DJ Kool Herc would "invent" hip-hop in the Bronx, New York City. Classic films like *The Exorcist* and *The Sting* would top the box offices by the end of the year, and Billie Jean King would beat Bobby Riggs in the exhibition tennis match dubbed "The Battle of the Sexes" in September. In world engineering feats news, the Sydney Opera House and the Bosphorus Bridge in Turkey both opened in 1973. As President Nixon was sworn into his second term in the White House (the first person to be sworn in as both vice president and president—twice—until Joe Biden in 2021), the top song on the radio was Carly Simon's "You're So Vain," a rollicking kiss-off to a narcissistic lover.

The number-one hit in the United States for 1973 was "Tie a Yellow Ribbon ('Round the Old Oak Tree")" by Dawn featuring Tony Orlando. While in contemporary American culture, a yellow ribbon immediately brings to mind the "support our troops" ribbons and car magnets that became popular during American involvement in the Middle East, the song's lyrics are about a man coming home from prison, not war. The narrator requests that his love tie a ribbon around the oak tree in front of their home as a sign that she's willing to take him back. It's a sweet enough song, but too soft rock–country sounding for my taste; February's "Superstition" (Stevie Wonder) and "Crocodile Rock" (Elton John) are more my speed. Americans had a variety of music tastes in 1970, per the charts, but also beyond them; in January alone, Kiss performed its first show and Aerosmith released its first album.

At the end of January, the Supreme Court ruled that state bans on abortion were unconstitutional, per *Roe v. Wade*, paving the way for women to have the right to control their bodies—well, paving the way for women to try to control their bodies while overly conservative (white) men fight them tooth and nail, at least. Also, at the end of January, former president Lyndon Johnson died at the age of 64 at his ranch in Texas; he had been out of office for only four years. Roberta Flack's gorgeous "Killing Me Softly" topped the charts by March, and Pink Floyd released *Dark Side of the Moon* on March 1, introducing progressive rock to the masses and becoming one of the best-selling albums of all time. The animated children's movie *Charlotte's Web* also arrived in March 1973.

At the end of March, the Watergate scandal sizzled with new information involving the directorial role that former attorney general John Mitchell played in the scandal, which was still a developing story. The remaining American POWs were released by March, and April's *Catch a Fire*, the fifth album by the Wailers, put reggae on the map as a musical genre. As Led Zeppelin embarked on a grand tour of the United States in May 1973, a band with similar hard edges, the Edgar Winter Group, scored a hit with the psychedelic–hard rock mix instrumental jam "Frankenstein."

In May, the American Indian Movement (AIM) and federal authorities ended a 71-day standoff at the Pine Ridge Reservation at Wounded Knee, South Dakota. The "Wounded Knee Occupation" stemmed from the frustrations of the Oglala Lakota people, who lived at Pine Ridge, with their tribal chairman, Dick Wilson, whose poor leadership was also racist, corrupt, and nepotistic. In an article memorializing Russell Means, an AIM leader who passed away in 2012, demonstrators at Wounded Knee recalled the harrowing events that stemmed from their peaceful protest:

To many observers, the standoff resembled the Wounded Knee Massacre of 1890 itself—when a U.S. cavalry detachment slaughtered a group of Lakota warriors who refused to disarm. Some of the protesters also had a more current conflict in mind. As one former member of AIM told PBS, "They were shooting machine gun fire at us, tracers coming at us at nighttime just like a war zone. We had some Vietnam vets with us, and they said, 'Man, this is just like Vietnam.'"[1]

The protesters surrendered after the Oglala Lakota persuaded AIM to stand down. Wilson would remain in power, and in the three-year wake of the protest, Pine Ridge boasted the highest per-capita murder rate in the country.[2] Native Americans, like Blacks, Chicanos, Puerto Ricans, and other minorities in the United States, remained poorly treated throughout the 1970s as the new decade tried to learn the civil rights lessons of the 1960s.

Come June, the "Summer Jam at Watkins Glen," featuring the Allman Brothers Band and the Grateful Dead, attracted 600,000 people to the Watkins Glen Grand Prix Raceway in upstate New York. Former Beatle Paul McCartney (with Wings, "My Love") and George Harrison ("Give Me Love [Give Me Peace on Earth]") made summertime hits in 1973, along with Jim Croce (the hilarious "Bad, Bad Leroy Brown") and Marvin Gaye (the classic "Let's Get It On"). By fall, Gladys Knight and the Pips released the legendary "Midnight Train to Georgia," which preceded another former Beatle hit, Ringo Starr's "Photograph."

In November, Congress reined in presidential powers with the War Powers Resolution (or War Powers Act). Essentially, Congress insisted that presidents consult Congress before deploying armed forces abroad; the Viet Nam War had taught the House and Senate that congressional approval should be part of the war equation—the president could not just send the troops out. President Nixon tried to veto the resolution, but Congress checked him. While Congress put together the Endangered Species Act of 1973, the president signed the Trans-Alaska Pipeline Authorization Act, which set in motion the construction of the Trans-Alaska Pipeline. The year 1973 ended relatively quietly, compared to the Christmas Bombing of 1972. The last number-one hit of 1973 on the Billboard charts was the appropriately sedate Jim Croce's minstrel-like love song, "Time in a Bottle."

I read an AP article recently about a painter embedded with the North Vietnamese Army. His paintings centered around those moving through the Ho Chi Minh Trail. Alongside a serious portrait of the artist (as well as North Vietnamese troops slogging through the jungle looking heartily determined) were some of the paintings. Watercolor and faded, they depict troops carrying on with the Lunar New Year (Tet) holiday. The article, published in the *South China News*, was filled with a kind of communist-y rhetoric, with special emphasis on the knowledge the Vietnamese had of the land and how they ate heartily off the roughage of the terrain while the Americans had C-rations flown in—that sort of stuff.

Because I study the Viet Nam War, I have willingly exposed myself to a lot of things that are, frankly, dissing America. It can be hard; most of us don't like admitting we as *individuals* did anything wrong ever, much less our entire country. It's hard to say sorry. And we, the United States, did some things worth being sorry for in Viet Nam. I don't think many people will quibble with that particular assertion. The massacre at My Lai. The lack of support post–1972 for our allies, the ARVN. The muddled evacuation and fall of Sai Gon. When having those conversations, it seems strange to ask: What value does art have in all this? What role do *depictions* of war play in our individual and collective memory?

Wandering through museums dedicated to the Viet Nam War, as with any museum dedicated to one theme, you will get bored. I've experienced a sort of museum burnout before, in Italy, where art and museums weave into the architecture and cinematic views of the countryside. I studied in Orvieto, Italy, for a month while getting my master's. It was one of the best times of my life, but, in this instance, I want to emphasize how this trip conditioned me for history, museums, and so forth. Our class spent a weekend in Florence and a few days in Rome; we quickly learned, while following our intrepid leader, that she was prepared to traverse as much of Italy as possible. We *had* to see all the art we possibly could. Dr. Alma Bennett didn't seem to tire of Renaissance art; she didn't seem to tire at all as she misread a map and reversed us 20 minutes to the left or dismissed *vaporettos* (waterbuses) in Venice in favor of us lugging our belongings up and over canal after canal. We saw many triptychs of fluffy white people, naked and eyes lifted toward the heavens. We craned our necks in the Sistine Chapel; we saw every rendition of David (the Michelangelo David is impressive, while the Donatello one has a funny hat) and marveled at the depictions of heaven and hell rendered in mosaic form. We gazed at portraits of men in frilly blouses and permed hair. And, while they don't bother me in any real way, statues or paintings of naked people—which is one of the hallmarks of a lot of eras of Roman art—get a bit tedious after a while. That's why Dr. Bennett poked fun at me at the Guggenheim in Venice—there, in the sinking city sitting atop submerged ruins, was modern art! I was visibly more animated and engaged with the new, strange art. It's one of the only museums where I bought a print.

Dr. Bennett lost her brother in Viet Nam. He died in the early years, I believe in an aircraft accident. The world lost her about ten years ago to a quick and harsh form of cancer. A draft of a piece of her doctoral portfolio—I call it a painting—hangs over my desk at work. Dr. Bennett combined classical composition (she was also a gifted pianist) with art she'd made in response to the war and her brother. The piece I have is slashes of blue and blue-black paint, under which some German opera lyrics are pasted. It looks painful, but also steady and firm. I never got to talk to Dr. Bennett about her brother; I only heard about him when she'd mention him in stories. There was always so much else to talk about with her—she was a delightful and remarkable woman.

I think even Dr. Bennett would get war-museum-weary with Viet Nam. The Ho Chi Minh Museum in Ha Noi is a good antidote to war-museum fatigue, mostly because of its ultra-modern displays. The museums I go to often think every bit of war hero ephemera—shrapnel, a button, a teacup—needs labeling and display. But what constitutes memory and art beyond tangible artifacts?

Some bits of the past that stuck around can be found in art. During my third visit to the War Remnants Museum in Sai Gon, I met (as I mentioned earlier in this chapter) Richard di San Marzano. Talking to him felt like talking to a sparkler: fizzy and quick, bright and crackling, but shining with new information. Richard, whom I've spoken to a few times since our meeting (thanks, Facebook), is the person I must thank for introducing me to art from the Viet Nam War.

When Lenin famously declared, "Art is not art unless it is propaganda," it is doubtful that he foresaw the artistic developments created by Vietnamese propaganda artists during the Viet Nam War. Under the guise of propaganda, Vietnamese artists created their works "quickly and in the field—paints and paper were often scarce [so] many [Vietnamese] posters from that time are produced on the back of any spare material, including maps and Soviet bloc posters."[3] The artists maintained a sense of individuality, courage, and aesthetic integrity while also helping out with the war effort. Many were classically trained, and evidence of their art school studies can often be found on the backs of original propaganda materials. Furthermore—and most interesting, considering the nature of propaganda art—these artists often signed their names or placed an individual signature or mark on their work.

Proud to be helping the war effort in some way, most Vietnamese propaganda artists were not aware that their art would be viewed as propaganda. Pham Thanh Tam, an artist interviewed for *Revolutionary Spirit: Vietnamese Propaganda Art from the Dogma Collection* (an exhibition held at the Ho Chi Minh City Fine Arts Museum in April 2015), "simply thought of [his art] as a means to help the public understand."[4] What artists understood about the Viet Nam War as individuals provides an example of unique human artistic expression, especially during an international conflict and in the brutal realities of war. Furthermore, these art pieces comment on a universal desire for bravery and the dominance of the human spirit and experience despite adversity.

So who were these artists? Resolute individuals, as their self-portraits suggest, but also committed freedom fighters. The majority of artists involved in creating propaganda for the unification of Viet Nam—as well as the end to the American War—saw their work as physical representations of the ideas of liberation and freedom. One painter featured in the Dogma Collection, Nguyen Thu, quoted Ho Chi Minh when asked what his role as an artist represented to him during the Viet Nam War: "Artists are also soldiers, soldiers on the culture front."[5] Another artist interviewed for the Dogma Collection's *Revolutionary Spirit* exhibit, Trung Be, elaborated on the idea of artists as soldiers of culture:

> I want to say propaganda posters have historical values, artistic values and political values in particular times. Therefore, we should respect them, and make the later generation understand the grand history of our forefathers. In terms of artistic value, particularly on the subject matter and style of propaganda posters, we can say that Vietnamese artists had proudly contributed a great deal to the resistance against France and America.[6]

It has long been debated whether art has any value or merit if it is politically charged, but the artists involved in Vietnamese propaganda creation believe their work to be historical artifacts and personal contributions to the war effort. And while propaganda art often works under imposed themes and messages, the ideas communicated by this art resonate beyond the historical document.

Cultural critic Herbert Marcuse argued that while "art has its own language and illuminates reality only through this other language,"[7] art remains bound to the historical and social denominators surrounding its creator and milieu. Marcuse called this phenomenon *Lebenswelt* and contended that art is able to transcend *Lebenswelt* the viewer's perspective collides with it, rendering art both "same" and "other" in terms of how the viewer perceives the art. Art, per Marcuse, reveals and conceals hidden truths about the human experience, particularly when tragedy is involved—and war is arguably pretty tragic on the grander scale of human experiences. Art can escape its *Lebenswelt* through its "reconstruction of society and nature under the principle of increasing human potential for happiness. The revolution is for the sake of life, not death. Here is the perhaps most profound kinship between art and revolution."[8]

The messages of Vietnamese propaganda art do indeed often point toward the hope for a better world, underscoring the belief that, for the Vietnamese, peace and unity were hopes represented in art that "ought not to remain mere ideal."[9] Much of Vietnamese propaganda art, following Marcuse's opinions, represented hope for a better tomorrow—a vision that the artists insisted could be realized with their assistance. Perhaps the trials of the times that create art remain inescapable and so terrifying that they must be part of the artistic record in order for a hopeful future to be imagined. George Orwell, in an address on the BBC radio series *Listener* in May 1941, noted that writers working in 1930 and onward "have been living in a world in which not only one's life but one's whole scheme of values is constantly menaced"[10]; while Orwell spoke to the aesthetic dilemmas of literature, his comments may also apply to other artistic endeavors. There could be, Orwell argued, no separation from the aesthetic and the political in times of war:

> You cannot take a purely aesthetic interest in a disease you are dying from; you cannot feel dispassionately about a man who is about to cut your throat. In a world in which Fascism and Socialism were fighting one another, any thinking person had to take sides, and his feelings had to find their way not only into his writing.... Literature had to become political, because anything else would have entailed mental dishonesty. One's attachments and hatreds were too near the surface of consciousness to be ignored.[11]

Per Orwell and Marcuse, the truthfulness and merits of good art stem from its ability to be honest (or at least as honest as it can be). The critically removed lens generally reserved for arguments on the aesthetic value of art does not work in times of great strife, war, and horror; removing oneself from these realities makes one's art unreal and untrue. So how did Vietnamese artists convey the horrible reality, yet enduring hope, of Viet Nam during the war?

One symbol of hope that Vietnamese artists could rely on was the benevolent figure of Ho Chi Minh. Ho was and remains the most cherished subject of Vietnamese propaganda art. He is depicted galvanizing the morale of troops, supporting education or agricultural endeavors. His famous "slogans" are heavily featured. These have entered the national psyche of the Vietnamese people, particularly his most famous quote: "Nothing is more precious than independence and freedom." The lotus flower is often incorporated into depictions of "Bac Ho" (Uncle Ho) and is an especially revered symbol of purity, elegance and sublime nobility. It was intended to convey diverse and sometimes quite profound meanings. The lotus of Thap Muoi, for example, is closely associated with Ho Chi Minh's father and with the province of the Mekong, where his father is buried and where this famed lotus grows.

Women also represent hope. A propaganda poster that caught my attention in the Dogma Collection states, "When war comes, even the women have to fight." The depiction of women taking up arms, and especially in action on the battlefield, is rare in the history of art outside of the Vietnamese oeuvre. There exists no comparable visual testimony on such a scale of the participation of women in warfare, or any similar series of images, excepting, perhaps, sculptural relief and painted ceramic depictions of the semi-mythological Amazons from early classical times. Images of women frontline soldiers in combat are samples of the scope and range of their presence in the art and the depictions of the many roles they played in the war.

While propaganda art definitely has its own style and methodology (form), it does tend to be a bit repetitive after a while, and the repression of individual artists' tastes and ideas cannot be discounted. Writer and art critic for the BBC, Alistair Sooke, upon viewing an exhibition of propaganda art in London, ultimately decided that "art commissioned by the state" could be "good." Sooke quoted Pablo Picasso during his reflection on the exhibit: "Art is something subversive. If art is ever given the keys to the city, it will be because it's been so watered down, rendered so impotent, that it's not worth fighting for." But Sooke argued that

> propaganda has been around for millennia—and much ancient art that we value today is a form of propaganda. The Parthenon Marbles extol the virtues of the Athenians at the expense of their enemies. Promoting the political values of a Greek city-state, these sculptures are the definition of art, in Picasso's words, "given the keys to the city"—and yet few people would describe them as "impotent."[12]

Few people would also describe the vivid, bold Vietnamese propaganda art as "impotent." The artists themselves see their work as part of a larger cultural movement, and they were often as subversive and potent as the war itself. Artist Kim Vinh asserted that his propaganda art represented "not just memories of difficult times" because the art was a product of the war itself. Vinh noted that much of his and other artists' work was done in the combat zone, underscoring the earlier idea that artists were also soldiers. Vinh recalled, "If the enemy plane arrives while you were drawing, you had to run. We were constantly on the go while drawing."[13] Vietnamese propaganda artists were thus literally drawing for their lives, "on the go" with the hopes that their work and message (which they very much identified with individually) would survive enemy fire. Messages like "the war must be at peace" surely resonate today, surely transcending the *Lebenswelt* of the Viet Nam War—perhaps if it does not, then we are not paying propaganda art proper attention.

15

1974 and 1975

The main reason I went to Viet Nam in 2012 was to see. I wanted to see what Viet Nam looked like; I wanted to see what the battlefields looked like. I hoped I would see thriving, healthy people, and, after experiencing a little bit of China for six weeks, I wanted to see the similarities and differences between the neighboring countries. One of my dissertation committee members wanted primary sources. His gauntlet thrown, I stepped up: I had spoken to veterans (and surveyed some anonymously about music), and I would now go to the country where the Viet Nam War had been fought. Easy-peasy.

Fast-forward into a slick car (I think a Mercedes), with the AC cranked up, in 2012. Mr. Anh, our guide, twisted his head around so that my friend Carrie and I could hear him clearly from the front seat. Carrie handled the iPad, which Mr. Anh would occasionally hand us so that we could see pieces of an old black-and-white documentary on the "American War" before getting to the site just shown on film. I feverishly took notes, not looking out of the windows much. We first went to Khe Sanh, which, aside from a victory monument marking the turn, I would've never found on my own. Mr. Anh, throughout the whole tour, would show us photos (which you can find in the archives of *Life*) of the DMZ sites during the war. He'd often hold them up once we got to places so we could look at, for example, Khe Sanh, simultaneously then and now.

When I think back on it now, I remember the deep red soil. Dark, fertile, sticking to everything—in the Carolinas we have a kind of sandy orange mud that does the same thing. American helicopters were parked, and a corridor of sandbag-lined trenches could be walked through. I kept touching the gritty walls, trying to look with my fingertips. The faux sandbags were concrete, and there was a guy hanging out near the entry area selling—and I was warned to expect this—fake relic Zippos. Mr. Anh waved him away, and after he showed us a map of how the base had been organized, we began to walk it. The only real surviving pieces of the old site were the helicopter bays, the concrete being taken over by bottle-green-colored grass, alarmingly bright against the rich dirt.

I'd never traveled to Asia before, so my quest to see all I could was limited by all the things I didn't know. As a (former) smoker, smells weren't really something I liked to latch on to; I preferred my dead sense of smell to the aromas of "Fish Street" in Jiujiang, China, where I taught English for six weeks. The curling tendrils of spicy scents from freshly unwrapped dishes were lost on my nostrils, so going overseas to try new culinary delights was never on my list—also, my first real travel experience was a semester abroad in London, a place not really known for its "indigenous" cuisine. British food— meat pies, random custards, deflated meat and peas (peas with every meal!)—did little to prepare me for the wonderland of world cuisine. Since 2012, the Food Network and

Travel Channels in the United States have made countless programs on world travel and food. But at that time, there was only one travel/food show: the masterful Anthony Bourdain's *No Reservations*. Bourdain loved Viet Nam. I trusted his judgment (though I don't recall whether Anthony Bourdain went to Viet Nam War sites).

In Khe Sanh, we stood on a bridge, which boasted a plaque denoting its generous funding from Fidel Castro, and Mr. Anh pointed to a creek running below: "That's part of the Ho Chi Minh Trail." I stared at the area, trying to imagine people, often under the cover of darkness, in flip-flops, shuttling supplies beside this creek. Maybe they stopped and cooled off or got some drinking water (was that safe?); it's fun to use your imagination in places like this.

One of the most interesting parts of the full-day DMZ tour, for me, was the Hien Luong Bridge, which spans the Ben Hai River at the 17th parallel. It's also known as the "Reunification Bridge"; originally a French construction, the 590.5-foot steel structure stood from 1954 until 1975 as a point of division. Today it stands as a testament to the unification of Viet Nam. Mr. Anh, as well as many Vietnamese and Viet Nam War scholars, agreed that the arbitrary splitting of the country by the Geneva Convention—made up of mostly Western powers with foreign interests, though there were Vietnamese represented—was a poor decision. Today the bridge sits parallel to Highway 1 and is marked with a typical yellow with red accents and a "cultural attraction" arch that you'll see around different things Viet Nam deems important. The big loudspeakers on the northern side of the bridge, aimed at the South, used to blare propaganda during the war. Mr. Anh told us that the bridge used to be painted and repainted as a continued act of hope; the North would paint the bridge red, for example, and at night folks from the South would paint their half of the bridge blue. The North then would paint its side of the bridge blue. And on the game went. Mr. Anh showed us some *Life* photographs of the area through the war. An aerial shot revealed that the bridge was also bombed; it collapsed into the water. During the war, there was no Highway 1, but scores of circular bomb craters pocked the northern side of the river. It's a ridiculous image, the bombing evidence. I know I'm too young to understand or whatever, but if you look at these photos, the pervading question is "*why?*"

I don't know what to make of the bridge-painting story. Mr. Anh's grandfather was a northern

Author in replica trenches, Khe Sanh, Viet Nam (2012).

Khe Sanh battle site, Viet Nam (2012).

guy, but his father fought with the South. The two didn't reconcile until the grandfather's final days; I didn't ask Mr. Anh for details, and he didn't provide more. To be a tour guide in Viet Nam, you need to have government clearance, and it's easier to get that permission if your family is favorably hooked up with the party. I don't think Mr. Anh does tours anymore, and his field of expertise was military history more than social and cultural history. Carrie and I were definitely his first "women only" clients; he told us about the older white men (usually Viet Nam War veterans from America or Australia) he usually took on these tours. His fondness for the Australians was partly linked to his English teacher; you could hear that his English had an Australian accent.

The Reunification Bridge has a museum next to it, featuring the typical waxen dioramas and murals of battle and war. In the paintings, the Vietnamese flag, as usual, is prominently displayed, alongside acts of heroism (soldiers helping the fallen, soldiers leading the charge, peasants helping in various ways, with emphasis on a woman sewing the Vietnamese flag). I found the reconstructed "negotiation house" comical, with stand-in dummies representing the Geneva-enforced "neutral observers" from India and Poland. Their costumes were like those you might see in a "color the countries" type of coloring book: the Polish delegate sported a gray suit, and the Indian representative had a turban, beard, and orangey robe. Their job was to watch the DMZ for any overt war crimes, as well as host the occasional delegation or discussion. I seriously doubt they lived together in this stilt house 24/7, but it's funny to think of them learning each other's languages or playing card games. Or running from bombs.

I found the Reunification Bridge a great portal into studying war on a broader scale.

As we walked around the site, I saw a water buffalo hanging out on the riverbank. The way cows chew—I grew up around lots of farms—has always been an equalizing thing; the whole world could be coming to an end, but cows will not chew any faster or with more thought in their glossy brown eyes. The greater symbolism of the bridge was lost on the water buffalo, which calmed me. Also, watching cars, trucks, and motorbikes whiz by on Highway 1 from the bridge, I noticed most of the drivers didn't bother to look over the side of the bridge. Like many historic sites all over the world, history blends into the landscape over time. But this is an important site, if for no other reason than it represents the possibility for reconciliation elsewhere in the world. I hope I see a world where there's a reunification bridge connecting North and South Korea, or somewhere in Iraq or Afghanistan, or between Israel and Pakistan. I know that war is more complicated than the eventual "smile on your brother/everybody come together" refrain from the Youngbloods' 1967 hit "Get Together," but it's heartening to think eventual reconciliations are possible in places that, in my lifetime, have always been divided.

◁▷ ◁▷ ◁▷

On Holocaust Remembrance Day, my friend Sten, who is German and also a cultural historian, sent me a tweet in which the U.S. ambassador to Denmark wrote that we should remember this day "when American soldiers liberated Auschwitz." Sten added his own postscript: "That would be the Red Army."

This message spurred a discussion of 21st-century Polish politics in the shadow of Poland's past, which is, to be most abbreviated, fucking awful. So many people (mainly Russia and Germany—it's always the neighbors) have been trying to get a piece of Poland, and the wars and suppression (I believe Polish masses were a rebellious act in the 19th century, as one example) have made the country a little hard around the edges. I have only been to the Silesia area, where I stayed in Katowice most of the time. A colleague, a native of Poland, upon hearing that I'd gone to his homeland, immediately noted that Katowice is "an industrial city." So did TripAdvisor.

Why talk about Poland at all in a larger book about the Viet Nam War? Two reasons.

First, the task of manning a UN lookout point on the DMZ in Viet Nam fell to delegates from Poland and India. I have a Polish colleague whose work involves looking at how public policy, propaganda, and anti-war history shape the narrative of the Viet Nam War in Polish history and culture. Being part of a live peacekeeping site is a pretty large role to play in a war—you're the most outwardly neutral, and yet …

Second: That time I went to Poland, I was there for a conference. My presentation had to do with Viet Nam veteran friends who'd gone back to Viet Nam with the specific task of trying to heal, as the theme of the conference was "Emotions: Engines of History." Somehow, though, my presentation riled a colleague, who insisted on turning the discussion to how, and I do quote, "the lost Confederates of the South have taken up the cause of Southern Viet Nam."

Say what?

Despite assuring my colleague that the recent removal of Confederate monuments had nothing to do with Lost Cause crusaders taking up the mantle of a democratic Viet Nam, he persisted. Because I was so gobsmacked by the question, I didn't get angry. I recall at one point tossing literature and historical evidence aside and using my Southern authority. I am the daughter of a Virginian, I have lived in three states that once belonged to the Confederacy (South Carolina, Kentucky, and Georgia), and I was born and raised in rural North Carolina—*believe me, man*, if "the South" was taking up the cause of the ARVN, I would know. I doubt many of my Southern brethren could find Viet Nam on a map (and to be fair, I couldn't tell you where Djibouti was until the last Olympics). But anyway: No, Polish man, this is not so. I will note that some South Vietnamese refugees in the United States flocked to the policies and antics of the Trump administration. I'm told this has to do with "strong man" rhetoric and anti-communist policies, but I don't see how Trump, who's met with Vladimir Putin and Kim Jong-un and famously shunned European allies, is the avatar of anti-communism. In my opinion, he's trying as hard as he can to turn the United States into a fascist state, but that's just what I think (what do I know?).

I've seen academic scuffles but had never been in one before this conference, so I was happy it was only slightly uncomfortable. I'd once seen a woman get so angry at another woman's presentation that she declared she must "share [her] ideas in [her] native French to fully say them"—only the woman to whom she directed her impassioned French diatribe didn't know French. It got huffy. This incident wasn't so bad, comparatively speaking, but I was bewildered by the question. An American college student studying at the university apologized afterward: "They're taught some strange things in Poland." I brushed it off with humor, but inside I was confused. Had I missed some Confederate–South Viet Nam connection? I know there were soldiers in both wars who employed the "rebel yell" (a sound Shelby Foote described in Ken Burns' 1990 documentary *The Civil War* as a cross between a banshee squall and a foxhunt yip), but that's as far as it went. Where had my Polish colleague gotten this idea?

Combining 1974 and 1975 made sense to me in that they represent interregnum years for Viet Nam. The country remained divided until 1975, as ARVN and PAVN military operations continued until April 30, 1975. The United States employed fewer than 100 Marines at the U.S. Embassy in Sai Gon; the overwhelming military presence was gone. Some journalists and private contractors remained, but everyone south of the Demilitarized Zone in Viet Nam knew there was an imminent threat from the North. The last U.S. troops hadn't even left before skirmishes broke out, automatically breaking the ceasefire agreement in the Paris Peace Accords. The war would continue between the South and the North, with U.S. support—political, military material, and economic—dwindling as President Nixon became embroiled in the Watergate scandal. Congress and the American public (and pocketbook) were also weary of committing more resources to Viet Nam. Even with a Hail Mary plea to Congress from President Gerald Ford in 1975 to support the flailing ARVN and South Vietnamese people, the House and Senate wouldn't budge.

Viet Nam, to the United States, was locked in a drawer to be ignored for several years. Even Viet Nam veterans would, as author and Viet Nam veteran Karl Marlantes articulated in the 2017 Ken Burns and Lynn Novick documentary *The Vietnam War*, keep quiet about their service; Marlantes likens Viet Nam to "an alcoholic father [whom] we don't talk about."[1] Veteran memoirs usually depict the early 1970s as a hazy time of dipping in and out of college, jobs, and relationships. No one got a hero's welcome on returning from Viet Nam, and no one wanted to talk about the war, which left some deep wounds in America's culture and psyche that took several years to begin to heal. Finally, PTSD (posttraumatic stress disorder) had yet to be defined, much like "moral injury," which are now open topics among veterans from many wars; the Viet Nam vets, as well as many other Americans, were adrift in the 1970s.

There were several important milestones in the United States in 1974. Muhammad Ali made his triumphant return to boxing in the "The Rumble in the Jungle" in Zaire, knocking George Foreman out in eight rounds. The sitcom *Happy Days* and the comedy show *Saturday Night Live* premiered on television, Hank Aaron tied Babe Ruth in home runs, and Bob Dylan went out on the road for the first time since 1966. Acts like the Ramones, Patti Smith, ABBA, and Joni Mitchell made their respective debuts—live or album—in 1974, and fan favorites like John Lennon, Elton John, Dolly Parton, and Eric Clapton were making headway in solo careers. Barbra Streisand's title track to the movie *The Way We Were* was the number-one song of 1974, but it only held the top spot for two weeks. Until the early 1970s, songs gained the "most popular song of the year" title by remaining in the charts, but by the middle of the decade, music was disseminated more widely and there were more artists to choose from; it was hard to hold the top spot in the Billboard charts for more than a few weeks by the mid–1970s.

Arguably the biggest news in the United States in 1974 was the impeachment and resignation of President Richard Nixon. The investigation of the Watergate break-in in 1972 slowly dismantled the Nixon administration. Multiple officials resigned, and during the hearings, on July 16, 1973, an aide to Nixon, Alexander Butterfield, provided the final domino to fall: Butterfield stated that the president had been recording his White House conversations since 1971. Over the course of the next year, Nixon would be embroiled in a bitter back-and-forth battle with the Senate Select Committee on Presidential Campaign Activities. The president dug his heels in, refusing to surrender the tapes, firing the special prosecution, and generally making himself look terribly guilty.

The Supreme Court eventually ordered Nixon to hand over the tapes—not transcribed or edited like the ones he tried to put forward in previous months—which immediately revealed that the president had been involved in covering up the Watergate incident from the start. The House Judiciary Committee prepared articles of impeachment, and a surly Nixon had to admit defeat. On August 9, 1974, Nixon addressed the nation, saying, in part:

> To continue to fight through the months ahead for my personal vindication would almost totally absorb the time and attention of both the president and the Congress in a period when our entire focus should be on the great issues of peace abroad and prosperity without inflation at home. Therefore, I shall resign the presidency effective at noon tomorrow.[2]

The country might not have been entirely shocked—the Watergate scandal had been playing out in the newspapers for two years, and many Americans already considered Nixon untrustworthy before he took office—but it was an international event, and quite the scandal. The president's insistence upon his innocence looks preposterous from my perch in the 21st century, but his emphasis on "personal vindication" does not look so unfamiliar in the wake of the 2020 presidential election. The heavy-handed, absolute power the presidency assumes is false, and 1974 was a watershed moment for the American government functioning correctly. President Nixon submitted a resignation letter to Vice President Gerald Ford, who assumed office and immediately pardoned his former boss. The United States, a country that only 30 years prior had been hailed as a great world power and victorious leader, deflated under the effect of years at war in Viet Nam and the downfall of a career politician.

In 1975, damage repair would need to begin immediately on what happened to the U.S. psyche in 1974. The music charts, at least, reflected a new era. This phase of American music took pieces from the socially conscious and groundbreaking music of the 1960s, but it used new sounds and moods to sing about themes that every Billboard chart reveals: love, heartbreak, joy, and sadness. The number-one song of 1975 was "Love Will Keep Us Together" by the Captain and Tennille. While the sentiment of unity wasn't new, the delivery wasn't either; the 1970s sound was more polished and wholesome than the 1960s' more innovative sounds, but production methods and hardware were improving steadily. The Bee Gees, Bruce Springsteen and the E Street Band, and David Bowie first appeared on the Billboard charts in 1975, the Sex Pistols had their first live show, and Elvis (a blast from the past) put on a huge show at the Silverdome in Pontiac, Michigan (I only know about this show because Elvis famously ripped his pants during the performance and had to leave the stage). Stevie Wonder's outdoor Human Kindness Day performance in May 1975 sounds more enjoyable than the return of Elvis, as does the opening of Broadway's *The Wiz* or *The Rocky Horror Picture Show,* both of which premiered in 1975.

In Viet Nam, the Northern campaign bore down. The Party Politburo in Ha Noi had a master plan, and the PAVN troops began moving south, taking the Central Highlands in March. President Thieu, abandoned by his U.S. allies, tried to save his people by evacuating them farther south in an event known as the "Convoy of Tears."[3] Thieu also called the military down to Sai Gon for protection, even though members of the South Vietnamese army had begun to defect, trading their uniforms for civilian clothes. On April 10, the Australian Embassy closed and evacuated its staff; the United States would wait until April 29, per the misguided leadership of the U.S. ambassador to South Viet Nam, Graham Martin. In the end, the United States would exit dramatically, via helicopter, as North Vietnamese tanks rode into Sai Gon, one pushing through the gates at the presidential palace.

President Thieu angrily resigned after addressing the Vietnamese public in a rather long speech. He did choose some careful words for the United States:

> [The refusal of help from the United States] is the US scheme to stop providing us with aid and to wash their hands of us. This is a scheme of people who have completely lost their conscience and humanity.... The US fought a war here without success and went home.... There was a promise [from the United States] that if the Communists intruded and invaded again, there would be a reaction [and there wasn't]. This amounts to a breach of promise, injustice, lack of responsibility and inhumanity to an ally that has suffered continuously—the shirking of responsibility on the part of a great power.[4]

Obviously, Thieu had expected (and former President Nixon had led him to believe) that the United States would come and help once the North violated the Paris Peace Accords (which Thieu, in the same speech, went to great lengths to trash). That help didn't come by way of money or airpower, and Thieu, in his resignation, admitted that the South Vietnamese government didn't have the resources to defeat the North on its own. President Thieu did not lie when he accused the United States of "wash[ing] their hands of [Viet Nam]," and images of Viet Nam from the last few weeks of April 1975 show that the South was desperate for some help, but, just as Thieu described, the United States instead "shirk[ed] responsibility" and displayed a "lost ... conscience and humanity" toward its "suffering ally." How great could a "great power" like the United States be if it ignored the suffering of a people whose nation, until quite recently, had received so much time, attention, manpower, and money? The CIA helped Thieu escape to Taiwan before the Politburo could get its hands on him, but it is easy to see that his point of view—that the United States betrayed its commitment to South Viet Nam—is valid. He died, in permanent exile from Viet Nam, aged 87 in Boston.

◁▷ ◁▷ ◁▷

I'm standing again across the street from the former location of the U.S. Embassy in Sai Gon; it is now the U.S. Consulate. It's only fitting that the embassy is no longer standing. I'm not sure how much the original area was modified, but the tall building, where the iconic images of America leaving via helicopter were caught on camera, is gone. I've heard you can beg for a tour of the consulate, as an American. But I've also heard your tour won't discuss the "fall of Sai Gon" in 1975, so I haven't tried. I did think it was weird that the *one* thing I couldn't photograph—aside from the embalmed Ho Chi Minh, who I have no desire to see or photograph—was something that somewhat belonged to the country I'm from. But that's what happens in communist countries; there are new rules to follow.

As I walked back from the old embassy site toward the Notre Dame Cathedral Basilica of Sai Gon, also known as Cathedral Basilica of Our Lady of the Immaculate Conception (like Ha Noi, you can orient yourself in part of Sai Gon/Ho Chi Minh City by remembering where a cathedral is), I thought about the various brands of communism I've seen. Laos, China and Viet Nam each present a different type of communism. The only time I've been shut down on a photo op in China was when I tried to get a picture of a tour guide talking about Chairman Mao's thoughts on Mt. Lushan; the guide shoved his hand in the way of my lens. I don't know what was inflammatory about the possible photo—you could take pictures of pictures of Mao just about everywhere else I went in China, so why that instance? As for Viet Nam, is the "no photo" policy at the old embassy site a power play? I'm pretty sure the guard knew I was an American; however, the Vietnamese have every right to dictate what gets photographed in their country. It was just strange to have a site blocked off, especially a site that carries such a story of American failure.

Let me be clear: I don't think American involvement in Viet Nam was an across-the-board failure. I think we lost the war, but I also don't think it was our war to win; rather, we perpetuated a problem that was already present. I think the bigger question we don't ask, regarding the war, is "What did Americans *learn* from being in Viet Nam?" Back to the "different communisms" point: In Viet Nam and Laos, you can use Twitter, Instagram, and Facebook. You cannot use those sites or apps in China. Is the lasting impact of America in Viet Nam things like 21st-century technology access? I think it's one of the more lingering effects of the war. American presence in Viet Nam changed aspects of the Vietnamese marketplace at the very least; you can't show people, say, the wonder of Ritz crackers or doo-wop hairdos and then snatch those things away. Free speech can be stunted, but the powers of American music and sports break through a lot of borders. I didn't find many Vietnamese (or Chinese or Laotian) people who listened to some of my favorite bands, but everyone knows who LeBron James and Beyoncé are wherever I've gone. Even the Chinese children I taught could sing Taylor Swift songs—some things cannot be contained.

Not far from the cathedral in Sai Gon, I bought another jug of water and a tasty but unknown origin pink juice from a street vendor, and then I sat down on a shaded bench in 30/4 Park. This park is named after the date April 30, 1975 (aka Viet Nam's Liberation Day). Some *viet kieu* refer to it as the National Day of Shame or National Day of Resentment; 20th-century Vietnamese history is either packaged nicely by the Vietnamese government or bundled under layers of personal history by the Vietnamese people. The straightest, "correct" answer is the one from the government, but I think it's important to look at the story from several angles.

In April 1975, it was becoming obvious that the NVA forces were going to take over Sai Gon. The only American military personnel left in Viet Nam were Marines employed at the embassy and a smattering of army and air force advisors near former U.S. bases; their job was to assist the ARVN forces. However, the ARVN forces had been telling their U.S. counterparts that things were going badly for over a year prior to April 1975. The weapons weren't working, there wasn't enough ammunition, and materiel was failing, in need of replacement or repair. President Ford's hands were pretty tied by a war-weary constituency and Congress, so any hope of funding a last gasp of the conflict became nearly nonexistent. By April, Americans in Viet Nam—military and civilians, which included contractors, journalists, and myriad peace workers—could see the writing on the walls. People started making plans to leave, including Vietnamese citizens who'd worked for or with the Americans; they didn't want to see what might happen to them if they stayed behind with the communists. The massacres in Hue, where residents were killed for not rising up against the Americans during the Tet Offensive, left scars in the Vietnamese psyche.

We watched about half of the Rory Kennedy documentary *Last Days in Vietnam* in class. The students were really keyed into the U.S. government's lack of preparation for the fall of Sai Gon, and the footage of people trying to get on boats, planes, and one particularly harrowing helicopter landing on a ship really struck them. It's interesting, because in the 21st century, refugees look poor. They walk miles to cross borders, or they board rickety boats and try to get away—in Viet Nam, in photos and film footage, the fleeing people look middle class.

Of course, per *Last Days in Vietnam*, there were a lot of sympathetic Americans trying to help the Vietnamese leave. The documentary describes people who worked with the United States closely, who tried to take off their ARVN uniforms in the street and blend in because they were afraid of the communists. They knew (better than we did) what was coming; Viet Nam portrays the entire decade of the 1980s as a time of rebuilding, but many Vietnamese spent the better part of the decade in "reeducation camps."

Two things stand out to me when watching *Last Days in Vietnam*: (1) the resistance to putting a real plan of evacuation in place, due to Ambassador Martin's dogged insistence on holding on to the American Embassy, and (2) the ineptitude of the American government.[5] The United States straight dipped on its allies in this situation. Sure, President Ford tried to get a surge of supplies and troops (ARVN soldiers had been reusing medical supplies and running out of ammunition for months), but war-weary America wasn't having any more to do with Viet Nam. And I can kind of understand, but the swaths of people surrounding the embassy on that fateful day in 1975, waving papers documenting their connections to the United States, should have been treated better.

The American evacuation from Viet Nam boils down to a logistics issue. The ARVN arguably got mowed down when the United States began withdrawing troops, because we hadn't given or left much material for them to use to fight off the incoming surge from the North (and much of what we provided was "stolen" in some way—about 30 percent of anything the United States sent to Viet Nam during the conflict went on the black market[6]). The images of Vietnamese soldiers walking nearly naked instead of wearing their ARVN uniforms always makes my heart break a little. They weren't able to get out of Viet Nam in time (which was also due to logistics gone wrong, per *Last Days in Vietnam*), and they did the best they could to avoid inevitable harm. We could have helped more, especially those who had jobs with the U.S. government and thus were prime targets for the communist "reeducation" labor camps.

Now the American departure from Sai Gon is only a problem if you go looking for it, as I did with my sneaky photos (which came out nonsensical at best). American presence in Viet Nam is now achieved through products like Starbucks, Nike, North Face, McDonald's, and KFC—a softer method of influence. Communist Viet Nam is an ally to the United States, which is perplexing after all the pearl-clutching America did over communism. I'm glad we can now visit, and that the country is unified, but I often wonder whether all the suffering could have been avoided or if it was necessary. Either way, it can't be undone, and the Vietnamese will not let anyone forget the American War in Viet Nam. And that's their right; it was, ultimately, their victory in a protracted, complicated war that they were determined to win at all costs. And they did.

Conclusion

"Oh, wow! What's this?" I exclaimed, pointing to a poster advertising a new book—and author reading event—by a Viet Nam veteran. It was my first week on the job as an adjunct instructor at Jefferson Community and Technical College and about two weeks into my doctoral program at the University of Louisville in 2008. I was green in terms of "being a researcher," but I knew I would be studying the Viet Nam War, so seeing this flyer was a jackpot!

"Oh yeah, he's a great guy," said a bearded gentleman I hadn't met. My colleague, Pat, rolled his eyes behind the bearded guy's head.

"Do you know him?" I asked, way too excited, likely in a high-pitched voice. I know I babbled on about my PhD program, how I needed to meet this man, and similar fangirl-y sentiments.

"I am him," he laughed. My jaw fell open and I blushed; he had let me go on and on, and now he was laughing at me. That is how I met Jim McGarrah: poet, prankster, Purple Heart USMC, and one of my favorite people on the planet.

Jim opened a lot of doors for me, including doors to bars, where we'd hang out and drink and talk about all kinds of nonsense. He showed me around Louisville, a city new to me, forcing me to try new things, like Irish food or martinis. My first real friend in Louisville, Jim also loved to jabber about things like music from the 1960s and 1970s, writing about war, and talking to Viet Nam War veterans. When we met, he'd just published a memoir, *A Temporary Sort of Peace*, which included his recent trip to Viet Nam, so he could also tell me about going to Viet Nam, which, until I met him, I hadn't considered as part of my research. When I moved to Savannah and started working at the University of South Carolina Beaufort, I missed Jim so much I figured out a way to bring him to campus, where he gave a dazzling talk to the community and entertained my classes. He's lived several lives (which you can read about in his many great books) and has retired to Georgia, where he still writes and sneaks the occasional whiskey.

When I first started writing this book, I intended to incorporate Viet Nam veterans' "musical memories" into the narrative, but then I decided that aspect would be better as a separate piece. How American soldiers heard music while they were in Viet Nam varied by their occupation. My lunch friend George Utter, whom I met through USC Beaufort channels, for example, graduated from West Point in 1966 and got to Viet Nam by 1967 (graduates needed 16 weeks/4 months in a stateside billet before going overseas). For the two years he was in Viet Nam, George saw only one big show, though he did recall the popularity of the Animals' "We Gotta Get Out of This Place" and a Filipino group's rendition of "Proud Mary." What I love about George's "musical memory" is that there are several Asian accents that replace the "R" sound (as in "rolling on a river") with an "L" sound, so the "Proud Mary" George remembers sounded like "lolling on a liver," which is a funny memory. While I've heard about veterans listening to tapes or the radio, George noted that it would have been dangerous to have a radio "in the bush," which seems obvious: you wouldn't want to literally broadcast your position. My friend Frank Gutierrez (Army) remembers hearing some *tejano* music while on base, while my new podcast pal, Mack Payne (Army), has a hilarious story about bouncing around in a helicopter to "No Sugar Tonight" by the Guess Who (we bonded over our love of the song). The variety of stories you'll hear, just in terms of what songs Viet Nam War veterans remember from their time in service, prompted me to keep some of the music in this book; I know some of you have your own memories of these songs, service member or not.

◁▷ ◁▷ ◁▷

I often get asked whether it's lonely traveling alone—whether it's difficult to be away (from my husband, our home, our pets) for long stretches of time. It *can* be lonely. But I am comfortable being alone (I know not everyone is). Also, to be honest, I'm often so consumed in my research that I'm not thinking of home—I'm thinking of the patterns I see in letters home from Australian GIs or the rhetorical devices used in museum exhibits in Viet Nam. These aren't necessarily the most interesting or romantic trips in which to include my husband or my friends. There's less "rent a motorcycle to drive into the mountains for a food tasting" activity and more of things like walking around in circles to find a monument or sitting in the basement of a museum, looking at archives. It's not the most glamorous itinerary.

My research inevitably takes me to veteran accounts of the war—before, during, and after—so I don't see loneliness so much as a sacrifice after I read letters from soldiers who never came back. I'm coming back. I'm sitting in archives in Canberra, *reading* letters from people who were in the jungles of Viet Nam, not *in* Viet Nam.

I have spent many a night in front of the Sai Gon Liberty City Point hotel, drinking, smoking, and staring out at the whirl of activity on Pasteur Street. A balcony overlooking someone's private yard in Hoi An, the curb outside my hotel in Ha Noi, the window looking onto a college quad in Canberra, the roof of a hotel in Dien Bien Phu—all of these places have been vantage points of reflection and learning. I do think of what I'm missing, but I'm also thinking of where I am, what I'm watching, and how what I'm looking at resembles—if at all—what this area looked like in 1956, 1966, 1976…. My hope is to imagine as much as I can while recognizing that what I'm seeing will never be the exact scene from the past. Time moves us forward.

In 2017, I took a picture of two Vietnamese teenagers, draped in ponchos and waiting out the night's rain by checking their cell phones, with a Starbucks sign in the background. I sent it to my Uncle Ron, who served in the navy during the war. I wanted him to see how different Viet Nam was, as well as the lasting effect of the American presence on Vietnamese life (Starbucks). I wanted him to see the difference we made—if Starbucks and cell phones count. I desperately want everyone involved in the war to feel like their time wasn't wasted. I want them to learn the world changed because of this war; Viet Nam taught us all something, no matter what role we played. My uncle laughed at the photograph: "Kids are kids everywhere, I guess."

We may have "lost the war" or found "peace with honor" with regard to the American experience in Viet Nam, but those sentiments don't end the experience of the war for those who lived through it. Nor does it end the experience of war in the earth that the war reshaped.

As I wrote in chapter 6, my visit to Project RENEW near Hue, Viet Nam, was a stroke of great fortune. I was set to visit with Mr. Nguyen Thanh Phu, RENEW's Mine Action Visitor Center manager and explosive ordnance risk education program officer. I think we even met on a Saturday, when the Visitor Center was closed, so I remain grateful to RENEW being so helpful and accommodating. It was one of those happy accidents that I had enough time—and that crucial multi-entry visa—to get back into Viet Nam via Da Nang. I hired a driver and was all set.

Let's just get it out of the way that I "waited" an unnecessary hour to meet with Mr. Phu, sitting outside, in the shade but still Viet Nam in June, next to a closed building. About 45 minutes into my pacing around the center (including passing the building in which Phu was waiting for me), an office manager tried to help, but my Vietnamese and his English did not conversation make. I am eternally grateful that he let me use the ladies' room, though. Eventually, with my driver now returned and idling outside, the office manager and I figured out that we should call "Mr. Phu" (this is like how my Southern—and very often Black—community says "Miss Erin" instead of "Dr. McCoy," and it's actually a familial form of respect). It turned out that he'd been within shouting distance *the whole time.* I showed up to the correct building in an effusion of apologies, asked the driver to wait, and introduced myself to Mr. Phu. Looking back through my photos, I remember, while talking to him, feeling ribbons of sweat run down my back, down my legs and neck—the heat, along with being surrounded by shrapnel and prosthetic limbs, had me agitated. When my host gently asked why I'd not asked the driver to call him on his cell phone, I almost burst into tears of frustration—not at him, but at myself, the intrepid scholar-traveler who doesn't know how to use a phone. I also mismanaged my cash funds and didn't adequately tip my driver, who waited two hours past the time we'd agreed, causing him to drive us back to Da Nang as if we'd robbed a bank. He was pissed over the tip, and the best I could do was bleat "I'm sorry" (in Vietnamese) to the back of his head as he peeled off onto General Vo Nguyen Giap Street into the bustle of Saturday night in Da Nang.

If Mr. Phu was angry about waiting for me for over an hour, he didn't show it. He spoke to me enthusiastically and proudly about Project RENEW, what they were doing, and what they planned to do. I'd spoken to Chuck Searcy about this subject a little over our lunch—he is RENEW's international advisor—but Chuck was the preview to the movie that was Phu. He was originally from the area, took a degree in hospitality and worked in the industry, but now he was giving back to his hometown via his work with RENEW. He explained to me what many of us don't know: the United States dropped *so many* bombs on Viet Nam, especially Quang Tri Province, where RENEW works. Of these bombs, about 8–10 percent of the explosives do not detonate, and thus they sit like … a bomb waiting to go off. Phu told me that over 81 percent of the land in Quang Tri was contaminated with explosive ordnance (EO), per a survey done through a collaboration between the Vietnam Veterans of America Foundation and the Vietnamese military. The de-mining program that RENEW runs is effective, with insistence on a data-driven methodology that relies on assistance from the citizens; the only hitch is that funding goes up and down for RENEW, so they often do much with very little resources.

Aside from active de-mining of EO, RENEW has educational outreach programs, which target children (who represent the majority of victims), farmers (50 percent of UXO casualties), scrap metal collectors, and (most likely to be looking for metal) dealers. A child's drawing stood before a display of rusted and detonated mortar shells; it was of a group of people sitting around a table, but, instead of heads, they had weapons: the cluster bomb, the incendiary bomb, the missile, and so forth. Phu translated the cartoon bubble over their heads to reveal what they were saying; each one was arguing how it was the best bomb, only for all to be beaten by the last guy at the table, the nuclear bomb. If asked to list types of bombs, it would take me a moment to even start, but this child—a budding artist— had to learn them as well as why you should never touch them, along with what to do if you see one. Phu told me that those running the outreach programs even incorporate risk education into soccer games; it enhances the "peer-to-peer" aspect of learning, which is simultaneously music to my teacher's ears and horror to

Prosthetic limbs at Project RENEW, Quang Tri, Viet Nam (2019).

my hidden id. What do our kids teach each other that's even comparable in the United States? Active shooter drills?

Quang Tri also is ninth in terms of high exposure to Agent Orange on a list of 58 provinces; Project RENEW coordinates medical support for those who suffer from various Agent Orange–related disabilities. RENEW's help is limited in that they cannot provide medical care, but they can improve the quality of people's lives. Phu told me that mental disabilities are far more common effects of Agent Orange, and he gave me an example how RENEW might help with the "safety and hygiene" areas in the life of a child who "can do nothing but lie on the floor all day and draw." My mind wandered back to the jars of deformed fetuses in the War Remnants Museum and to the persons with hearing impairments and physical disabilities in Hue and Hoi An, on the bus to Hoa Lu, on the streets of Ha Noi....

When you look purposefully for wounds of war, like the aftermath of chemical weapons, it can quickly become overwhelming. Phu, however, could keep things positive. He spoke excitedly about a mobile outreach program that helped people upgrade prosthetic limbs, which could be a result of both Agent Orange and EO. He pointed out a 500-pound piece of shrapnel "we found last week," which lay mangled and still vibrating with menace near the front of the Visitor's Center. They display the more recent pieces, Pho explained, to illustrate the constant work Project RENEW and its primary partner, Norwegian People's Aid (one of the leading humanitarian mine action and disarmament organizations from Norway), are doing. When discussing different sources of funding for RENEW, Phu underscored that the United States working with Viet Nam was a "win-win" situation for everyone involved.

◁▷ ◁▷ ◁▷

While the Viet Nam War is fascinating, it is not as captivating as Viet Nam as a destination. My research in Viet Nam didn't only expand my scholarly pursuits; it also, and more important, opened my mind. Traveling in Europe (where I can blend in) or Latin America (where I can at least understand the language) did not challenge me as much as Southeast Asia did. Being uncomfortable—with subject matter or food—teaches you a lot about yourself. You have to face your biases and fears, and, more often than not, you meet people who would rather help you than harm you.

I thought the Vietnamese, Laotians, and Cambodians would hold grudges from the war, but no one ever expressed any to me if they did. Instead, from the United States to Viet Nam to Australia, people wanted to talk. It is important to keep the lines of global communication open, on issues of the past and present, as we collectively cope with and heal from the traumas of the Viet Nam War.

Or perhaps *healing* is too ambitious a term; we need to collectively work together to keep talking about what war does to people, both those who lived through it and those who deal with the repercussions in the form of generational trauma. Most important, like all war tourists, my hope is that war sites and scenes teach us to avoid conflict whenever we can. The pain of the Viet Nam War is still palpable, no matter how modern Viet Nam becomes or how many commemorative bricks are laid at the memorial in Angel Fire. We need to honor that pain and explore its roots, even if that means facing some uncomfortable truths. We must also seek out individual stories so that we have a fuller, more comprehensive story of what it is like to be at war, to go to war, to come back from war. We have to look at the anti-war movements, hopefully learning that individual voices do matter, even if their beliefs go against the norms of national identity and popular opinion. War is hell, a wise veteran once said—let's try to avoid going there when we *know* that we know better.

Chapter Notes

Introduction

1. Le Van Bang, former Vietnamese ambassador to the United States, quoted in "Vietnam Passage, a Teacher's Guide" 2017.
2. Brummer 2018.
3. Nguyen 2017, 116.
4. Johnson 1965.
5. Kennedy 1956.
6. Brinkley and Nichter 2015, 361.

Chapter 1

1. Phụng 2005, 23.
2. Ibid., 75.
3. Lederer and Burdick 1958, 124–25.
4. Rusk 1966.
5. Pormus, D., & M. Shuman. (1960). "Save the Last Dance for Me." Perf. by Ben E. King and the Drifters. *Save the Last Dance for Me*. Atlantic Records.
6. Scanlan and Loescher 1983, 120.

Chapter 2

1. King 1943.
2. Lewy 1978.
3. Burns and Novick 2017.
4. Sedaris 2000, 56.
5. Eisenhower 1961.
6. Cf. Williams' book *Negroes with Guns* (1962).

Chapter 3

1. Mitchell 2012.
2. McNamara quoted in Morris 2003.
3. Nixon 1962.
4. Glass 2013.
5. McPeak 2017.

Chapter 4

1. Bowden 2017.
2. Daddis 2017.
3. Burns and Novick 2017.

4. *Ibid.*
5. *Ibid.*
6. "Selma March" 2010.
7. King 1963.
8. Langguth 2002.
9. X 1963.
10. "Vietnam, Diem, the Buddhist Crisis" 2010.

Chapter 5

1. X 1964.
2. "Viet Cong Troops Overrun Town—July 20, 1964" 2016.
3. Michals 2007.
4. *Ibid.*
5. Kearns-Goodwin 2015.
6. Lumet 1964.
7. "Transcript of CBS Broadcast with Walter Cronkite" 1963.
8. Quoted in Polner and Woods 2008, 236.

Chapter 6

1. Bates 2020.
2. "Selma to Montgomery March," n.d.
3. "March on Washington" 2016.
4. LBJ Presidential Library 2015.
5. "Pacifica Radio/UC Berkeley …" 2020.
6. Johnson 2007.
7. Gregory 2016.
8. Oglesby 1965.
9. Lynskey 2012, 95.
10. James 1997.
11. Cf. Marcuse 1978.
12. Lynskey 2012, 91.
13. Quoted in Polner and Woods 2008, 235.
14. "Simple Gifts" 2018.
15. Barga 2018.

Chapter 7

1. "World War 2 Trail" 2019.
2. Sadler and Moore 1966.
3. Young 2020.
4. Binyon 1914.

Chapter 8

1. Chow and Bates 2020.
2. Goodacre, n.d.
3. Strange and Hager 2012.
4. "Muhammed Ali Refuses Induction …" 2019
5. "Taylor Swift on 'Lover' and Haters" 2019.
6. Muldar 2002.

Chapter 9

1. Bowden 2017.
2. King 2018.
3. Beschloss 2012.
4. Small 2004.
5. Halbertstam 1993, 574.

Chapter 10

1. Nixon 2017.
2. "A Boy Named Sue" 1969.
3. "Jimi Hendrix on Performing the National Anthem …" 2019.
4. Cush 2016.
5. Aronowitz quoted in Moores 2019.
6. Morley 2017.
7. Blake 2014.
8. Burns and Novick 2017.
9. *Ibid.*
10. Richards quoted in Giles 2017.
11. Jagger quoted in Block 2012.
12. "Murder at Altamont …" 2009.
13. Andresen 2003, 105–6.
14. Viet Nam veteran Gene Leroy quoted in Andresen 2003, 109.
15. Haggard, M. (1970). "The Fightin' Side of Me." Perf. M. Haggard and The Strangers. *The Fightin' Side of Me*. Capitol Records.
16. Andresen 2003, 106–7.
17. *Ibid.*, 107.
18. *Ibid.*, 109.
19. *Ibid.*, 111–12.
20. *Ibid.*, 112.
21. Appy 2000.
22. Wright 1970.
23. Kennedy 2014.
24. Brown 1969.
25. McCoy 2015.
26. Mariscal 1999, n.p.
27. Roberts 2016.

Chapter 11

1. Gilbert 2016.
2. Starr 1970.
3. Cohen 2015.
4. "Mexican-American March" 2015.
5. Sterba 1970.
6. Fitraikis 2003.

7. "'Ohio'—Neil Young Lyrics Analysis," n.d.
8. Fitraikis 2003.
9. Quoted in "'Ohio'—Neil Young Lyrics Analysis," n.d.
10. *Ibid.*
11. *Ibid.*
12. *Ibid.*

Chapter 12

1. Nguyen 2017, 162.
2. Brinkley and Nichter 2015.
3. Ayres 1975.
4. "Calley Apologizes …" 2009.
5. Stur 2018.
6. "Washington DC Protests …" 2012.
7. Pentagon Papers 2009.
8. "Edward Snowden" 2013.
9. "The 10 Greatest All-Time Speeches …" 2015.
10. Brinkley and Nichter 2015, 70.

Chapter 13

1. Pelley 2002, 124–25.
2. Wilbanks 1993.
3. "Story Behind the Terror of War" 2019.
4. "Transcript of Kissinger's News Conference …" 1972.
5. Glass 2018.
6. "Paris Peace Talks …" 2017.
7. Brinkley and Nichter 2015.
8. *Ibid.*, 70.
9. *Ibid.*

Chapter 14

1. Chertoff 2012.
2. *Ibid.*
3. Irvine 2015.
4. *Ibid.*
5. Dogma Collection 2015.
6. *Ibid.*
7. Marcuse 1978, 23.
8. *Ibid.*, 56.
9. *Ibid.*, 57.
10. Orwell 1941.
11. *Ibid.*
12. Sooke 2014.
13. Dogma Collection 2015.

Chapter 15

1. Burns and Novick 2017.
2. "President Nixon's Resignation Speech" 1974.
3. "The Vietnam Center …" 2013.
4. Thieu 1975.
5. Kennedy 2014.
6. *Ibid.*

Works Cited

Andresen, L. (2003). *Battle Notes: Music of the Vietnam War*. Superior, WI: Savage Press.

Appy, C. G. (2000). *Working Class War: American Combat Soldiers in Vietnam* [Kindle]. Chapel Hill, NC: The University of North Carolina Press.

Ayres, B., Jr. (1975, December 26). 1976 Surprise: Carter Is Running Well. Retrieved November 14, 2020, from https://www.nytimes.com/1975/12/26/archives/1976-surprise-carter-is-running-well-carter-is-running-well-for.html.

Barga, M. J. (2018, March 05). "The 'Bonus March'(1932): The Unmet Demands and Needs of WWI Heroes." Retrieved November 14, 2020, from https://socialwelfare.library.vcu.edu/eras/great-depression/bonus-march/.

Bates, J. (2020, February 20). "The Mystery Surrounding Malcolm X's Assassination." Retrieved November 14, 2020, from https://time.com/5778688/malcolm-x-assassination/.

Beschloss, M. (2012, December 04). "In His Final Days, LBJ Agonized Over His Legacy." Retrieved November 13, 2020, from https://www.pbs.org/newshour/politics/lbjs-last-interview.

Binyon, R. L. (1914). "For the Fallen." Retrieved November 14, 2020, from http://www.greatwar.co.uk/poems/-laurence-binyon-for-the-fallen.htm.

Blake, J. (2014, October 18). "How Jimi Hendrix Stopped Being Black." Retrieved November 14, 2020, from https://www.cnn.com/2014/10/18/showbiz/jimi-hendrix-invisible-legacy/index.html.

Block, M. (2012, November 16). "Mick Jagger on The Apocalyptic 'Gimme Shelter.'" Retrieved November 14, 2020, from https://www.npr.org/2012/11/16/165270769/mick-jagger-on-the-apocalyptic-gimme-shelter.

Bowden, M., & T. J. Brennan. (2017, May). "The True Story of 'The Marine on the Tank' and One of the Most Emblematic Images of Vietnam." Retrieved November 13, 2020, from https://www.vanityfair.com/news/2017/05/the-true-story-of-the-marine-on-the-tank-vietnam-war.

"A Boy Named Sue" [Recorded by J. Cash]. (1969). On *Live at San Quentin* [MP3]. (1969, February 24).

Boys Who Said NO! Draft Resistance and the Vietnam War excerpt. Retrieved November 14, 2020, from https://www.youtube.com/watch?v=dHsa_vRBO-E.

Brinkley, D., & L. Nichter. (2015). *The Nixon Tapes: 1971–1972*. Boston, MA: Houghton Mifflin Harcourt.

Brummer, J. (2018, September 25). "The Vietnam War: A History in Song." Retrieved November, 2020, from https://www.historytoday.com/miscellanies/vietnam-war-history-song.

Burns, K., & L. Novick. (Directors). (2017). *The Vietnam War* [Motion picture on DVD]. USA: Florentine Films.

"Calley Apologizes for Role in My Lai Massacre." (2009, August 22). Retrieved November 14, 2020, from https://www.nbcnews.com/id/wbna32514139.

Chertoff, E. (2012) "Occupied Wounded Knee: A 71-Day Siege and a Forgotten Civil Rights Movement." *The Atlantic*. 23 October 2012. https://www.theatlantic.com/national/archive/2012/10/occupy-wounded-knee-a-71-daysiege-and-a-forgotten-civil-rights-movement/263998/.

Chow, A., & J. Bates. (2020, June 12). Black Vietnam Veterans on Injustices They Faced: Da 5 Bloods. Retrieved November 14, 2020, from https://time.com/5852476/da-5-bloods-black-vietnam-veterans/.

Cohen, S. (2015, August 26). "Women's Equality Day: The History of When Women Went on Strike." Retrieved November 14, 2020, from https://time.com/4008060/women-strike-equality-1970/.

Cronkite, W. (1963, September 02). "Transcript of CBS Broadcast with Walter Cronkite." Retrieved November 14, 2020, from https://www.jfklibrary.org/asset-viewer/archives/JFKPOF/046/JFKPOF-046-025.

Cush, A. (2016, September 12). "Remember When Jimi Hendrix Protested the National Anthem on a National Stage?" Retrieved from https://www.spin.com/2016/09/remember-when-jimi-hendrix-protested-the-national-anthem-on-a-national-stage/.

Daddis, G. (2017, July 31). The Fallacy of "The Turning Point"—A Critical Look at Mark Bowden's History of the Battle of Huế. Retrieved November 13, 2020, from https://lareviewofbooks.org/article/the-fallacy-of-the-turning-point-a-critical-look-at-mark-bowdens-history-of-the-battle-of-hue/.

"Dogma Collection Gallery." (2015) *Dogma Collection Gallery*. Retrieved14 Mar. 2016, from www.dogmacollection.com.

"Edward Snowden: The Whistleblower behind the NSA Surveillance Revelations." (2013, June 11). Retrieved November 14, 2020, from https://www.theguardian.com/world/2013/jun/09/edward-snowden-nsa-whistleblower-surveillance.

Eisenhower, D. (1961). "Transcript of President Dwight D. Eisenhower's Farewell Address" (1961). Retrieved November 13, 2020, from https://www.ourdocuments.gov/doc.php?flash=false.

Fitraikis, B. (2003). "Why Four Died in Ohio." *Dissident Voice*. 23 April 2003. 31 July 2010 http://www.dissidentvoice.org.

Gilbert, E. (2016). *Committed: A Love Story*. New York, NY: Riverhead Books.

Giles, J. (2017, October 27). "Keith Richards Recalls Making the Rolling Stones' 'Gimme Shelter.'" Retrieved November 14, 2020, from https://ultimateclassicrock.com/keith-richards-making-gimme-shelter/.

Glass, A. (2013). "Mike Mansfield delivers Assessment of Vietnam, Dec. 2, 1962." Retrieved November 13, 2020, from https://www.politico.com/story/2013/12/mike-mansfield-delivers-an-assessment-of-south-vietnam-dec-2-1962-100505.

Glass, A., & N. Cook. (2018, November 07). Nixon Reelected in Landslide, Nov. 7, 1972. Retrieved November 14, 2020, from https://www.politico.com/story/2018/11/07/this-day-in-politics-november-7-963516.

Goodacre, G. (n.d.). Vietnam Women's Memorial. Retrieved November 14, 2020, from http://www.vietnamwomensmemorial.org/memorial.php.

Gregory, H. (2016). "McNamara's Morons: Salvaging the Deficient for the War Effort." Retrieved November 14, 2020, from http://vvaveteran.org/36-3/36-3_morons.html.

Halberstam, D. (1993). *The Best and the Brightest:*. Bridgewater, NJ: Paw Prints/Baker & Taylor.

Hendrix, J. (2019, April 22). "Jimi Hendrix on Performing The National Anthem at Woodstock | *The Dick Cavett Show*." Retrieved November 14, 2020, from https://www.youtube.com/watch?v=VGf9PTYyJ4A.

Irvine, D. (2015) "Vivid Propaganda Posters of Vietnam's War-Torn Era." CNN. Cable NewsNetwork, Mar. 2015. Web. 14 Mar. 2016.

James, David E. (1997). *Power Misses: Essays Across (un)Popular Culture*. "American Musicand Viet Nam." New York: Verso Books.

Johnson, L. B. (2007). "Editorial Note." Retrieved November 14, 2020, from https://history.state.gov/historicaldocuments/frus1964-68v03/d97.

Johnson, L. B. (1965, August 03). "Remarks to the International Platform Association Upon Receiving the Association's Annual Award." Retrieved November 13, 2020, from https://www.presidency.ucsb.edu/documents/remarks-the-international-platform-association-upon-receiving-the-associations-annual.

Kearns-Goodwin, Doris. 2015. *Lyndon Johnson and the American Dream*. New York: St. Martin's Griffin.

Kennedy, J. F. (1965). "Remarks of Senator John F. Kennedy at the Conference on Vietnam Luncheon in the Hotel Willard." Washington, D.C. Retrieved November 11, 2020, from https://www.jfklibrary.org/archives/other-resources/john-f-kennedy-speeches/vietnam-conference-washington-dc-19560601.

Kennedy, R. (Director). (2014). *Last Days in Vietnam* [Motion picture on DVD]. USA: American Experience Films.

King, J. (Director). (1943). *The Spirit of '43* [Motion picture on VHS]. United States: Disney.

King, M. L., Jr. (1963). "Letter from a Birmingham Jail." Retrieved November 13, 2020, from https://www.africa.upenn.edu/Articles_Gen/Letter_Birmingham.html.

_____. (2018, April 04). "The Speech Martin Luther King, Jr. Gave the Night Before He Died." Retrieved December 14, 2020, from https://www.cnn.com/2018/04/04/us/martin-luther-king-jr-mountaintop-speech-trnd/index.html.

Langguth, A. J. (2002). *Our Vietnam: The War, 1954–1975*. New York: Simon & Schuster.

LBJ Presidential Library. (2015). Retrieved November 14, 2020, from http://www.lbjlibrary.net/collections/on-this-day-in-history/april.html.

Lederer, W. J., & E. Burdick. (1959). *The Ugly American*. New York: W.W. Norton.

Lewy, Guenter (1978), *America in Vietnam*. New York: Oxford University Press, pp. 442–453.

Lumet, S. (Director). (1964). *Fail Safe* [motion picture on DVD]. USA: Columbia Pictures.

Lynskey, D. (2012). *33 Revolutions per Minute: A History of Protest Songs, from Billie Holiday to Green Day*. London: Faber.

"The March on Washington." (2016). Retrieved November 14, 2020, from http://michiganintheworld.history.lsa.umich.edu/antivietnamwar/exhibits/show/exhibit/the_teach_ins/national_teach_in_1965.

Marcuse, H. (1978). *The Aesthetic Dimension: Toward a Critique of Marxist Aesthetics*. Boston: Beacon.

Mariscal, G. (1999). *Aztlán and Viet Nam: Chicano and Chicana Experiences of the War*. Berkeley: University of California Press.

McCoy, E. (2015, May 16). "*Yo Protesto!* Puerto Rican Anti-Vietnam War and Pro-Independence Protests." Retrieved November 14, 2020, from https://unionpenumbra.org/article/yo-protesto-puerto-rican-anti-vietnam-war-and-pro-independence-protests/.

McPeak, M. A. (2017, December 26). "Bombing the Ho Chi Minh Trail." Retrieved November 13, 2020, from https://www.nytimes.com/2017/12/26/opinion/bombing-the-ho-chi-minh-trail.html.

"The Mexican-American March against the Vietnam War." (2015, August 25). Retrieved November 14, 2020, from https://www.bbc.com/news/av/magazine-34006603.

Michals, D. (Ed.). (2007). "Fannie Lou Hamer." Retrieved November 14, 2020, from https://www.womenshistory.org/education-resources/biographies/fannie-lou-hamer.

Mitchell, F. (Director). (2012). *ESPN 30 for 30: Ghosts of Ole Miss* [Motion picture on DVD]. USA: Disney.

Moores, S. (2019, August 15). "Patriotism or Protest? Army Vet Jimi Hendrix had the 'Most Electrifying Moment' at Woodstock." Retrieved November 14, 2020, from https://www.stripes.com/news/special-reports/vietnam-stories/1969/patriotism-or-protest-army-vet-jimi-hendrix-had-the-most-electrifying-moment-at-woodstock-1.594315.

Morley, J. (2017, September 26). "6 Times National Anthem Protests Rocked America." Retrieved November 14, 2020, from https://www.salon.com/2017/09/26/6-times-national-anthem-protests-rocked-america_partner_partner/.

Morris, E. (Director). (2003). *The Fog of War: Eleven Lessons from the Life of Robert S. McNamara* [Motion picture on DVD]. USA: Sony Pictures Classics.

"Muhammad Ali Refuses Induction, Opposing Vietnam War April 28, 1967." (2019, April 29). Retrieved from YouTube, https://youtu.be/dHsa_vRBO-E.

Muldar, M. (Director). (2002). *Smothered: The Censorship Struggles of the Smothers Brothers Comedy Hour* [Motion picture on DVD]. USA: New Video Group.

"Murder at the Altamont Festival brings the 1960s to a Violent End." (2009, November 13). Retrieved November 14, 2020, from https://www.history.com/this-day-in-history/the-altamont-festival-brings-the-1960s-to-a-violent-end.

Nguyen, V. T. (2017). *Nothing Ever Dies: Vietnam and the Memory of War*. Cambridge, MA: Harvard University Press.

Nixon, R. (1962). 55 Years Ago—"The Last Press Conference." Retrieved November 13, 2020, from https://www.nixonfoundation.org/2017/11/55-years-ago-last-press-conference/.

_____. (2017, January 19). "Richard Nixon Inaugural Address: Jan. 20, 1969 | CBS News." Retrieved November 14, 2020, from https://www.youtube.com/watch?v=ipyhSEvfaUs.

Oglesby, C. (1965). "The Speech Given by Charles Oglesby, President of SDS at the November 27, 1965 March on Washington." Retrieved November 14, 2020, from http://freedomarchives.org/Documents/Finder/DOC30_scans/30.sds.carloglesbyspeech.pdf.

Orwell, G. (1941). "The Frontiers of Art and Propaganda." Listener. BBC. BBC Overseas Service, London, 29 May 1941. Radio. Transcript.

"The Pacifica Radio/UC Berkeley Social Activism Recording Project." (2020). Retrieved November 14, 2020, from https://guides.lib.berkeley.edu/c.php?g=819842.

"Paris Peace Talks and the Release of POWs." (2017). Retrieved December 14, 2020, from https://www.pbs.org/wgbh/americanexperience/features/honor-paris-peace-talks-and-release-pows/.

Pelley, P. M. (2002) *Postcolonial Vietnam: New Histories of the National Past*. Durham, NC: Duke UP.

"The Pentagon Papers." (2009). Retrieved December 14, 2020, from https://www.upi.com/Archives/Audio/Events-of-1971/The-Pentagon-Papers/.

Phụng, V. T. (2005). *Dumb Luck: A Novel* (N. N. Cẩm, Trans.; P. Zinoman, Ed.). Ann Arbor, MI: University of Michigan Press.

Polner, M., & T. E. Woods. (2008). *We Who Dared to Say No to War: American Antiwar Writing from 1812 to Now*. New York, NY: Basic Books.

President Nixon's Resignation Speech. (1974). Retrieved December 14, 2020, from https://www.pbs.org/newshour/spc/character/links/nixon_speech.html.

Roberts, S. (2016, March 26). "Santiago Erevia, Once Denied Medal of Honor Over Ethnicity, Dies at 69." Retrieved November 14, 2020, from https://www.nytimes.com/2016/03/26/us/santiago-erevia-once-denied-medal-of-honor-because-of-ethnicity-dies-at-69.html.

Rusk, D. (2010). "Memorandum from Secretary of State Rusk to President Johnson. Retrieved November 13, 2020." from https://history.state.gov/historicaldocuments/frus1964–68v04/d38.

Sadler, B., & R. Moore. (1966). "Sgt. Barry Sadler—Ballad of the Green Berets 1966." Retrieved December 29, 2020, from https://www.youtube.com/watch?v=8kj9qv6rmG8.

Scanlan, J., & G. Loescher. (1983). "U. S. Foreign Policy, 1959–80: Impact on Refugee Flow from Cuba." *The Annals of the American Academy of Political and Social Science, 467*, 116–137. Retrieved November 1, 2019, from http://www.jstor.org/stable/1044932.

Sedaris, D. (2000). *Me Talk Pretty One Day*. Little, Brown.

"Selma March." (2010). Retrieved November 13, 2020, from https://www.pbs.org/wgbh/americanexperience/features/wallace-selma-march/.

"Selma to Montgomery March." (2018, June 27). Retrieved November 14, 2020, from https://kinginstitute.stanford.edu/encyclopedia/selma-montgomery-march.

"Simple Gifts." (2018, February 03). Retrieved November 14, 2020, from https://songofamerica.net/song/simple-gifts/.

Small, M. (2004). *Antiwarriors: The Vietnam War and the Battle for America's Hearts and Minds*. Wilmington, DE: Scholarly Resources.

Sooke, A. (2014). "Can Propaganda Be Great Art?" BBC Culture. BBC.com. 21 Oct 2014.

Sterba, J. P. (1970, June 14). "Monsoon Mud Mires U. S. Tanks." Retrieved November 14, 2020, from https://www.nytimes.com/1970/06/14/archives/monsoon-mud-mires-us-tanks.html.

"Story Behind the Terror of War: Nick Ut's 'Napalm Girl' 1972." (2019). *About Photography Blog.* https://aboutphotography.blog/blog/the-terror-of-war-nick-uts-napalm-girl-1972.

Strange, E., & B. Hager. (2012, February 19). "Emily & Barb—Incoming | Vietnam War Song Project." Retrieved December 14, 2020, from https://www.youtube.com/watch?v=nB6Tj6riqAc.

Stur, H. (2018, January 04). "The Beatles of Vietnam." Retrieved November 14, 2020, from https://www.nytimes.com/2018/01/04/opinion/beatles-of-vietnam.html.

"Taylor Swift on 'Lover' and Haters." (2019, August 25). *CBS Sunday Morning.* Retrieved November 14, 2020, from https://youtu.be/nDzhoofkRJI.

"The 10 Greatest All-Time Speeches By 10 Inspirational Women." Retrieved November 14, 2020, from https://www.marieclaire.co.uk/entertainment/people/the-10-greatest-all-time-speeches-by-10-inspirational-women-79732.

"The Terror of War: Nick Ut's Napalm Girl." (2019, January 12). Retrieved November 14, 2020, from https://time.com/4485344/napalm-girl-war-photo-facebook/.

Thieu, N. V. (1975/2010). "Text of Thieu's Resignation Speech." Retrieved November 14, 2020, from https://www.cia.gov/library/readingroom/docs/LOC-HAK-244-10-4-5.pdf.

Toczek, D. M. (2007). *The Battle of Ap Bac, Vietnam: They Did Everything but Learn from It.* Annapolis, MD: Naval Institute Press.

"Transcript of Kissinger's News Conference on the Status of the Cease-Fire Talks." (1972, October 27). Retrieved November 14, 2020, from https://www.nytimes.com/1972/10/27/archives/transcript-of-kissingers-news-conference-on-the-status-of-the.html.

"Viet Cong Troops Overrun Town—Jul 20, 1964." (2017). Retrieved November 14, 2020, from https://www.rallypoint.com/deployments/vietnam-war/shared-links/viet-cong-troops-overrun-town-jul-20–1964-history-com--2?loc=similar_main.

"The Vietnam Center and Sam Johnson Vietnam Archive: Exhibits—The Fall of Saigon." (2013, October 23). Retrieved November 14, 2020, from https://www.vietnam.ttu.edu/exhibits/saigon/1975.php.

"Vietnam, Diem, the Buddhist Crisis." (2010). Retrieved November 13, 2020, from https://www.jfklibrary.org/learn/about-jfk/jfk-in-history/vietnam-diem-the-buddhist-crisis.

"Vietnam Passage, a Teacher's Guide." (2017). Retrieved November 13, 2020, from http://www.pbs.org/vietnampassage/Teacher/.

"Washington, D.C. Protests Against the War in Vietnam (Mayday), 1971." (2010). Retrieved November 14, 2020, from https://nvdatabase.swarthmore.edu/content/washington-dc-protests-against-war-vietnam-mayday-1971.

Wilbanks, J. (1993). "Thiet Giap! The Battle of An Loc, April 1972." Retrieved November 14, 2020, from https://www.armyupress.army.mil/Portals/7/combat-studies-institute/csi-books/thiet-giap-the-battle-of-an-loc-april-1972.pdf.

Williams, R.F. (1962). *Negroes with Guns.* New York: Marzani & Mansell.

"World War 2 Trail." (2019, January 04). Retrieved November 14, 2020, from https://www.athertontablelands.com.au/world-war-ll-trail/.

X, M. (1964). "The Ballot or the Bullet." Retrieved November 14, 2020, from http://www.digitalhistory.uh.edu/disp_textbook.cfm?smtID=3.

_____. (1963) "Malcolm X, 'Message to the Grassroots.'" Retrieved November 13, 2020, from https://www.blackpast.org/african-american-history/speeches-african-american-history/1963-malcolm-x-message-grassroots/.

Young, B. (2020, November 10). "Elite Vietnam Fighting Unit Pushes for Canungra Memorial—'Not Another Concrete Plinth.'" Retrieved November 14, 2020, from https://www.abc.net.au/news/2020-11-11/vietnam-veterans-push-for-memorial-outside-canberra/12867480.

Index

anti–Viet Nam War activities 8,
 18, 47, 61, 62, 70, 71, 72, 73, 76,
 77, 85, 90, 104, 105, 107, 118,
 119, 122, 123, 124, 125, 126, 127,
 128, 129, 131, 140, 141, 143, 144,
 145, 152, 154, 155, 159, 161, 168,
 179, 190
Ap Bac 24, 25, 51

Baker, Deane-Peter 85, 86, 87
Brummer, Justin 7, 8
Butler, Rick 67, 81, 82

Cat Ba 58, 60
Chicano Rights Movement 133,
 142, 171
Civil Rights Movement 1, 20, 53,
 61, 62, 63, 70, 72, 90, 100, 104,
 107, 113, 115, 118, 121, 143, 145,
 152, 160, 171
Cu Chi Tunnels 26, 27, 28, 29,
 30, 31, 149

Da Nang 68, 69, 71, 74, 90, 98,
 110, 188
de Heer, Derrill 87
de-militarized zone (DMZ) 14,
 27, 42, 45, 47, 91, 97, 99, 176,
 177, 178, 179
Diem, Ngo Dinh 17, 18, 24, 25,
 41, 46, 52, 53, 56, 57, 61, 75,
 152
Dien Bien Phu 13, 14, 15, 16, 17,
 21, 22, 23, 45, 149
Dien Bien Phu Museum 13, 16,
 17, 21, 23

Eisenhower, Dwight 17, 19, 20,
 32, 33
Engelmann, Ted 68, 156

Ford, Gerald 180, 181, 184

Giap, Nguyen Vo 16, 69, 75, 156
Gutierrez, Frank 37, 134, 187

Ha Long Bay 58, 59, 60, 68
Ha Noi 7, 11, 12, 23, 34, 35, 36,
 37, 38, 42, 43, 44, 45, 55, 67,

75, 76, 78, 97, 98, 102, 130, 156,
 157, 158, 163, 172, 182
Hall, Bob 87
Ho Chi Minh Museum, Ha Noi
 166, 172
Ho Chi Minh Museum, HCMC
 165, 166
Ho Chi Minh Trail/Troung Son
 Museum 8, 42, 43, 44, 45, 75,
 117, 135, 137, 171, 177
Ho La Prison/"Ha Noi Hilton"
 37, 156, 159
Hoi An 80, 109, 110, 111, 112
Houng, Duong Thu 9, 26, 102
Hue 36, 45, 47, 48, 49, 50, 55,
 56, 75, 90, 113, 114, 130, 184,
 188

Johnson, Lyndon B. 10, 41, 53,
 61, 62, 63, 64, 65, 66, 69, 70,
 71, 89, 90, 91, 105, 107, 113, 114,
 115, 117, 118, 126, 128, 150, 170

Kennedy, John F. 10, 14, 19, 20,
 32, 33, 39, 41, 53, 57, 66, 150,
 152
Khe Sanh 14, 45, 113, 117, 176,
 177, 178

Long Tan 67, 79, 80, 81, 83, 84,
 85, 90

Mai, Nguyen Phan Que 26, 102
Marlantes, Karl 100, 180
McCain, John 4, 158
McGarrah, Jim 47, 186
McNamara, Robert 40, 62, 65,
 71, 105, 128, 129, 150
Minh, Ho Chi 11, 13, 16, 17, 36,
 38, 45, 66, 67, 75, 98, 117, 131,
 149, 157, 158, 165, 166, 167,
 173, 174
My Lai 109, 110, 117, 124, 131, 141,
 142, 151, 154, 163

Native American Rights
 Movement 142, 170, 171
Nguyen, Nathalie 67, 87, 102
Nguyen, Viet Thanh 8, 9, 26, 149

Nixon, Richard M. 10, 17, 19, 20,
 32, 41, 117, 121, 122, 123, 124,
 126, 128, 141, 142, 143, 144, 145,
 150, 151, 152, 154, 159, 160, 161,
 162, 163, 170, 171, 180, 181, 182

O'Brien, Tim 8, 30

prisoners of war (POWs) 3, 71,
 104, 158, 159
Project RENEW 67, 68, 140,
 156, 157, 188, 189, 190
Puerto Rican Rights Movement
 62, 132, 133, 134, 142, 153

Reagan, Ronald 76, 103

Sai Gon (Ho Chi Minh City) 7,
 24, 26, 28, 29, 42, 46, 57, 62,
 64, 67, 91, 95, 111, 120, 129, 130,
 131, 151, 160, 165, 167, 169, 172,
 180, 182, 183, 184, 185
Searcy, Chuck 156, 157, 188

Tet Offensive 47, 48, 49, 75, 113,
 114, 117, 150, 184
Trang, Thomas 81, 83, 84

Utter, George 29, 186, 187
UXO (unexploded ordnance)
 Cambodia 29, 137, 138, 140
UXO (unexploded ordnance)
 Laos 29, 135, 140
UXO (unexploded ordnance)
 Viet Nam 29, 110, 156, 157,
 167, 189

Vietnam Veterans Memorial
 (Angel Fire, New Mexico)
 3, 5
Vietnam Veterans Memorial
 (Washington DC) 33, 85, 99,
 100
Vietnam Women's Memorial
 (Washington DC) 101, 108
Vietnamese Ethnography
 Museum, Ha Noi 38, 42
Vietnamese History Museum,
 Ha Noi 38, 130

Vietnamese Military History
    Museum, Ha Noi 76, 167
Vinh Moc Tunnels 27, 28, 45,
    46
Vung Tau 83, 84

War Remnants Museum,
    HCMC 76, 111, 130, 167, 168,
    169, 172
Westmoreland, William 49,
    71, 105

Westphall, Victor "Doc" 4
Women's Rights Movement 1,
    72, 77, 104, 107, 108, 118, 142,
    150, 153